THE NEW
INTERNATIONAL
POLITICAL

THE NEW
INTERNATIONAL
POLITICAL
ECONOMY

edited by
Craig N. Murphy
Roger Tooze

Lynne Rienner Publishers · Boulder

International Political Economy Yearbook, Volume 6

Published in the United States of America in 1991 by
Lynne Rienner Publishers, Inc.
1800 30th Street, Boulder, Colorado 80301

Library of Congress Cataloging-in-Publication Data
The New international political economy / Craig N. Murphy
  and Roger Tooze, editors
  (International political economy yearbook, v. 6)
  Includes bibliographical references and index.
  1. International economic relations. I. Murphy, Craig.
II. Tooze, Roger.
HF1359.N46 1990   90-19266
337—dc20   CIP
ISBN 1-55587-180-1
ISBN 1-55587-261-1 (pbk)

Printed and bound in the United States of America

The paper used in this publication meets the requirements
of the American National Standard for Permanence of
Paper for Printed Library Materials Z39.48-1984

Published and distributed outside North and South America and Japan by:

Macmillan Education Ltd.
Houndmills, Basingstoke, Hampshire RG21 2XS, England

British Library Cataloguing in Publication Data
The New international political economy
  1. Economics
  I. Murphy, Craig N. II. Tooze, Roger
  330
ISBN 0-333-55857-X
ISBN 0-333-55858-8 (pbk)

Contents

Acknowledgments

We are grateful to the series editors of the International Political Economy Yearbook, William P. Avery and David P. Rapkin, for giving us the opportunity to edit this volume, and to the yearbook's Board of Editors, who helped us identify and review contributions. The board's members are Jonathan D. Aronson, Richard Ashley, Thomas J. Biersteker, James A. Caporaso, Christopher Chase-Dunn, Peter F. Cowhey, Robert W. Cox, Ernst-Otto Czempeil, Alain de Janvry, Judith Goldstein, Keith Griffin, Hans-Henrik Holm, W. Ladd Hollist, Raymond F. Hopkins, Takashi Inoguchi, Harold K. Jacobson, Robert O. Keohane, Stephen J. Kobrin, Stephen D. Krasner, Bruce E. Moon, Heraldo Muñoz, Lynn K. Mytelka, E. Wayne Nafziger, Guillermo O'Donnell, Dieter Senghaas, Susan Strange, William R. Thompson, F. LaMond Tullis, Laura D'Andrea Tyson, Raimo Varyrynen, and Mark Zacher.

We also wish to thank Christina Lui for her help in producing the final manuscript.

Craig N. Murphy
Roger Tooze

Introduction

Craig N. Murphy
Roger Tooze

Today few people would question the importance of understanding the linkages between politics and economics at the international level. Iraq's invasion of Kuwait, with its threatening implications for global stability and prosperity, made the importance of those links all too clear. Similarly, the economic aftermath of the collapse of Soviet power and the resurgence of nationalism in the less-well-off parts of Europe demonstrate that international politics and economics cannot be separated. And the inventory of today's significant issues of international politics and economics still includes older, but just as pressing problems of widespread indebtedness, monetary instability, and a crisis-ridden trade system. All these issues demand new understanding, new explanations to inform more effective action.

Unfortunately, many of the explanations offered by scholars of what is called "international political economy" (IPE) have proven insufficient. One purpose of this book—its critical purpose—is to try to explain why. But our main purpose is to go beyond that criticism to introduce a new IPE that provides more adequate explanations of the changing global political economy.

What Is IPE?

International political economy has developed as a field defined more by agreement among scholars about what to study than by agreement about how to study it. One of us has previously argued that IPE "denotes an area of investigation, a particular range of questions, and a series of assumptions about the nature of the international 'system' and how we understand this 'system'" (Tooze, 1984: 2), as opposed to denoting the application of a specific methodology or theory. This conception of IPE as a "set of questions" is now widely accepted as a correct characterization of the field. For example, Robert Gilpin in his *Political Economy of International Relations* states "I use the term 'political economy' simply to indicate a set

1

of questions to be examined by means of an eclectic mixture of analytic methods and theoretical perspectives" (Gilpin, 1987: 9).

Of course, scholars still debate what exactly should be included in the set of questions that defines IPE. For Gilpin the questions concern the relationship between the state and market because, "The tension between these two fundamentally different way of ordering human relationships has profoundly shaped the course of modern history and constitutes the crucial problem in the study of political economy" (Gilpin, 1987: 11). Similarly, Susan Strange has entitled her introduction to international political economy *States and Markets*. However, for her, the defining characteristic of IPE is that "It concerns the social, political and economic arrangements affecting the global systems of production, exchange and distribution, and the mix of values reflected therein" (Strange, 1988: 18). Thus, the mix of values—security, prosperity, freedom, and justice—within the market-authority nexus is the core of the field for Strange, and this give rise to her concern with delineating and explaining structures of power in the world economy. Gilpin's problematique, on the other hand, produces a slightly different set of broad research questions concerning "the causes and effects of the world market economy, the relationship between economic and political change, and the significance of the world economy for domestic economies" (Gilpin, 1987: 14).

These two overlapping conceptions of the problematique of IPE focus on questions that lie within the fusion of not just two, but four previously distinct academic domains: (1) international politics, (2) international economics (3) domestic (national) politics, and (4) domestic economics. In fact, it was only by breaking down traditional distinctions between the international and the domestic, and between politics and economics, that IPE scholars were first able to understand some of the complex linkages between international and economics that are still with us today.

The Context and Origins of IPE

It is important to bear in mind that today's IPE is not all that old, even if today's scholars borrow liberally from much older traditions. Today's IPE has its roots in the academic field of international relations (IR) as it developed in the countries of the Western bloc throughout the Cold War. In the early era of the bipolar nuclear system, during the 1950s and 1960s, IR was dominated by a form of "realism" that defined all aspects of international relations, and all its own subsidiary concepts, in terms of power and security, where "power" was primarily military power and "security" was essentially territorial integrity. The realist problematique was appropriate to its time. That it evolved from and legitimated the interests of the dominant power in the Western bloc should be expected. Of course, this fact was rarely discussed in realism's canonical texts, which were (and still are), not surprisingly, mainly U.S. products. Two of the central elements of realism at this stage were the conceptual separations of economics and politics and of the international and the domestic. In assuming a separation of economics and politics, realism borrowed from and supported the concept of a "liberal" economic order, that is, an order in which economic activity was separated from political activity for the purpose of maximizing the common wealth. In terms of international politics itself, realism helped support the liberal elements of the international economic order established over the Western bloc and the dependent Third World after World War II. The question of whether or not this "liberal" system maximized global welfare is not particularly relevant here, but three consequences of the maintenance of such a system from 1944 Bretton Woods negotiations onwards are relevant.

First, the liberal system clearly did facilitate the enormous growth of the world economy and thereby created the context for the globalization of economic activity that is so much a part of economic life today. In this, the system certainly served the joint interests of all the national economies of the Western bloc, and perhaps even those of the dependent Third World. However, sometime between 1968 and 1971 the interests of the U.S. government and those of the liberal system as a whole began to diverge. Economic growth in the United States began to slow. Other Western bloc countries began to overtake the United States in many fields. One OPEC member began to push up the price of oil. Finally, the U.S. government began to abrogate responsibilities for maintaining the system as a whole. The "formalization" of the crisis in the Bretton Woods system by the announcement of President Nixon's "New Economic Policy" on August 15, 1971, clearly demonstrated to scholars and practitioners alike that the world was no longer understandable in terms of the enforced separation of economics from politics.

Yet, initially, it was difficult for many observers to fully comprehend these events. The difficulty can be explained, in part, as a result of the way in which the successful liberal international system had helped to reinforce the legitimacy and academic dominance of the discipline of economics, the system's second significant consequence for our purposes here. When the power structures that underpinned the liberal system (the United States) began to have problems—partly as a result of changes in the system itself but primarily because of U.S. domestic policy—economics, to which most scholars and policymakers turned for an explanation, was not able to contribute that much. Of course, given the division among the disciplines, traditional political science and IR fared no better than economics.

Paradoxically, a final consequence of the postwar liberal order helped bring the separate fields back together. The liberal international system rested upon the idea that there could be an international economic order separated from politics and governed by the application of technical rules and norms.

What spurred much of the initial IPE research in the early 1970s was a search for new technical rules and norms that could preserve the division between the political and the economic, even if the distinction between the academic fields of political science and economics had to be sacrificed. Thus, a process of *relinking* the studies of IR, economics, and politics began, a process driven, to some extent, by the potentially conflicting desires to reinforce the postwar "liberal" economic order and to reinforce the position of the dominant state, but, in any event, to do so through "expertise"—through the discovery of new technical rules and norms that would keep the world economy functioning as it had in the 1950s and 1960s.

Toward Consolidation of an Orthodoxy

While conventional IR rested upon the twin separations of politics from economics and the international from the domestic, many social science traditions never incorporated these distinctions. For example, neither Marxian political economy nor the nationalist economics championed by many industrializing states had ever accepted the division between politics and economics. Analysts of dependency have always questioned the ultimate utility of the domestic/international distinction. But these traditions had no answers to questions about inventing new rules and norms to preserve the liberal economic order or the power of the United States, and so they did not become the main foundations of the resurgent IPE of the late 1970s and 1980s.

Instead, the IR community first approached the "new" problems of the world economy in a way that preserved as much of the economics/politics and domestic/international distinctions as was possible. First, the new problems were defined as *international*, that is they were defined as problems located within the relationships of (nation) states and national economics. Second, they were defined as primarily *economic*, that is they were derived, ultimately, from the pursuit of wealth as distinct from the pursuit of power. The problems had only become "political" due to the breakdown of rules and norms. Thus, contemporary IPE began as the study of "the politics of international economic relations" (PIER), and its philosopher's stone became the identification of effective "regimes" that could *de*politicize international economic relations once again.

From the very beginning, the journal *International Organization* played an important catalytic and defining role in the resurgent field of IPE. Intellectual historians trying to trace the history of IPE could do worse than to track the changing contents of this journal from 1975 though 1990. One pattern they would find would be an increasing breakdown of the distinctions between economics and politics and, slightly later, between the domestic and the international, and therefore, an increasing inability to maintain the PIER framework. Intellectual historians would also see a periodic openness to learning from the social science traditions that have long maintained a political economy perspective, especially the Marxian and dependency traditions. All of this would suggest that IPE had constituted itself as a fairly dynamic and open-ended field.

Yet, IPE has never really fulfilled the practical goals that scholars and policymakers began with 15 or 20 years ago. We do not know much more about how to reconstitute the political bases of the postwar liberal economic order, but the fear of the imminent demise of that order, or at least of U.S. dominance, has abated. Yet, strangely, even though the reassertion of U.S. supremacy was not informed by lessons learned from IPE, and even though the institutional foundation of the liberal world economy may be as shaky today as it was in 1975, few IPE scholars have spent much time critically reflecting on these failures. Instead, the period of relative calm in the world political economy in the second half of the 1980s was used by many scholars as an opportunity for strengthening the scholastic rigor of IPE without questioning its, often unstated, foundations. Many of us have not been particularly open to rearranging the hierarchy of the substantive issues that IPE studies, nor have we been happy to muck about with the hierarchy of values attached to those issues. Many have been interested only in seeing that scholars reach "better" conclusions about the same old issues—conclusions influenced by a clearer and more rigid view of methodology.

Unfortunately, perhaps, these urges have combined to consolidate an orthodoxy in IPE. This orthodoxy combines a fairly narrow view of what are the most important questions in the field—the continued focus on regimes that might secure a liberal international trading system—with a view of scholarly "rigor" that is not only quite narrow, but, arguably, is also outdated; it ignores significant developments in the philosophy of social science in favor of a very simple model of the accumulation of knowledge, one rarely employed in other branches of the social sciences, even in economics, the field that many students of IPE still insist upon treating as the one social science to be emulated.

Breaking Out of the Orthodoxy:
The New International Political Economy

This orthodox IPE, while easily identifiable, has never become ubiquitous. Heterodox analysis has flourished, albeit it usually only when it steers clear of the mainstream. But that is not the tack of the authors collected here. Our purpose is to bring IPE back into the broader mainstream of social science discourse as a whole. All of the authors collected here want to place IPE on broader theoretical foundations and all want to expand the field's agenda of research.

The contributors to this collection deviate from the orthodox perspective on theory and methodology in three ways: (1) They are willing to recognize and confront the necessary subjectivity of the social sciences, our essential inability fully to stand outside the global political economy in order to view it with disinterested "objectivity." (2) The contributors are all open to considering a wide variety of forms of historical and social explanation, as well as their combination, as persuasive, rather than acting as if the scholar's work is never done until things have been "explained" as the rational, egoistic action of some axiomatic "individuals," as some economists might. Further, the authors included here all demand that an "explanation" tell us something more than common sense would—a criterion that many IPE explanations in terms of egoistic rational action do not meet. Finally, (3) the authors all desire to examine the many explanatory frameworks offered in IPE on their own terms, with their own historical specificity, rather than try to force them into the tripartite pedagogical framework (mercantilism versus liberalism versus Marxism) so often inappropriately used by scholars as something more than a tool for the beginning student.

Our deviations from the orthodoxy's research agenda are more complex: Most of us (due to citizenship, if nothing else) are less interested in issues of U.S. economic statecraft and the consequences of waning U.S. power than are most of the proponents of our field's orthodoxy. Similarly, many of us (as J. Ann Tickner might point out, due to gender, if nothing else) are more concerned with the involvement in the global political economy of people who are often ignored because they are considered less powerful. Finally, almost all of us (due to otherwise intractable problems we have confronted in our own research, more than anything else) are concerned with the historical development and influence of concrete "private" interests in the world economy—for example, firms, representatives of sectoral interest groups, groups of intellectuals, individual inventors, and political entrepreneurs.

Ultimately, the relative success of the new international political economy will depend not only on our ability to explain and inform effective action around the private interests and supposedly less powerful people that have been our particular concern, we also will be judged by our ability to understand the orthodox issue agenda, and, perhaps most significantly, by our ability to shed light on new questions raised by unforeseen changes in the world political economy. This collection is organized in a way that, we hope, will help the reader make those judgments. The first section of three chapters explains the orthodox perspective and the reasons for developing a new IPE in more general, theoretical terms. The second section concentrates on a central issue of the orthodox issue agenda, the constitution of a liberal international trading order. The chapters in this section help answer the critical questions about the contemporary liberal economic order that the orthodoxy has overlooked: why the liberal trading order remains on such a shaky institutional basis and why the reassertion of U.S. supremacy in the

1980s was little informed by orthodox IPE. The final section expands the issue agenda of IPE, demonstrating how the integration of insights from other social science traditions can help students of IPE understand and anticipate problems in the world political economy that we would otherwise ignore.

PART 1

THEORETICAL FOUNDATIONS OF A NEW IPE

The chapters in Part 1 explore the necessary conceptual foundations for a "new" IPE. It is worth emphasizing that we are not arguing for one particular new perspective, for that is to argue for the replacement of one orthodox privileged view by another. What we are arguing is that IPE needs an effective evaluation of its philosophical and related conceptual bases in order to move toward a greater understanding of a complex global political economy. And, that greater understanding is possible only through an opening up and challenging of the analyses that are produced by the practice of orthodox IPE. The opening up of orthodoxy should allow a number of competing subjects rather than the imposition of one universal view.

It seems to us that a necessary part and first stage of this process is a thorough evaluation of the practice of what we identify as orthodox IPE. Here, it is not sufficient merely to evaluate the products of orthodox IPE, because that can only proceed to a limited extent. Orthodox IPE has to be considered as a fusion of theory and practice—as a social product—before any comprehensive evaluation can be undertaken. Our first chapter attempts such an extended evaluation of the practice of orthodoxy in IPE. It makes no apology for being firmly and necessarily based upon a consideration of the philosophical bases of IPE, although not only on these bases. Any attempt to discover the power of orthodox thinking must start with epistemology and ontology: how we know what we know and how we configure that which we want to know.

Chapter 2, by Susan Strange, is part of a longer-term project of heterodox thinking that she has presented throughout the last twenty years. In this she further develops her pragmatic and eclectic analysis of the global political economy and presents a multilevel synthesis. For us Strange's strength is in the constant challenge she poses for orthodox IPE in her articulation of an alternative view and in her continuing skepticism regarding the claims of orthodox theory. She challenges the orthodox issue agenda head

9

on, particularly in her analysis of the financial system as a core structure and her relegation of trade to a secondary position in political economy.

Chapter 3, by Stephen Gill, presents a similar challenge to orthodox IPE. Gill has developed a strong historical materialist form of analysis from the work of Antonio Gramsci and, in his chapter, uses this as a basis of critique. Like us, Gill considers it absolutely necessary to begin to evaluate conventional views from their philosophical bases. Like Strange, he offers a synthetic, open-ended theory of the world economy that provides greater historical and sociological understanding of the global political economy than the narrow framework of the orthodoxy.

Collectively, the three chapters offer a means of evaluating the existing foundations of IPE and illustrate similar paths forward.

1

Getting Beyond the "Common Sense" of the IPE Orthodoxy

Craig N. Murphy
Roger Tooze

For many of our students, and for too many of our colleagues, another essay on IPE theory will not be particularly welcome and may even be regarded as irrelevant, or marginal at best. After all, there is already a lot of "theory" in IPE even though politics and economics at the international level appear not all that difficult to understand. That is why even though the media flood us with new information every day, analysts usually fall back on the same set of century-old theories to explain what has happened. All we really need is a bit of common sense to sort out the useful information from the noise—a bit of common sense to figure out which theories are most valuable and when this is so.

Common sense has it that theoretical discussion in IPE, if it must occur at all, should center around the appropriateness of the instrumental categories and theories employed to "make sense" of the changing "reality" of a global political economy. It is a straightforward matter to use and to test different theoretical analyses against "reality" as given and understood by conventional, common sense, means. This reality is somehow known prior to any theoretical understanding; at least that is the view confirmed by the practice of most of us "doing" IPE as a social practice, as professionals or academics, most of the time.

Nevertheless, we have good reason to be skeptical of all common sense about human society, including what is taken as such in our own field. Antonio Gramsci even considered such skepticism of common sense to be the necessary starting point for progressive social change (Augelli and Murphy, 1988: ch. 1). Our progressive credentials may not be as grand as Gramsci's, but we agree with his suggestion that we look closely at common sense in order to (1) reveal the specific ways in which an often-unacknowledged level of "theory" determines what are taken as "facts," (2) uncover inconsistencies among the accepted preconceptions of popular orthodoxies (and see how that orthodoxy draws our attention away from those inconsistencies), (3) provide insight into the historical and practical reasons

11

for the development of a particular configuration of common sense ideas, and finally, (4) help answer the question "Cui bono?" Who is served by what commonly is taken as sensible? And, who is not?

Our purpose in this chapter is to bring together the elements of such a critique and to identify the ways in which that critique can lead to a new, more open, IPE. We contend that analysis of the deeper epistemological foundations of IPE is not merely a whim or merely the desire of those who "do" theory; it has become a necessity recognized by scholars who are trying to keep the field from stagnating.

Our task in making this case is neither easy nor straightforward. The reception and response to the arguments we make in this chapter, and to the range of arguments articulated in the book as a whole, will be governed, in part, by the prevailing conception of "theory" we seek to challenge. The common sense view, after all, gives theory a particular, limited, role and function. It separates those who theorize from those who do not (Tooze, 1988). We, along with the other authors represented here, find that division untenable.

In this chapter we argue a substantive claim of "newness" for the variety of analyses presented in the book. We argue that it is constructive to view the collection of interrelated practices that constitute the core of the recent academic study of IPE as a practice of *orthodoxy*. The configuration and the dimensions of this orthodoxy will be examined in some detail. From this analysis the corresponding contours of a "new" IPE can be identified. These, in turn, allow us to identify a deeper connection among the common themes and objectives of a variety of innovations in the field. We do not, and would not, argue that any of the new approaches represented in this volume "solve" the problem of explanation in IPE, but we do claim that they all have the *potential* for taking us beyond the common sense understanding of the global political economy, which has been reinforced by the practice of orthodox IPE.

The Configuration of Orthodoxy:
A Preliminary Identification

It is instructive to remind ourselves that even at the fundamental level of "paradigm shift" in international relations what is claimed is often revealed to be mistaken. John Vasquez, among others, has shown that the products of the "behavioralist revolution" were merely extensions of an already constructed "power politics" paradigm (Vasquez, 1983). Although scholars have yet to declare a paradigm shift within the narrower confines of the younger field of IPE, research has been characterized by the existence of a profusion of possible approaches and research programs. The appearance of a range of competing approaches is, however, deceptive, for the global political economy of the production of IPE knowledge has, over the past fifteen years, delivered a clear orthodoxy of values, theory, and interpretation of policy. It is in opposition to this orthodoxy that we posit a "new" international political economy.

We identify orthodoxy not just as a set of values and theories, but as a particular mode of production of IPE knowledge that specifies a particular relationship between the objective and the subjective and uses appropriate epistemological and ontological categories to support this relationship. The view of knowledge and knowledge production that we hold is close to that articulated by Robert Cox when he argued: "Theory is always for someone and for some purpose. . . . There is . . . no such thing as theory in itself, divorced from a standpoint in time or space" (Cox, 1981: 127). This conception of theory demands an investigation into the conditions of knowledge production and reproduction: knowledge for whom and for what purpose. We must ask who benefits from the production and reproduction of the IPE orthodoxy.

At an immediate, intuitive level, IPE certainly does not seem to be a narrow field based on a conventional wisdom of theories and values and serving some readily identified interests. It has all the appearance and possesses all the characteristics of a broadly based and highly contested area of knowledge. Disagreements are rife, and differing interpretations are evident for all to see. The field seems full of new work and important developments that appear to add to our understanding of the complexities of the global political economy every year. Critical views are cogently expressed by many, and are tolerated and even encouraged by the scholarly consensus.

Yet the question should be asked, "What impact have these 'critical' views had?" Consider, for example, the impact of Susan Strange's (1982) critical analysis of the concept of "regime" in an article that appears on the (now) standard list of references that everyone must cite on regime theory. Those who cite the article rarely acknowledge, let alone confront and refute, her contentious and disturbing claim that the concept, as conventionally used, is not particularly fruitful because it derives from a political interest in the question "How to keep order?" at a time when the politically more salient question is "How to achieve change?" The apparent lack of impact of this and other critical views that are, nonetheless, widely cited is understandable in terms of a general practice of an orthodoxy that nurtures divergent views only to either incorporate them into prevailing explanations or to ignore them, thus marginalizing the heterodox analysis and/or its author(s).

Beneath the surface impression of a contentious field where many voices are heard, this clear and important orthodoxy shapes much of the substantive output of IPE—the explanations of the global political economy that are offered and the policy judgments that are based upon those explanations. Most of the work proffered as IPE is produced within the context of a number of intellectual assumptions and practices that form a framework of "paradigm production." These assumptions and practices are such that large amounts of knowledge are produced forming a number of different paradigms: the range of contesting frameworks and ideologies in IPE. But each of these frameworks is produced and developed within the same larger theory of knowledge production. So, although at one level the frameworks are contesting (liberalism versus Marxism versus neorealism), at another they—or, more properly, their adherents, individually and collectively—maintain and reproduce a particular way of producing a particular form of knowledge. A specific epistemological and ontological foundation allows orthodox IPE to resolve the essentially contested differences among these three positions to be resolved, usually producing a "realist/liberal" synthesis.

Of course, orthodox ideas are not agents. They cannot reproduce themselves, no matter what the cohesive power of their epistemological foundations. An appreciation of how a particular form of knowledge is reproduced can come only from understanding the social realization of the philosophical principles that form the basis of that knowledge. To understand the process of "intellectual production" (Cox, 1979) we must take into account the material and ideological bases of knowledge.

Such a statement is, no doubt, incompatible with the views of knowledge and knowledge production that many scholars hold. This is the root of the problem. Orthodox IPE is firmly based in positivist thought and as such sees knowledge production as purely an intellectual process. In this, orthodox IPE accepts and sustains the positivist separation of subject and object, what Gramsci calls the "traditional intellectual's" view that he or she is unaffected by material concerns that affect all other citizens, or by the political battles of the day. However, to be realistic, the production of knowledge must always be considered a social process linking subject and object.

Thus, in summary, the current IPE "orthodoxy" cannot be identified solely with a particularly range of theories and empirical referents. We must look for a distinct ontology and epistemology that, together with a particular range of theories and empirical referents, form a specific *culture* of orthodoxy. This culture has its material base, and it encompasses not only the production and dissemination of knowledge, but, critically, also the creation of consensus around or upon the knowledge so produced.

The reader may be forgiven for thinking that in the preceding paragraphs we sometimes lose sight of what IPE is, but this judgment is itself reflective of orthodox, positivist IPE. It is the very purpose of our analysis to suggest that an understanding of IPE must necessarily include the kinds of considerations we have discussed. Similarly, we may be accused of forcing yet-to-be-named authors into the "straitjacket of orthodoxy." But, as we have endeavored to stress, the orthodoxy of IPE is not exclusive at the level of its substantive analyses. All of us who "do" IPE, no matter how heterodox our substantive analyses, are likely to participate in the social process of the orthodoxy's reproduction, especially if we do not pause to consider the deeper theoretical foundations of our work. An orthodoxy cannot be exclusive or narrow if it is to succeed in its broader goals. Finally, in case it is felt that we have somehow created or imagined this orthodoxy, it is worthwhile to briefly consider an example of what we define as constituting the orthodox.

In a recent and authoritative critical review essay published in *International Organization* (regarded by many as one of the leading journals in the field), Benjamin J. Cohen (1990) presents a formulation of what he labels "the research agenda of international political economy." It is interesting to consider some of the things Cohen treats as common sense. For instance, he identifies the basic research agenda as focusing on

> two broad sets of questions. One set has to do with actor behavior—meaning, in particular, government behavior, since the fundamental unit of authority in the international system remains the sovereign nation state. . . . The other has to do with system management—coping with the consequences of economic interdependence. . . . Methodologies used to seek answers to these questions vary, depending both on the disciplinary training of the individual scholar and on the nature of the specific issue-area under consideration. International trade, of course, is one of the most central of the issue-areas explored in the IPE literature. (Cohen, 1990: 264)

Cohen then analyzes a number of works of IPE, all by North Americans (within the context of a field defined almost exclusively by U.S. writings), and offers suggestions for future productive work, the substantive and critical part of his analysis. For example, "If economists would take a cue from political scientists and open up the analysis of state motivations to include equally relevant noneconomic interests, this certainly would help the real world conform more to theory" (Cohen, 1990: 272).[1] In the same vein, he argues that political scientists make a vital contribution by "endogenizing" questions (of power and conflict) into the agenda and theoretical apparatus of economics, and "it is also necessary to build a formal structure to the interactions between market and politics that appear to be most pivotal in the trade area."

Consider some of what is taken as common sense, even in Cohen's critical arguments about what the IPE research agenda *should* be.

First, consider *actor behavior*—where the actor is the state. Well, yes, the state is important, but what kind of state? Much of the empirical work ever done in the field has indicated that in the contemporary global political economy it is essential to consider a large number of other nonstate social and economic actors. Just because it is possible to say that the state is still the "fundamental unit of authority" does not mean that state action will explain change; it does not even mean that the behavior of other actors will explain less. A focus on actor behavior as advocated by Cohen ignores the fundamental problems of agent-structure of relationships and denies the existence of structure as a focus of research in itself. This is a fundamental ontological weakness.

Second, issues of *system management* provide the next broad set of questions for Cohen. Again, there is no doubt that system management is important, but again it is much too narrow a focus, particularly when that system is defined in the way Cohen defines it, as managed by the state. Could Third World debt be treated as simply an issue of global "interdependence" managed (with more or less success) by various states? Could we account for the ability of the banks to offset their exposure to sovereign debt (incurred as a result of the banks' own decisions) through transferring some of the costs onto the taxpayers of their own states? This is only possible through analysis that disaggregates the state and encompasses a broad understanding of society.

Finally, to say that *international trade* is the most central issue-area explored in the IPE literature is to ignore completely an increasing number of works that argue that trade is, at most, a secondary activity in terms of the dynamics of the contemporary global political economy.

For Cohen, the research agenda of IPE is defined in terms of the economics first and then the political practices and consequences that follow from it. The ultimate "problem" of IPE is generated by a central contention of liberal economics—the desirability of free trade. The first political problem is that of assuring that a liberal trade regime is maintained (system management). States and government policies become important only because they are assumed to be the key agents maintaining or undermining such management; liberal economics leads to the importance of trade and realist politics leads to a concern with the state. Perhaps this agenda is to be expected; given that Cohen is a professor of international economic affairs, he needs to be concerned with the politics of international economic relations. But this definition of the research agenda of IPE is more widely shared; it is treated as common sense, even amongst those who consider themselves as "realists" focusing on statecraft. Most of the time, those of us who "do" IPE also make little attempt to consider the political issues at the top of our research agenda, let alone to develop an integrated political-economy analysis.

Cohen's common-sense identification of the variation in methodologies in IPE is also illuminating: "Methodologies used . . . vary, *depending both on the disciplinary training of the individual scholar and on the nature of specific issue-area under consideration*" (Cohen, 1990: 264, emphasis added). To consider these two factors as determining methodology is to adopt a relatively narrow and particularistic conception of methodology as scientific technique, along with a wholly positivist conception of the possibility and desirability of objective analysis prefigured by the separation of subject and object. Cohen's rhetorical strategy at this point indicates that he believes his readers will consider this position unexceptional. He does not need to argue the point. We agree. He is simply stating orthodox views.

However, perhaps the clearest confirmation of orthodoxy lies not in Cohen's research agenda itself, nor in his comments about how it should be pursued, but in an assumption underlying the way he carries out his review. As an initial comment (one that will, perhaps, seem to be belabored throughout this book), it seems that for Cohen (as a representative of orthodoxy) IPE is defined "by Americans for Americans as American." Of course, this does not seem that all American scholars of IPE are part of the orthodoxy, or that non-U.S. scholars of IPE are heterodoxical. What it does mean, however, is that, as Cohen demonstrates in his critical review, there is a dominant ontological posture (interstate material relationships) coupled with an accepted epistemology (positivist), which form the foundation of a particular view of what and who (by virtue of practicing the aforementioned) constitute the legitimate study of IPE. And the production of this view is the core of a self-identified U.S. "supremacy" in the scholarly fields of international relations and IPE; that is, the typical adherence of U.S. scholars to the orthodoxy implicitly explains to orthodox scholars why U.S. products of IPE are all that need be considered (Tooze, 1988).

From the above outline of what one representative of mainstream IPE treats as common sense, and from our preliminary metatheoretical considerations, we can now explore the ramifications of orthodox IPE in more depth. The practice of orthodoxy incorporates a number of methodological dimensions and a range of substantive issue concerns. The two complementary sets of orthodox practices share the same genealogy but are not logically derived from one another.

The Methodological Range of Orthodoxy

We turn first to the methodological dimensions, of which there are at least three of significance. These dimensions define ranges over which the methodology of orthodox IPE may vary. The first, and most restrictive, dimension flows from positivism. At a fundamental level the epistemological and philosophical basis of orthodox IPE is avowedly positivist and empiricist, separating subject and object and claiming legitimacy from a notion of science (primarily and initially derived from mainstream economics). The second dimension reflects orthodox IPE's ultimate predication on a radical form of methodological individualism, although there is disagreement about whether "economic man" or the "state as individual" should be treated as the final locus of explanation. Finally, the third dimension reflects the way orthodox IPE identifies the basis of explanation and the core of theory as lying within the opposition and contest of three "ideologies" and their respective concepts, theoretical constructs, and forms. These ideologies are treated as constituting the *totality* of possible explanations, and they are usually treated as mutually exclusive.

Within the methodological range defined along these dimensions, orthodox IPE produces a highly specific form of knowledge, one characterized by its qualities of exclusion. This key point will be taken up after we consider each of these dimensions in greater detail.

Positivist Epistemology

It is not our intention here to explicate the minutiae of positivism but to consider its meaning within its incorporation into orthodox IPE. Briefly, the separation of subject and object that is the basis of positivism produces the possibility of objective knowledge by creating a category of phenomena that can be manipulated. Manipulation consists of creating hypotheses concerning these phenomena and testing the hypotheses against a (presumed) objective reality—a process which produces explanation.

We are not arguing that positivism has no value as the epistemological basis of IPE, and we are fully aware of the difficulties that the denial of positivism creates. However, different epistemologies are clearly "linked to different modes of knowledge" (Cox, 1986: 242), and the knowledge produced by the practitioners of orthodox IPE is clearly problematic in a number of ways.

Positivist IPE knowledge, although claiming a legitimacy derived from following a "scientific" process, denies the possibility that any form of (nonmaterial) intersubjective meaning may be part of *the* international political economy. It denies the possibility that beliefs and values are themselves just as real as the material structures and powers of the global political economy (Tooze, 1988; Cox, 1986). For example, in the context of the Bretton Woods system, the "liberal" separation of economics and politics (into rational economics and nonrational politics) enabled international economic relations to be presented by the supporter of the system as technical and scientific. Economic issues were resolvable on the basis of rational economic knowledge and the resolution of technical problems. Acceptance of the system of meaning by participants in the international economy entailed the acceptance of what constituted legitimate economic knowledge and legitimate political action. Acceptance also externalized the system of meaning from the dominant state(s) into an objective part of the external reality faced by the participants: it became just as real as the material conditions facing them. This point cannot not be grasped by the IPE orthodoxy because the orthodoxy excludes this heterodox argument's ontological presupposition—the reality of intersubjective meaning in the structure of the global political economy.

Through the same form of exclusion, positivist IPE prevents the development of a *reflexive* practice, a practice of IPE that explains its own emergence and purpose. It is a core assumption of positivist thought that social action can be understood universally over time and space and therefore objectively. Hence, the production of academic (and other) knowledge is characterized as an attempt to apply objectively generated concepts to an objectively understood external reality that is somehow separate (or can be separated) from the academic as observer (for example, see Gilpin, 1987). This process configures the production of knowledge as the search for scientific truth and academics as nonsocial participants. Yet this is clearly not the case. More important, it does not allow us to integrate the production of knowledge (orthodox IPE in this case) into the processes of the international political economy itself.

Finally, positivist IPE, because it excludes certain phenomena that are not captured by its ontology, produces inadequate explanation *whatever the derived explanatory framework actually is*. This point has been fairly well discussed by Kratochwil and Ruggie (1986) in their consideration of regimes, but the inadequacy of positivist ontology is for us not confined to regimes. All the global political economy is constituted by the reciprocal interaction of meaning and material capability, and not just regimes.

Ultimate Methodological Individualism

Now let us look more closely at the range of explanations permitted by orthodox IPE. Orthodox IPE scholarship displays a clear, if often unstated, commitment to explaining events in terms of the rational action of individuals or of state actors treated as individuals—a commitment to a relatively radical form of methodological individualism that denies ultimate validity to contextually bound explanations as well as explanations in terms of concrete social wholes. This commitment leads to some typical orthodox *mis*understandings of heterodox explanations, which include a concatenation of differences among different theories outside the orthodoxy; that is, an inability to distinguish among many nonorthodox positions. The problem does not arise from a commitment to methodological individualism per se, but to the exclusiveness of that commitment—the lack of openness to other forms of explanation.

In contrast, consider Marx's view of explanation as revealed in *Das Kapital*, at least as interpreted by Daniel Little (1985). Little points out that a number of the explanations that Marx offers display the conviction that explanations in terms of individual rational action are persuasive, a conviction as strong as that of many of today's neoclassical economists. Typically, Marx draws conclusions about the aggregate social consequences of the actions of a host of individual rational capitalists operating in the context of particular historical social institutions. But, as Little sees it, these explanations operate only within a larger explanatory framework of "the logic of institutions," one that provides explanations in terms of the prominent social institutions of a particular place and era. In *Das Kapital*, Marx rarely takes pains to explain the origins of the social institutions he uses as part of his explanations, and he certainly does not bother to do so in terms of individual rational action, although Marx provided historical and structural explanations in his earlier and contemporary works of historical materialism.

Similarly, other theories of action—other accounts linking issues of agency and structure, of individual action and social causation, in a single explanatory framework—display a similar, limited commitment to methodological individualism. Consider the classics of sociology, Weber's account of the rise of capitalism or Parson's theory of modern society, as well as more contemporary theories like Giddens's account of the "structuration" of the link between the modern state and violence. As Chapter 6 by Douglas Nelson illustrates, even those who have elaborated game theory as a means of explaining concrete social action typically overcome an exclusive commitment to methodological individualism and offer supplementary explanations of real-world games in terms of concrete social structures, evolving norms, historically unique conjunctures, or culturally specific communities. The last part of Anatol Rapoport's (1962) classic, *Fights, Games, and Debates*, explained why this would be necessary long before orthodox IPE scholars began to think about iterated prisoners' dilemmas or two-level games.

Orthodox IPE displays a different attitude toward uniting explanations in terms of individual (or state as individual) rational actions with contextual, historical explanations in terms of concrete institutions and social wholes. Consider what is taken as common sense (as not necessary to argue about) about explanation in Stephen Krasner's (1982b) seminal essay, "Structural Causes and Regime Consequences: Regimes as Intervening Variables." The essay summarizes the explanatory schemes proffered in each of the essays in the volume that also contained Strange's critique, mentioned above (all the explanatory schemes except, perhaps significantly, the one employed by Strange). Regimes—which are historically specific, concrete, social institutions consisting of intersubjectively meaningful norms—can be "explained" as a consequence of the strategic interaction of rational individuals (pp. 195–200) and/or as influenced by (almost "logically entailed by") *broader* historically specific, concrete, social institutions, including intersubjectively meaningful norms (pp. 200–204). But Krasner, in this essay, is silent about the possibility that what we take as "individuals" and what we take as "rational" at any time could be explained as *constituted* by historically specific, concrete, social institutions. In contrast, the one thing that unites the different melanges of explanation provided by Marx, Weber, and Parsons (and anticipated by Rapoport) is an abandonment of methodological individualism in order to explain the historically contingent constitution of certain significant "rational individuals" (e.g., capitalists and modern states).

In the concluding essay of this important volume, Krasner (1982c) gets close to allowing this possibility, discussing sovereignty as "the constitutive principle of the existing international system," only to back away immediately with an explanation of "sovereignty" as a consequence of the strategic interaction of rational local governments in early-modern Europe (p. 508). The book closes by privileging explanations in terms of the rational action of individuals as "more conventional" (p. 510).

The craving of orthodox IPE scholars for ultimate explanations in the "conventional" form, explanations in terms of the rational actions of axiomatically given individuals, can lead to an extremely unproductive *mis*understanding of the explanatory schemes offered by scholars who do not share this urge—a misunderstanding evidenced even by the orthodox scholars who are the most open to other forms of explanation.

Consider Robert O. Keohane's (1988: 392) concatenation of a vast array of often contradictory, heterodox research traditions in IPE, many of which share a willingness to explain the social constitution of individual actors in a contextual and historical way. Keohane calls them all "reflectivist" and argues:

> The greatest weakness of the reflective school lies not in deficiencies in their critical arguments but in the lack of a clear reflective research program that could be employed by students of world politics. Waltzian neorealism has such a research program; so does the neoliberal institutionalism, which has focused on the evolution and impact of international regimes. Until the reflective school . . . [has] delineated such a research program . . . they will remain on the margins of the field, largely invisible to the preponderance of empirical researchers, most of whom explicitly or implicitly accept one or another version of the rationalist premises.

Our point, simply, is that there is not *a* unitary reflectivist research program in IPE any more than there is in the study of the emergence of capitalism where Marx and Weber, at least, developed different research programs. There are, in fact, a variety of research programs in IPE that do not share the explanatory predilections of neorealism or neoliberalism: There is Alker's program (1981) for investigating the dialectic of world orders, which differs fundamentally from Cox's (1987) world order research program rooted in historical materialism, which differs fundamentally from the more sociopsychological research program (equally rooted in historical materialism) exemplified by Benedict Anderson's (1983) and Partha Chatterjee's (1988) work on the political economy of nationalism, which differs from Giddens's (1981) neo-Weberian project exploring the economy of violence and the modern state, which differs from Bremer and Hughes's (1990) research program, also focusing on the state and violence, which only shares a distant relationship to Giddens's—going back to Weber through Karl Deutsch and Talcott Parsons.

Contesting Ideologies

This orthodox concatenation of differences among heterodox positions is supported by the range of explanations permitted along the third methodological dimension. Orthodox IPE explanation, and the core of theoretical activity, lies within the realm of the contest of three dominant ideologies, each of which is derived from a set of practices that, taken together, are seen as constituting an approximation of the totality of contemporary political life. Again, here we are not interested in the detailed interpretation of the possible content of the three ideologies (and any possible synthesis), but we are concerned to explore the reasons for and the implications of such a construction of theoretical activity.

Part of the impetus to configure IPE this way comes from the relationship that IPE as a set of practices has with the academic study of international relations and, in turn, the relationship that IR has with social and political science. Each field has in different ways "necessarily been exposed to the problems of enquiry and explanation that are general to the social sciences" (MacLean, 1981). This has meant coming to terms (or not coming to terms) with contemporary problems in the philosophy of social science, issues of scientific explanation, and the Kuhnian "shift" in thinking about the production of scientific knowledge. However, orthodox IPE has accommodated "paradigmatism" (Lapid, 1989) only to a limited extent. The incorporation of ideologies into IPE analysis has not been allowed (by practitioners of orthodoxy) to invalidate the positivist epistemological basis of IPE.

The shift to a conception of socially produced scientific knowledge, widespread in the early 1970s, was itself part of a broader change in understanding social forms. At the same time as its epistemological basis was being challenged, IR and its "new" subfield of IPE,[2] began to reflect an increased skepticism about the possibility of purely objective and scientific explanations. This skepticism was supported by changes in the articulation and perceived role of ideologies and values in the structure of the international political economy. In particular, ideology seemed important to many Western scholars and policymakers trying to understand the New International Economic Order (NIEO) and the "irrational" support given by Third World states to the Organization of Petroleum Exporting Countries. Given the speed and direction of change in the now global political economy of the 1970s, values clearly had to be taken into account in the process of generating explanation.

Orthodox IPE thus embraced ideologies as part of the reality of political economy: "Over the past century and a half, the ideologies of liberalism, nationalism and Marxism have divided humanity" (Gilpin, 1987: 25). Yet the way in which ideologies have been incorporated into orthodox IPE is itself contradictory. For one thing, ideologies are not allowed to explain anything fundamental in the realm of action in the world political economy. They only explain differences within the community that reflects on those actions. As Gilpin suggests, "It may not be an exaggeration to say that every controversy in the field of international political economy is ultimately reducible to differing conceptions of these relationships" (p. 25)—the relationships being society, state, and market. Yet, "these perspectives [ideologies] can neither be proved or disproved through logical argument or the presentation of contrary empirical evidence" (p. 41).

Thus, it would seem that if one were to say that Third World support for OPEC is explained by Third World acceptance of a particular ideology, one could not also conclude that Third World was "wrong." But remember, orthodox analysis accepts only an ideographic role for ideology, useful in terms of interpretation, but not an integral part of a material reality. Nor are ideologies an integral part of any orthodox attempt to *explain* that reality. Thus, for example, in the orthodoxy a statement such as, "From the liberal point of view, Third World support of OPEC was wrong," is allowed. It is the statement, "Third World ideology explains Third World action" that is not allowed. Instead the explanation must come from positing something like an egoistic interest in "state power" or "wealth" that is merely "masked" by an ideology that is fundamentally inexplicable because it is not one of the privileged three. Thus, having embraced and considered ideology, orthodox IPE consigns it to a peripheral role and continues to pursue a positivist conception of the place and ideas in the explanation of social life.

To further complicate this contradictory understanding of ideology: even though the orthodox position is that the ideologies can neither be refuted or validated (in accord with one interpretation of Kuhnian paradigms), one role of the ideologies in the production of positivist IPE knowledge is usually to suggest alternative hypotheses about the origins of some state of affairs—a notion that contradicts this particular interpretation of Kuhn. Despite statements like Gilpin's about the incommensurability of ideologies, the rhetoric of many contributions to IPE looks like a case being built that only one (or, sometimes, a combination of two) of the ideologies gives a more valid picture of the world.

The contradictory position of ideology in the explanatory framework of orthodox IPE is for us without doubt the most important feature of this configuration, but a number of other problems are also apparent. The delimitation of the arena of analytical discussion to the interpretation and contestation of the three identified ideologies not only privileges the substantive content of each ideology, it precludes other ideas. If other ideologies are ever considered, they are subordinated to the three privileged ideologies and considered only from their vantage point. Finally, each of the three—liberalism, nationalism, and Marxism—is treated as equivalent by orthodox IPE. The particular history of each, the social and political context of their emergence, are ignored.

The Issue Agenda of Orthodoxy

The issue agenda of orthodoxy shares the same genealogy as its methodological dimensions, but is not logically derived from its methodology. Here, the assumptions and values that give rise to a particular hierarchy out of concern are derived from a specific set of ideological and material conditions (a context that is also examined by Richard Higgott in Chapter 5). For us, orthodox IPE is articulated on the basis of the privileging of certain issues within a universe that is constructed so as to exclude a number of other important questions and issues.

The Universe of IPE

In a fairly straightfoward way, the construction of the universe of IPE reflects the policy concerns of the government of the United States throughout the era of U.S. global supremacy and, especially, contemporary concerns about various challenges to that supremacy. This is not a new observation, but it is still an important one. Moreover, the interpretation of problems located within the universe of orthodox IPE tends to reflect U.S. values. We do not argue that this is necessarily either good or bad, only that these values *must* be made explicit and be put on the global context, rather than be presented as scientific academic analysis that is universally applicable in space and time.

At a more abstract level the universe of orthodox IPE takes much of its form from the nature of post-1945 industrial society. As such as it presents a Western, male, privileged, and largely materialist view of the totality of the questions that IPE is (and should be) concerned with. It is not necessary to expand on these characteristics here, but only to note that the universe of IPE can be conceived of much more broadly than it is within the orthodox view. It is not just that the agenda of orthodox IPE does not include questions that come from challenging the orthodox definition, but that other values and perspectives are not even part of the universe within and against which orthodox analyses are located and evaluated.

One key assumption that forms an integral part of the universe of orthodoxy, and plays an important role in the maintenance of the orthodox, is the (presumed) distinction between what is labeled "economics" and what is labeled "politics." This distinction, derived from the emergence of an economics ideologically separated from political economy, is based on the definition of "economics" as the science investigating wealth production and distribution under scarcity, where wealth is somehow separate from "politics," and "politics" takes place where the realm of economics stops. In accepting this distinction, orthodox IPE has incorporated a peculiarly ahistorical conception of the relationship between politics and economics, one clearly derived from the political and ideological influences of liberalism in the eighteenth and nineteenth centuries. Such a distinction incorporated into IPE produces the analytical disjunction of a value-based political economy utilizing a closed set of economic techniques and analytical schemes.

Privileging Particular Issues

Within the specific universe of orthodox IPE, certain issues are privileged in a number of linked ways. First, in both theory and policy terms, the privileged issues are automatically assumed to be more important than other issues; therefore, other issues are marginalized. Second, the privileged issues form the constituted basis of evaluation for all other issues. In other words, the first question the analyst must address when confronting a nonprivileged issue (e.g., the significance of the uncompensated labor in both industrialized and less industrialized countries) becomes, "How does it affect————?" where the blank is filled in by privileged issues like "international trade" or "development." Third, overall explanation in IPE necessarily incorporates the processes and structures of these privileged issues and the actors associated with these issues.

The principal issue so privileged in orthodox IPE is trade. That this is the case partly reflects the prestige of economics as a discipline and the consequent incorporation of liberal economics into IPE. Liberal international economics is predicated on a view of the global political economy as an international economy of trading states. Consequently, liberal international economics has developed a tradition of elegant theorizing about trade relations, and it is on the basis of models of trade among states that other interactions in the world political economy are understood. That is, international economy is the principal structure, and the international economy is trade between and among national economies.

The assumption of the limitation of economic interaction among states to trade has been thoroughly discredited (Michalet, 1982) by the incorporation of international production into the analysis of the global political economy. However, as we might expect given the resistance of any orthodoxy to change, this seems to have had little impact upon the privileging of trade in IPE.

To explain the continuous privileging of trade we need to look at domestic political economy, particularly the domestic political economy of the United States. Trade, and especially trade in consumer goods, is highly visible within the common-sense, pluralist ways that much of the United States understands its politics. The visibility of the "trade issue" can easily be translated into political pressure by classes, sectors, and firms seeking to change government behavior, where government is perceived to be the mediator between the international economy and its results. Not surprisingly, therefore, as Nelson argues in Chapter 6, and elsewhere at greater length (Nelson, 1989a, b), U.S. postwar dominance of the world economy was predicated upon a unique, probably temporary, *de*politicization of the trade issue in domestic politics that gave the president control over making international trade policy. Similarly, and not surprisingly, those who fought for (and gained) executive control over the trade issue in the United States saw the problem of restructuring the world economy after World War II through the lens of that issue. As one senior Roosevelt administration official put it, "In the last analysis, every problem in the field of economic relations resolves itself into a problem of trade" (*U.S. Department of State Bulletin*, 10 October 1942: 821). At the time, this U.S. view was treated as strange, if not just a tiny bit ridiculous, by John Maynard Keynes and many of the other officials negotiating the postwar order for other states, where faith in liberal trade economics was not as great and where the lack of a domestic political system of divided power made unified economic policy a bit easier to achieve.[3]

In the era of contemporary orthodox IPE—the era of challenge to the postwar economic system under U.S. supremacy—concern about the U.S. executive's ability to "control" the trade issue has resurfaced. For government and politicians, trade is particularly suited as an issue in today's complex world economy: it directly affects specific groups, it can easily be identified and illustrated through the media, and it is one of the few aspects of the world economy that states can still control (to some extent) because trade involves the physical crossing of borders. Trade is a good common-sense issue. Moreover, because of these factors trade issues can be "won" in a narrow political sense.

A brief consideration of the U.S.-Japan trade issue makes the point well. The way in which the issue has been presented and debated both within the broader realm of U.S. political discussion as a whole, and within the narrower confines of orthodox IPE, clearly reflects the view examined above. However, if international production is included in the U.S.-Japan relationship, the significance of the trade imbalance is drastically reduced, particularly given the recent growth of Japanese inward investment in the United States. But public political concern is still with the trade figures, despite all the problems of measurement and interpretation, and orthodox IPE follows by treating the problem of maintaining a liberal or "open" world economy (in the face of the increasing political pressure for protection to reduce this imbalance) as a central issue for research. Cohen is quite accurate when he says, "International trade, of course, is one of the most central of the issue-areas explored in the IPE literature" (Cohen, 1990: 264), if the centrality of an issue is to be measured by the number of publications on the topic.

Orthodox IPE not only privileges trade as an issue, it presents a particular hierarchy of other, less-valued, issues. Again, one of the reasons for this is that IPE has taken the construction of its agenda largely from orthodox economics and initially translated this into the "politics of international economic relations," where the predefined universe of international economic relations provided the issues to be studied. An integral part of this hierarchy is the separation and subsumed role of security. Here both the concept and the practice of security are separated from issues of orthodox IPE (as the emergence of "strategic trade theory" goes some way to demonstrate). More significant is that the international political economy of security, Susan Strange's "security structure" (see Chapter 2) is often not a part of the analysis offered by orthodox IPE. Similarly, other issues, such as technological change, population dynamics, and resource depletion—the "master variables" in Choucri and North's (1975; North, 1990) integrative, but heterodox, and therefore less often cited, analysis of the international political economy of security—suffer subordinate status as a result of the privileged focus of orthodox IPE. This is somewhat ironic because changes in technology ("the division of labor") play a more fundamental role in Adam Smith's analysis than an open world trading system ("the extent of the market"). It is perhaps even more ironic that Smith's ultimate concern— fostering human dignity and the ethical life—appears even lower on the orthodoxy's hierarchy of issues.

Four Steps Beyond the Orthodoxy's Common Sense

Smith's views, needless to say, significantly predate today's orthodoxy and the problems of the era of challenge to U.S. supremacy. To recognize that there is a new IPE that shares some of Smith's concerns is to recognize that today's orthodoxy represents a break in a longer tradition. The new IPE has begun to develop in reaction to the contemporary orthodoxy's inability to provide persuasive explanations for much that goes on in the world political economy now, as well as much of what has gone on before the present era. Explanations, if they do nothing else, should illuminate more than common sense does. But the explanations we can produce through the orthodoxy often fail that simple test. Sometimes they fail because the orthodoxy does not let us raise issues. Orthodox IPE, for example, can say nothing more than common sense can about the pursuit of the ethical life because that is not constructed as an issue of IPE. Orthodox IPE can say very little more than common sense can about the primary questions about the global political economy raised by most people—questions of dependency, fundamental insecurity, powerlessness, and, above all, the question of how to identify opportunities for fundamental change. The orthodoxy can say very little about these questions, in great part because it has few organic links to those who would raise them.

The first three steps taken by practitioners of a new IPE quickly overcome these particular limitations of scope and audience. The chapters in this volume by Strange, Gill, Johnston, Ofuatey-Kodjoe, and Tickner all illustrate the first step. All reject the orthodox hierarchy of IPE issues. Trade and the management of an "open" trading system do not become the primary focus of their political economy.

The same can even be said for the authors in this volume whose chapters concentrate on the trade issue (Tussie, Higgott, and Nelson). They join the other authors in taking what is a logical next step: rejecting or ignoring the orthodoxy's means of constructing the universe of issues of IPE. All the authors are suspicious of the ultimate usefulness (for explanation) of an ahistorical distinction between politics and the economy. All contextualize and recognize the historical specificity of the particularly "American" cultural values, which have had such an impact on the institutions of the contemporary world political economy (and on orthodox IPE).

For a number of the authors, taking this second step was necessitated simply because the questions they wanted to answer were simply not part of the U.S. policy agenda. Recognition of that fact led many to ask about the implicit purposes served by the orthodoxy, and by their own analysis, a third step beyond the orthodoxy. Thus, for example, Higgott explicitly recognizes a connection between his own "antipodean" perspective on IPE and the issues central to Australians that is similar to the connection between orthodox IPE and the U.S. policy agenda. The difference is that Higgott's self-consciousness of this connection allows him to see the problems of objectivity that practitioners of the orthodoxy often ignore.

Such self-consciousness can lead heterodox scholars to contemplate a fourth step beyond the orthodoxy: the step of confronting the deeper epistemological difficulties with orthodox methodology. Each of the three methodological dimensions presents its own key problem, and some of the problems have been confronted in more than one way.

First there is the problem of trying to maintain positivism's incoherent distinction between subject and object in order to achieve objectivity—the guarantee that the scholarly community's work actually is truth seeking and not just a strategic attempt to persuade others (or itself) of a preconceived position. Many of those who practice a new IPE offer an alternative guarantee of truth seeking: their self-conscious identification with a group that has compelling interest in transforming the world political economy. The feminist scholar, the Marxist scholar, or the scholar organically connected to the periphery of the world economy *needs* to understand the world in order to change it. Thus, those who practice a new IPE reflect multiple sources of objectivity, rather than the orthodoxy's one (often unrecognized) real guarantee of truth seeking—its commitment to order, to management, to maintaining certain aspects of world political economy as they were in the heyday of U.S. supremacy. Taken together, scholars constructing a new IPE can be thought of as resolving the problem of objectivity in a way that individual postmodernist scholars, such as Deborah Johnston in this volume, try to do by themselves—by recognizing and reflecting multiple "interested" points of view, by giving voice to many voices.

Criticism of orthodox IPE along its second methodological dimension has also yielded multiple voices sharing an underlying unity: specifically, a willingness to investigate and try to explain the contingent historical social construction of agents or actors, which, at other times, may be treated as axiomatic in explanations in terms of individual rational choice.

Agreement upon the admissability of contextual, social, and historical explanations does not, however, mean agreement on specific explanations of specific historical phenomena, as is illustrated by the essays in this *IPE Yearbook*. For example, Tussie's characterization of the postwar trade system and her account of its origins differs significantly from Nelson's. What indicates that they are part of the same enterprise (and that it is an enterprise that differs from the IPE orthodoxy) is the similar way in which both authors would handle a critique of the other's position, and the similar way in which they respond to the problems along the third methodological dimension of orthodoxy. We have evidence in their chapters that Nelson would *not* try to squeeze Tussie's argument into one of the ill-fitting boxes of theory—liberal, Marxist, or realist—nor would Tussie try to do the same with Nelson's argument. This is not because they both inhabit the same box[4]; they simply do not use those categories as a way of limiting what they need to understand about different social scientists' arguments, theories, or research programs.

Accepting, and not trying to reduce, the diversity of research programs, theories, and arguments that IPE scholars actually offer does lead, almost immediately, to confronting a central issue of postpositivist philosophy of science: the problem of inherent limits to communication across research programs. None of the heterodox positions represented in this volume solves every aspect of that problem. No author tries, for example, to argue that the particular point of view that guarantees his or her objectivity should guide all IPE; none suggests that his or her key issues should be everyone else's. All, however, do appear to have implicit faith that open discussion in common language can to lead to wide agreement on matters of shared interest.

Three of the chapters (Strange's, Gill's, and Nelson's) point to or provide different conceptual schemes that can serve as ways of integrating knowledge across research programs and across disciplines. What Nelson's presentation of game theory, Gill's presentation of different versions of Gramscian historical materialism, and Strange's presentation of her own, consciously eclectic, theoretical synthesis have in common is a desire to provide a common language in which the insights of otherwise separate research traditions can be preserved. They also make clear that their ultimate aim is not the development of one, unitary, all-encompassing theory of international political economy. Rather, their aim is to support multiple points of synthesis among different perspectives.

This aspiration reflects both the philosophical approach of the emerging new IPE as well as a particular "culture" that differs from that of the orthodoxy. The same can be said of each of the other typical solutions that practitioners of a new IPE offer to the epistemological problems that emerge along each of the orthodoxy's methodological dimensions. Earlier we argued that the IPE orthodoxy cannot be identified solely with a particular range of theories and empirical referents, but that we must look for a distinct philosophical approach that, together with a particular range of theories and empirical referents, forms a specific *culture* of orthodoxy. The same can be said of the emerging new international political economy. In fact, it is the philosophical approach and culture that distinguish this new IPE the most, because those who practice a new IPE share a culture of openness to different theories and empirical referents. What the new IPE demands in return is an increased theoretical consciousness and a more direct confrontation with the theoretical foundations of the field, as well as greater reflection in the social constitution of IPE knowledge itself. Finally, and perhaps most significantly, the culture shared by the heterodox positions that make up a new IPE not only values openness, it equally values honest attempts at synthesis and judges them by both their ability to preserve older insights and their ability to truly explain more than common sense.

Notes

1. We assume that Cohen is being ironic when he suggests that it is the real world that needs to correspond to theory rather than the reverse.

2. That IPE was a "new" subfield of IR developed in the late 1960s or early 1970s is a widespread belief held by both orthodox and heterodox scholars (see, e.g., Strange, 1988: 20). In some ways that is true: today's organizations of scholars studying IPE date from that time, as do most IPE degree programs or specialties in IR degree programs. However, accepting that history without comment may help reinforce the practice of contemporary orthodoxy. Adam Smith was certainly "doing" IPE in the 1770s. Closer to the present, UNESCO's predecessor, the International Institute of Intellectual Cooperation, supported a series of studies of "the international political economy of peace," all but forgotten by IR scholars who came to maturity in the cold war years. The economic problems of the late 1960s and early 1970s, exemplified by the end of the fixed exchange rate system and by the oil crises, triggered the reinvention of IPE within the institutions that have become the most significant centers of the orthodoxy.

3. See Murphy (1984: 13–40).

4. In *Distinction*, Pierre Bourdieu (1985) investigates the vast human capacity to make common-sense distinctions like the placing of arguments into the orthodoxy's three boxes. He suggests that capacity is almost unbounded. Thus, we would hazard a guess that IPE scholars could "code" Nelson's and Tussie's work into the three boxes and, furthermore we have a good guess as to how they would be coded. Nelson would be a liberal and Tussie would be either a realist or a Marxist. The point of Bourdieu's analysis is to illustrate that such

codings into closed-ended schemes always turn out to be invidious, if only due to their attenuated cognitive links to other codings in which the hierarchy of values is more explicit. This, as Bourdieu illustrates, is one (often invisible) way that common sense serves to maintain the legitimacy of other social structures. Within the discourse community of practitioners of orthodox IPE, boxing Nelson and Tussie as liberal versus realist/Marxist would privilege Nelson and fit appropriately with other distinctions that are part of orthodox common sense: "American" IPE is better than "non-American" IPE, economists are better than other social scientists, and so on. We easily move beyond the orthodoxy when we become skeptical of such distinctions and when we compare contributions to IPE on their own terms.

2

An Eclectic Approach

Susan Strange

Stage 1: Openness to Insights from Many Disciplines

Some years ago I wrote the preface to an edited collection of essays called *Paths to International Political Economy*, in which I argued strongly for openness in the development of what was then still seen as a new branch of international relations (Strange, 1984). In reaction to the fencing off of the social sciences into smaller and smaller *chasses gardees*, each reserved for specialized insiders, I suggested that the study of international political economy would do well to stay as an open range, like the old Wild West, accessible—as the classical study of political economy had been—to literate people of all walks of life, from all the professions and all political proclivities. At all costs it must avoid the narrowness of much neoclassical economics and econometrics, which was apt to produce, as the late Lord Robbins said, nothing but "a lot of one-eyed monsters"—one-eyed because they were oblivious of politics; monsters because they were so arrogant towards all outsiders.

That preface was written through a fortunate (and fruitful) association with a demographer, a trade diplomat, an international lawyer, an economic historian, and colleagues in international relations who had specialized, respectively, in technology, ecology, monetary history, and theory. My plea for openness was reinforced by the experience of writing international monetary history to which the insights of commercial and central bankers had contributed more than books on monetary theory.

Stage 2: An Open Conceptual Synthesis

Being open to the concerns and insights of a variety of disciplines and professions, however, I now regard as only the first step in the development of a truly eclectic approach to international political economy. The next step was to find a way to effect a synthesis of some kind, to provide some unifying concepts that would allow connections to be made and dialogues to be begun between the disciplines. A decade of teaching experience in Great Britain, the United States, and Italy suggested how this might be done and why it needed to be done. The conventionally accepted paradigm of the politics of international economy relations (PIER) was where I had started teaching in London in the early 1960s. As I had soon discovered, it was—and still is—far too narrrow and stultifying (Spero, 1985; Blake and Walters, 1976; Gilpin, 1987)

There were three reasons for taking this second step. The first was that to define the subject in the conventional way too often meant limiting it, consciously or unconsciously, to consideration of those issues considered important and worth debating by governments in their relations with other governments. The second reason was to introduce into the field a serious discussion of ends as well as of means. In view of the overwhelming weight of numbers of U.S. as opposed to, say, Soviet or Latin American scholars in the field, the PIER approach encouraged students to take as given the policy goals, together with their underlying assumptions about value-preferences, favored by U.S. policymakers in and out of government. The "alternative" concerns and value preferences of Third World scholars, or feminists, or environmentalists, or radicals of any kind were automatically ruled out of order. The third reason was the crying need (of students more than teachers) for some analytical framework that would end the mutual isolation of the three standard paradigms of international relations, which so far had produced only a dialogue of the deaf.

I thought I had found this in the notion of enveloping structures that, rather than the overt conscious decision or action of any actor in the system, set the agendas and determined the range of options within which states and other groups and individuals contested all the major who-gets-what issues of politics, both within the state and in the world economy. This notion developed from Marxist, or in Robert Cox's case, Gramscian, perceptions of the importance in international political economy of the relations of production as an important determinant of power relations (Cox, 1987). It was fairly obvious that whoever or whatever determined what was to be produced by what combination of labor, land, capital, and technology; by what productive methods; where; and on what sort of terms and conditions for the workers was exercising structural power. And that this structural power was often more decisive than the outcome of relational bargaining—between management and unions, for example, or between producers and their distributors or subcontractors—for such bargaining took place only within a certain social, economic, and political context of market demand for the factors of production and for the product.

The who-gets-what implications of power over the nature of the production structure were obvious enough. Moreover, unlike the liberal paradigm, this structural analysis could just as easily be applied to relations of production in noncapitalist states (Solzhenytsin's *A Day in the Life of Ivan Denisovitch*, besides its literary value, would make an excellent case study of complex power relationships among a team of construction workers).

What has been much less obvious to IPE scholars, even those to the right of Cox, Michalet, or Gill and Law, was the structural power exercised by whoever or whatever determined the financial structure, especially the relations between creditors and debtors, savers and investors (Michalet, 1982; Gill and Law, 1988). This had been impressed on me by work for two commissioned pieces of research: one on the politics of a declining international currency (Strange, 1971) and the other on the politicoeconomic history of international monetary relations among developed countries in the the 1960s (Strange, 1976).

By the financial structure, I mean something different from what is usually described as the international monetary regime, which refers to the arrangements that govern relationships between national currencies. By the financial structure, I mean the system under which credit is created, allocated, and put to use. When I say, "whoever or whatever determined the financial structure," I am deliberately inferring that, in a capitalist system in which the use of money is fully developed, the "whatever" may well be a market rather than a government or an international organization. This is important because it then raises the question of who made (or unmade) the rules for the buyers and sellers and the intermediaries in that market. In the early 1970s, I once wrote a long-lost paper for an International Studies Association conference on the Eurodollar market as an actor in the international political economy. I suspect that few of the listeners understood the point of the paper. It was that the U.S. and British governments, by allowing the growth of the Eurocurrency markets in London in the 1960s, had enlarged the profit-making opportunities for international banks—at that time predominantly British or U.S. owned and based with only a few Dutch, German, and Swiss banks among them. Without deliberately intending to do so, these two governments had also incidentally been the midwives at the birth of a new factor in the financial structure, one that not only affected the who-gets-what in it but also increased the instability and volatility of exchange rates between currencies, thus affecting the trade-off of values in the production structure.

The winners from this financial innovation had been the banks as intermediaries; the depositors—at first corporate and later individuals—who could get a higher price for the money they lent; and the borrowers—mostly transnational corporations but also developing countries who were able for the first time to get access to credit in large amounts anonymously and without restraining political strings attached. This was a newfound freedom that all appreciated, although not all used wisely. The price was an increased vulnerability, not to any one actor in the conventional sense, but to the market and its vagaries. And this new actor—the market—did not exist in a political vacuum but would respond much more strongly to choices and policy changes made by the U.S. government than it did to choices and policies made by, say, the German government. For example, it responded very strongly to the decision of the Reagan Administration to change its policies for financing government spending by switching from monetary management by price to management by supply. At that point the line-up of winners and losers was changed, not by direct action of the U.S. government but indirectly and usually unintentionally, via the global financial structure. The indebted developing countries became the losers, whereas the banks who might also have been losers were saved from the financial disaster they had courted through their extravagant lending by the intervention of governments—the U.S. government in Mexico and the Japanese government in Korea.

As for the system, the structural power exercised over the international financial structure certainly shifted the preferred trade-off of values and their allocation among different interest groups. The system suffered some loss of security and stability, and also of equity inasmuch as the debtors were made to suffer substantially more than the creditor banks and as their freedom of choice was constrained whereas that of the banks was, on the whole, enlarged, for example, by such innovations as leveraged buy-outs (LBOs), junk bond issues, and debt-equity swaps.

No less important for a nonpartisan analysis of the who-gets-what questions in the international political economy are two other major structures; they, too, powerfully influence both the trade-off of values for the system as a whole and their allocation among interest groups, whether national or transnational. They are the security structure and the knowledge structure. Both have also been subject to change—change that shuffled and redealt the cards for the actors, redistributing such bargaining power as they had in dealing with each other and changing the degree and the nature of their vulnerability to the system. The security structure underwent sudden, unpredicted, and fundamental change, dramatically epitomized by the fall of the Berlin Wall, and rhetorically dramatized—perhaps overdramatized—as "the end of history." The security structure based on the balance of aggressive, destructive military power between the United States and the Soviet Union suddenly became an asymmetric security structure in which the risks to security within both of the superpower states became greater for individuals, and the risks to individuals from conflict between the superpowers became markedly less.

This security structure, by the way, accords with a good deal of current rethinking among scholars in strategic studies about the nature and definition of security. As states are obliged by popular pressures to show concern for food security, for energy security, even for environmental security, and to act accordingly in their domestic as well as their external policymaking, the value of the concept of a global or transnational security structure becomes clearer. It is both more flexible and less state-centered than the international political system, which Cox has characterized as the significant intervening variable between the relations of production in the world economy and the individual state (Cox, 1987).

The fourth—last, but not least—structure within which relational power is exercised, bargains are struck, and who-gets-what is finally decided is the realm of ideas, or, as I called it in *States and Markets* (Strange, 1988), the knowledge structure. By that I meant to combine two rather different structural phenomena: At the abstract level there are the belief systems and their associated value preferences that inhibit or validate some kinds of actions rather than others. A good illustration of the dynamics of this realm of ideas is to be found in John Mueller's *Retreat from Doomsday* (1989). Whether or not you accept his conclusion about the obsolescence of major war, the two historical case studies he includes—of dueling and slavery—are both excellent illustrations of the dynamic power of ideas over actions and choices, and thus over bargaining relationships. A more recent one in which structural authority has been exercised not by states, for once, but by scientists is the shift in the primacy of values in the exploitation of natural energy resources. Instead of efficiency in the production of wealth as the prime consideration guiding policy choices, scientists have told governments they should look instead to the protection of the environment from pollution and global warming. And governments in response to public opinion are beginning, reluctantly and perhaps too slowly, to act accordingly; their choices in policymaking have been shifted by the dynamics of power based on legitimate authority, within the knowledge structure.

But besides this abstract level of ideas, the knowledge structure can also be seen as a source of structural power at the practical or operational level; this is no less important for some bargaining relationships than the abstract level. For when systems of accumulating, storing, or communicating information change, the change is apt to have a direct and sometimes quite a substantial effect on the bargaining power of actors as well as on the prioritized values of the system. Who or what decides what kind of information shall be collected or discovered, how it is to be stored, and to whom and by what means it may be communicated exercises no less important a form of structural power than that exercised within the production structure or the financial structure.

At the operational level the technologies that are collectively described as "the information revolution" have taken away from governments their former control by censorship and their former monopoly power through state ownership and operation of postal, telephone, and telegraph services, and have given it to private corporate actors of various kinds. The former system of state-dominated communications was—within certain limits set by states—accessible to the rich and poor alike at prices that were often progressively subsidized for the sake of social cohesion; however the new structures of transnational and intranational communication—telephone calls, both local and intercontinental are a typical example—shift bargaining power in favor of the rich and powerful at the expense of the poor and weak consumer.

Here technology has been a more dynamic force for structural change than either the actions of states in the international political system or the condition of markets. It is technology that has altered both the trade-off in values for the system and the allocation of values within the structures—more wealth for producers and some consumers through more but cheaper communications, and less equality and less security for states.

Thus, if we draw a diagram to represent stage 2 (as I see it) in the evolution of an eclectic analytical framework for the study of IPE, it might look like Figure 2.1. Two other major factors, technology and markets, both exogenous to the international political system, are added to states (for short) as the determinants of change in the major structures. These four major structures are the intervening variables affecting the range of options open to states, firms, labor unions, or others. It is not therefore determinist, in the way in which much past social science has been. But it does represent the ways in which structural change in the international political economy can weight the dice for those who make choices.

In Figure 2.1, the three major sources of structural change—and thus of who gets what—have been drawn as equal circles. But in the example mentioned of the information revolution, it was said that technology was a more dynamic source of change than either markets or states. So perhaps for that example, the third circle should have been drawn larger, or its arrows made bolder than those of the other two. Similarly, when we consider the end of the cold war, the larger circles might be states because, as most people would agree, the system of states in which there is a duopoly of the superpowers is the predominant source of change.

In other situations, such as U.S. trade relations with Japan, for example, it might be that the markets circle would be larger, having a dominant dynamic effect through demand for, among other things, Japanese semiconductors, cars, motorcycles, cameras, on so forth.

A more complicated diagram could also show some feedback loops from the four structures to each of the circles, to the system of states, to markets, and to technology. It also would be more realistic to show the four structures as overlapping with each other, capable of interacting and of mutually supporting or counterbalancing each other. But for the present purposes, the simplified diagram is sufficient to make my point, which is to show how the choices of actors—whether governments; corporate enterprises; social classes; age, sex, or occupational groups; or just individual human beings—have the range of choices open to them determined by the basic structures of the international political economy and how the system of states is not the prime

Figure 2.1 Determinants of Choice

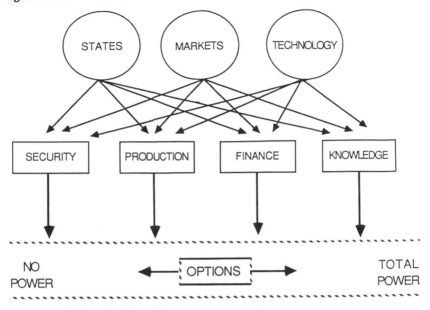

factor, the sole source of significant change, that the PIER writers tend to assume it to be.

Because the intellectual roots of so many writers in the IPE field have been in the study of international relations, informed by a realist perception of the international system, their attentions have focused on the power relations of states, and have ignored the two exogenous factors of technology and markets. Technological change can rob a country of demand for its exported products. It may be that chemicals replace guano as fertilizer, or that optic fibers capture the market in power supplies from copper, or that corn syrup or artificial sweeteners replace sugar in soft drinks and cakes. In each case, the comparative advantage of the producers within a market economy is gravely reduced, risks are incurred in the process of adjustment to the change, and costs and benefits are redistributed. Technical change can also affect security structures based on a particular balance of military power between states. Or it can affect the balance of power in the financial structure between state regulators on one side and innovative banks on the other—as when the automated systems of money transfer (ASMT) made obsolete the restriction on interstate banking imposed by the New Deal administration under the Glass-Steagall Act in the 1930s, especially when such transfers were conducted by nonbanks like Sears Roebuck or American Express.

Market forces can also alter bargaining situations even without the intervention of any new technology. Oversupply and surplus productive capacity can—and have—robbed cartels of their oligopoly power, just as shortage in the face of rising demand has conferred unexpected bargaining power on the very same producers. It did just that, for instance, in the 1971–1973 period for the foreign exchange earnings of the oil producing states and (although much less fuss was made about it) for the profits of the oil companies. Then, later in the 1980s, market forces again robbed the OPEC states of their bargaining power. The oil companies, however, had prudently resorted to diversification and had thus made themselves less vulnerable than the OPEC states to the same market forces.

Mention of oil reminds us that a good deal of the best empirical work in IPE in the last decade or so has been done at the sectoral level: Cafruny (1987) for shipping, Frieden (1987) for banking, and Mikdashi (1976) for oil, among many others. All such sectoral studies have an important bearing on theory, sometimes overlooked by pure theorists. Each of the above authors, and many others, serve to endorse and underscore the contention that although some states have power consciously or unconsciously to shape structures, so do technology and markets. The resulting structures can then create an environment within which states bargain with each other but also within which governments bargain internally with interest groups (social, political and economic), and within which political, and economic interest groups contest the arenas of policy.

Stage 3: The Role of Firms

It was indeed awareness of the great effect of market forces and of technological change that explains why I think that stage 2 is only a necessary step on the way to stage 3. In this stage, an important part in the evolution of an eclectic approach to IPE is played by recognition of the role of firms in the evolution of structures and of both partners and adversaries of states in a variety of bargaining relationships. Firms are becoming important to states both in alliance with governments and in conflict and competition with them. This seems to me a necessary—although possibly not always a sufficient—condition for the mental liberation of the next generation of IPE scholars from the restrictive corset of the state-centered PIER version of IPE.

I shall therefore try to explain why we need to look at IPE from the standpoint of the enterprise as well as that of the state or the class (political or occupational—that is, as peasants, pilots, sailors, or computer programmers) or the gender, or indeed, the generation.

The need for a framework of structures is still there, as well as for a method of analysis that makes the researcher ask questions about the value mix or trade-off produced by the structures and about the distribution of values and entitlements to them among individuals, groups, and institutions, including states.

What has happened in the second half of the twentieth century is an acceleration of structural changes that were at first referred to as interdependence. This was misleading because the interdependence also was not at all symmetrical; and it was imprecise because the loss of control by the state was not so much a loss to other states as to a world market economy under much less political control than national economies had been in the past. What had really happened that was in the long run more significant was that the name of the game for most states and for an ever larger number of economic enterprises had changed. The name of the new game was competition for world market shares. Only by winning and holding on to a good share of world markets for high value-added goods and services could the governments of states—or the management of firms—survive successfully. As the civil revolutions of Eastern and Central Europe have dramatically shown, governments will not survive long if they have not somehow made sure that the national economy is able to earn or borrow enough foreign exchange to pay for the imports of capital goods, of raw materials, and of technology necessary to maintain economic growth and higher material standards of living. Popular demand insists on material improvement and on political participation sufficient to prevent (among other things) the undue appropriation of the national product by the *nomenklatura*. Thresholds of tolerance for elitist privilege, for ethnic discrimination, for denial of free speech and free association, and even for social and economic inequality will be lowered when growth rates are poor and raised when they are good. South Korea, Malaysia, Singapore, or Taiwan are none of them above political criticism. Only fast economic growth has extended the political life of their ruling groups.

The imperative necessity of production and sales beyond the market provided by the territory of the state is much better understood in the world of business than among scholars in international relations. A whole literature has been devoted to explaining the rapid growth of the phenomenon of international production: Vernon (1977), Meyer (1978), Michalet (1976), Drucker (1986), Stopford (1972), and Dunning (1985). But much of it got off on the wrong foot by assuming that off-shore production was a U.S. phenomenon and that it was primarily driven by the pursuit of greater wealth through the maximization of profit. Rent was to be derived from the comparative advantage or advantages developed within the firm and extracted first from the national and then from foreign markets. Vernon's product cycle theory gained very wide currency and held it even after its weak points had been exposed.

Now it is clear that international production is a global phenomenon and that there are European, Japanese, and Third World multinationals as well as U.S.-based ones; and the driving force pushing enterprises into it is the fear of extinction for the firm that fails to produce and sell on a wider-than-national market. It is the search for security more than the pursuit of profit that motivates firms to engage in international production. By 1985, the estimated total of international production—that is, the value of goods and services produced according to a global strategy and sold outside the territory of the home economy—for the first time exceeded the value of international trade—that is, goods and services exchanged across national frontiers between buyers and sellers whatever their individual nationality. (Much international trade, varying from a quarter to a half of recorded trade, it should be remembered, is intrafirm trade, which means that buyer and seller belong to an enterprise with a common national headquarters.)

Three major structural changes have made it imperative that all sorts of enterprises that hitherto were content to sell their goods or services locally now seek to secure a niche on global markets. They range from art dealers and management consultants to fast food franchisers, fashion designers, construction companies, and producers of such specialized sporting goods as skis and tennis racquets.

The first structural change was in the methods of production and its fundamental cause was the nature and the accelerated pace of technological change—a feature of the knowledge structure, you could say. Accelerating technical change meant that each new manufacturing plant, each new advance in agricultural production, each operating system in a service industry, cost more in real terms than the one it replaced and was destined to become obsolete in less time. It cost more because technology was devoted to the replacement of uncapitalized (i.e., unskilled) labor with capital, whether in the form of machinery or of human capital and information. Technology allowed—indeed demanded—a change in the organic composition of capital. In many sectors this has raised the barriers to new entrants and preserved the interests of established enterprises.

The second structural change was in the greater transnational mobility of capital, making it far easier for the foreign-owned firm (FOF) to get ready access to the capital needed to keep up in the technical race in whatever country it chose to locate all or part of its production process. Of course, capital had always been far freer to move than labor, inhibited as it had been for half a century by immigration controls. But the changes in international banking and the integration of Western capital markets, beginning in the 1960s, extended in the 1970s, and consolidated in the 1980s, had made the process of investing abroad so much easier, quicker, and cheaper that the enlargement of the number of players in the competitive game for market shares has taken place with breathtaking speed.

Third, there have been changes in transport and communication, both of which were a necessary condition for the execution of global strategies by corporate managers. The significance of falling real costs of transport—for example, of air freight across the Pacific—have been generally overlooked or underestimated by international political economists. A part of the benefit of technical change in communications (satellites, computers, and fax machines) undoubtedly went to international business. At the same time, some part also stuck to the fingers of the operating firms. Maintaining a quiet cartel arrangement among themselves, these firms—some state-owned, some private—made record profits for 1989: a 22 percent increase over the previous year for Mobile Communications Corporation of America and a 12 percent increase for AT&T (*New York Times*, April 19, 1990; *Financial Times*, April 2, 1990).

Each of these three structural changes, in my estimation, owes a good deal to policy decisions of states—especially the United States, which initiated both financial deregulation and telephone communication deregulation while giving strong financial support through the space program to satellite development. These are not, of course, the only factors; the role of television in increasing transnational awareness of growing divergence in material standards of living is just one of the other subsidiary contributing factors. But these are the three that were both necessary and sufficient to explain the convergence of states and of enterprises in the same overlapping game of competition for world market shares.

The result has been to add two new dimensions to the practice of diplomacy in the international political economy. Besides the familiar interstate negotiating—some of it played in multilateral organizations like the International Monetary Fund (IMF) or the United Nations, but most of it still played on a one-to-one basis of bilateral bargaining—there are now two equally important kinds of transnational diplomacy. One is the diplomacy between governments and firms; the other is the diplomacy conducted between firms (see Figure 2.2).

In order to gain and hold a share of the world market for goods and services, governments have had, increasingly, to bargain with firms. This is no longer an imperative confined to bargaining over the exploitation of natural resources by an FOF. There the bargaining between states and oil companies, or copper or aluminum companies, has a long and well-documented history. Now states also have to negotiate with FOFs in most sectors of industrial manufacturing and services. Such bargaining forms part of national industrial policy—even when, as in the United States, the bargaining is conducted more at the local or state than at the federal level. For many states, industrial policymaking is more critical than foreign policymaking. A government must negotiate over the conditions by which it gives market access to the FOF, and over the conditions by which the enterprise collaborates in supporting and furthering macroeconomic or macrosocial policies. For example, FOFs get better bargains from the Malaysian government if they conform positively to the new economic policy goal of encouraging *bumiputra* (ethnic preference) enterprises in services and manufacturing.

Figure 2.2 Dimensions of Diplomacy

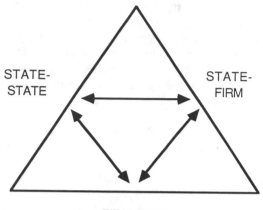

The state also has to negotiate with its own national enterprises. Governments are no longer in quite the same authoritative position to dictate where national firms shall locate their production nor even how much tax should be paid; on both counts, the firm often has other options. And although the negotiating process takes place within global structures, it is also much affected by the domestic structures of its host governments. Some recent collaborative research I have been doing with John Stopford and a great deal of contemporary work by the World Bank and other international organizations, as well as by independent development economists, has stressed the importance to the partner-firm of the infrastructural efficiency of the host country. This involves not just the efficiency of its transport and communications systems but equally the efficiency of its educational system and its administrative competence in processing requests for, for example, import licenses or profit remittances.

The result of getting involved in this second dimension of diplomacy for the state is substantial, greatly complicating the calculation of costs and benefits, of risks and opportunities that have to be weighed against each other in the making of state policy. But the importance of such negotiations should be abundantly evident to anyone who has followed the economic and financial news over the past decade. The importance to Colonel Gaddafi, for instance, of his alliance with Occidental is hard to overestimate. For Fiat, the "old alliance" with the Soviet Union is one of the few strong cards it still holds in the fight to hold off not only Japanese competition but also its European rivals, Volkswagen and Ford. Matsushita's contribution to Malaysian development has not been without costs to the government, as has

Nissan's contribution to the British economy. In some situations, it is the firm that holds the whiphand; in others, the state.

Moreover, the influence that firms now have on government policy as they wake up to the imperative of fighting their competitors for world market shares is not to be doubted. To take just two examples, we see the intervention of firms in pressing the South African National Party to do an about-turn on apartheid, and we see European firms pushing the European Community toward the creation of a single European market. In the first case, the divestment by U.S. firms in South Africa took effect only when the Big 4 South African trusts, hit by the massive devaluations of the rand and the closing of foreign markets to South African citrus, wine, and other exports, decided that apartheid was too great a handicap in their own efforts to develop world market, as well as national market, shares. Similarly, the push for a single European market undoubtedly came not just from commission officials and ambitious politicians like Jacques Delors but more significantly from an organized pressure group of twenty or so major European companies who began, about 1984, to threaten that their new investments would go outside Europe unless they could anticipate faster progress toward a real common market at home. And in Canada, the fears of Canadian manufacturing firms and Quebec-based banks of being shut out of the rich U.S. market and facing Japanese competition alone certainly played a part in getting the U.S.-Canadian Free Trade Agreement accepted in Ottawa.

The change in political attitudes brought about by the interest of firms in developing a global strategy with which to hold their competitors at bay has also been noted in developing countries. When the UN Centre on Transnational Corporations (UNCTC) was set up in New York in the early 1970s at the request of the Group of 77 developing countries, it saw its role as the hammer of the multinationals. Its first report (UNCTC, 1973) was highly critical of the failure of firms to transfer technology, of their practice of transfer pricing, and of their lack of commitment to the long-term economic development of their Third World hosts. Its fourth report (UNCTC, 1988) is almost an apologia for the transnational corporations (TNCs). Pointing out that their relations with their host had become "much less conflictual" over the past decade, it argued that the contribution of TNCs to development was not to be judged by their foreign investment alone. Some developing countries already had benefited, and others could also benefit from nonequity arrangements by TNCs, whether by producing for them under license or subcontracting to produce components. In either case, there was some transfer of technology and some job creation as well as the most important gain—a foothold in foreign markets.

Meanwhile, the third dimension of the new global diplomacy is that conducted between enterprises. The increased costs of product development, building distribution systems, and the increased specialization of technical experts led in the 1980s to a veritable spate of corporate alliances. To any scholar brought up in international relations, these seemed strikingly similar in many respects to the alliances formed by states. Allies have typically always been competitors as well as cooperators. Alliances crumbled if common threats disappeared. Within alliances, fierce arguments developed over the allocation of risks and costs, over who should lead and who should follow. Some were proposed but never consummated. Some underwent subtle change as the balance of bargaining power shifted from one side to the other. Some were issue-specific; and some were merely temporary collaboration for a particular purpose. It is just the same with the corporate alliances of the late 1980s—Daimler-Benz and Mitsubishi, AT&T and Olivetti, Vitro and Anchor Glass in opposition to Corning, AT&T and Sun Microsystems, Honda and British Leyland. The list is long, and growing, and the mix of failures and successes much as it always has been in interstate relations.

Implications for the Study and Teaching of IPE

Although some political scientists have begun to perceive the significance of the changing roles and goals of states, there has been much less attention among most economists or in business schools to the significance of the "foreign relations" of the firm. Rosecrance (1986) wrote of the rise of the trading state in place of the territorial state. Cerny (1982) wrote with more awareness of the importance of industrial policies of the "competition state." But in the literature developed in and used by the business schools, these new interfirm relations are poorly researched and analyzed. Theories of the firm, like theories of the state, are essentially inward looking. They ask how "the firm" functions and what motivates its management to act as it does. This reflects a body of theoretical literature built around two basic hypotheses: the enterprise operates as a hierarchy and the hierarchy's use of power is justified by the end to which it is put, which is the maximization of profit for the enterprise, enhanced, if possible, by internalizing benefits and externalizing costs. By this means the managers, the shareholders, and the workers could acquire wealth and security. Whether consumers too would benefit was of little concern to business schools, although this has received some attention from economists interested in oligopoly and contestable markets.

Very little attention has therefore been given in the standard literature to the external relations of firms with other hierarchies, whether with other economic enterprises or with political hierarchies like parties, governments, or international organizations. Some recent research on international business associations has made a start but only as an outgrowth of the comparative study of neocorporatism within states. Similarly, the transnational relations of political parties or labor unions has received scant attention and has not been well integrated into the IPE literature. A notable exception was Jeff

Harrod's (1972) early work on wage bargaining in the Jamaican aluminum industry.

What needs to be developed in the interests of future MBA students is a series of courses that would concentrate on developing a perception of the firm in its transnational context—as a political actor developing and nurturing relationships with governments, with international agencies, with other enterprises, with its bankers, and with university research centers. These would include courses on the political economy of international finance and capital markets, with some emphasis on international financial history as well as institutions. As far as international trade goes, students find it just as useful to study comparatively the evolving trade policies of major industrialized, developing, and formerly state-planned economies as to spend time on the intricacies of the General Agreement on Tariffs and Trade (GATT) and the multilateral trade negotiations at Geneva. They would also find useful a course on the political economy of conflict and cooperation in the management of natural resources—not only oil and nuclear power, but also water, air, and forests. Perhaps more than ever in the 1990s, it would be important not to leave out the political economy of security and defense— concerns that will not disappear altogether with the end of the Cold War.

All such courses require a secure grounding on the part of the teachers in something other than business studies and business management. It may be international relations, international history, or international organization; or it may be political science, development economics, or economic history— in my opinion, any of these more than neoclassical economic theory as it is taught in most economics departments. At present, only a minority of business schools engage in such "outside" recruiting. And only a minority of business school scholars have made significant contributions in teaching and research in these directions (e.g., Vernon, Dunning, and Stopford). But for the most part, business schools, and even business historians, have been reluctant to break out of their old, comfortable state-bound view of the firm's environment. Nor, again with some individual exceptions, have they been much concerned with the development of innovative research. Most of their students, having gained an MBA, hasten to put it to work in enlarging their career opportunities. Consequently, doctoral candidates are rare, and professors are constantly distracted by lucrative invitations to act as consultants.

But because of the transnationalization of finance, of knowledge, and of production and trade, there is now a growing but still largely unfilled need for research ventures that overflow state boundaries and transcend the divisions between international business and international relations. Let me briefly pose just three questions, randomly chosen.

- Who, in the international political economy, taxes whom? Are governments more effective at appropriating resources (information,

property, finance) from the system or are enterprises? And how do each apply such resources?
- What technological risks are internalized, both by states and by enterprises?
- How in practice are disputes over contracts settled between states, between states and enterprises, and between enterprises?

There are also implications for the teaching of international relations. Presently, only a minority of major universities with strong interests in teaching the subject at all have in some way tried to incorporate or adapt to the development of international political economy as a new dimension (or framework) for the old subject. How should they now proceed if they were to accept the arguments for stages 2 and 3 in the eclectic approach?

First, they should include not only courses on international financial history and institutions (as most do now), but also courses on international business history and practices. Students should be introduced at least to the theoretical questions about the motivations and management of firms and about the internationalization of production. As with the business schools, there is a case for looking for outsiders to do the teaching—perhaps people with close familiarity with individual firms and their corporate background and character, or people with practical experience of one or more major sectors of the world market economy. The underlying questions, as always, are the who-gets-what questions, not what the government in Washington ought to do about it in the (too often undefined) U.S. national interest. Good questions still ask, Who is the hammer and who is the anvil? And whose ox gets gored? Who carries the risks? Who gets the opportunities for greater wealth, more freedom, more security, more justice? It must also be understood that "Who?" does not only include states, but groups defined by sex, class, occupation, age, and size.

The point of incorporating the individual enterprise, identified by name, product, and form of organization, into the study of international political economy is simply to get better answers to all these basic questions. Enterprises exercise power in many ways, and not just internally within the firm. Because the aim in IPE is to look for the sources of power and the consequences of the exercise of power, it cannot rationally exclude firms. Firms, like states, play a role in markets and in technological development. Like states, they are affected by change in any of the four major structures, and can sometimes deliberately or unwittingly restrict, or enlarge, the range of options open to policymakers in government and in other firms. Or, conversely, their own options may be enlarged or restricted. Analyzing which, and how, is the task of IPE.

If we are looking for change, of whatever kind, we need to answer such questions. The efforts to do so inevitably reunite domestic politics and economics with international politics and economics. Moreover, it cannot realistically be done without locating both governments and enterprises within the ever-changing structures of power that make up the international political economy at any one time. Of course, there are problems, difficulties, even danger, in pursuing an eclectic approach such as this. But the problems, difficulties, and dangers of not doing so are even greater.

3

Historical Materialism, Gramsci, and International Political Economy

Stephen Gill

This chapter introduces new developments in historical materialism that might offer a means of broadening and deepening our concepts of international political economy as a field of study. My argument is that we need to develop a new historical materialist analysis in order to transcend the subject/object and agent/structure dichotomies that undermine the plausibility of the generally positivist epistemologies and ontologies that constitute the majority of studies within IPE, especially in the United States. This would enable the elaboration of a historically integrated, dialectical form of IPE analysis appropriate to the conditions of the late twentieth century.

The approach introduced in this chapter assumes that the central task of social science is to explain social action, social structure, and social change. Further, with respect to epistemological questions, it assumes that "there is no symmetry between the social and natural sciences with regard to concept formation and the logic of inquiry and explanation" (Gunnell, 1969: 168).

A further assumption is that there is not, and logically cannot be, a single language of scientific explanation. The key contrast between social and natural science is that the structure of social relationships and the meaning of social events are not principally functions of the scientist's theory, since what the social scientists confronts is "not a first but a second order reality." The "world" of the social scientist is a second-order one because it has been logically pre-ordered by its participants, "in whose terms action is conducted and is justified." As will be argued below, this implies that social scientific explanation entails limited generalizations and a conditional vocabulary (Gunnell, 1968: 179; 180). In order to avoid conceptual reification, this entails continual interaction between social scientific constructs and "social reality." "Such a requirement will be viewed as a limitation only it if is assumed that the science of physical mechanics must somehow serve as a standard of all explanation" (Gunnell, 1968: 186).

Underlying this contention is the argument that social science explanation cannot develop if it rests either upon a Cartesian dualism concerning subject and object or theorizes in terms of cause and effect. Of course, there is no single way in which the Cartesian dichotomy can be overcome. This essay simply introduces explanatory possibilities.

In this light, the chapter discusses recent literature in IPE and IR, partly to highlight and critique a widespread tendency to use transhistorical theorizations based upon sets of *a priori* categories that appear to take on an ontological autonomy. This is a characteristic associated with both American neo-realism and what might be called mechanical, economistic Marxism. Second, since the orthodox approaches are constructed upon subject-object and agent-structure dichotomies, while they may be *socially effective* (in that they inform the construction of the social world and of certain policy initiatives at any given moment) they fail to meet the criteria introduced above: that is they cannot provide social scientific *explanation*.

A Gramscian School of IPE?

As there is no single Marxism (Marx himself denied he was a Marxist), neither is there any agreed-upon interpretation of Gramsci's thoughts concerning social theory. Instead there are clusters of scholars working in ways that address some of the questions raised and posed in Gramscian terms, across different disciplines, in a large number of countries. These scholars have begun to communicate and to participate in joint conferences, and have thus begun to form the embryo of a global research community. Some research is of practical consequence insofar as it is linked to different ways of supporting the activity of socialist and progressive political parties and social movements.

In common with the objectives of the *IPE Yearbooks*, some initial work from this perspective has entailed a constructive dialogue with, as well as critique of, prevailing—or in Gramscian terms, hegemonic—theorizations (e.g., Gill and Law, 1988). The need for this, in my view, is occasioned by at least two important factors. First, while Marxism has always offered an integrated political economy approach, in large part because of the orientation and predominance of U.S. theory in the field, historical materialism has tended to become marginalized from many of the major debates in modern IPE. This marginalization in no small part is occasioned by the limitations of a rather mechanical and ahistorical application of many Marxist ideas and theories, some of which are linked to the tendency among what might be called "Marxist fundamentalists" to generate the condition of "ever-increasing expectations of the collapse of capitalism" (whereas Gramsci pointedly argued that there was no necessary relationship between economic and political crises, or vice versa). This theoretical pathology has led to a lack of appeal of Marxist ideas to a new generation of students in Western academies. This also seems to have been the fate of orthodox Marxism in Japan during the last twenty years or so. Particularly in the context of the capitulation of the Leninist and post-Stalinist systems of rule in Eastern Europe, as well as the collapse of dogmatic Marxism-Leninism as a social doctrine, we can perhaps now look forward to the moment when this pathological, mechanical Marxism can be consigned to its proper place as a macabre exhibit in a museum of twentieth century history.

The latter observation reinforces my second point in favor of dialogue. The 1980s and 1990s have witnessed a secular, and in some cases spectacular, decline in the salience and theoretical appeal of left-wing ideas. Notwithstanding Western triumphalism and propagandists who, forgetting both their Hegel and Marx, proclaim the "end of history," developments in Eastern Europe and the Soviet Union have reinforced the claims of credibility, positional power, and vigor of the hegemonic discourses in the West. Moreover, such historic developments emphasize the obvious fact that Marxist ideas developed in a theoretical ghetto will suffer irrelevance and morbidity. There is much to be gained from a constructive dialogue with arguments and theories from different perspectives. This is of crucial importance to assess the status of new theoretical ideas: to be persuasive these ideas must provide more comprehensive, consistent, and reflexive explanations than those that predominate. Indeed, only through an open exchange between, and competition of, ideas is progress of theoretical maturation likely to develop so that the field can advance beyond what Susan Strange once described as its "infantile stage," a point she claimed it had reached by the early 1980s (Strange, 1984).

Thus many of the scholars cited in this chapter have the common undertaking to rethink creatively historical materialism and to chart a path toward a new theory of IPE and IR. A Gramscian approach is seen as offering a promising (but by no means the only or necessarily the superior) avenue because its theory and concepts are understood to be generalizable in a coherent way across a range of current fields of study and individual disciplines:

> Gramsci's theory provides a relatively universal and complete approach to international relations, one that transcends the current debates dividing the field while preserving the insights of the major traditions, whether "realist" or "idealist" whether "structural" or "historical." . . . Thus, in his commentary on the history of modern Italy, Gramsci is able to treat both the Renaissance state system and politics within the twentieth century state within the same framework and with the same concepts. (Augelli and Murphy, forthcoming)

Of course, most of Gramsci's substantive work focused upon the analysis of national social formations, particularly Italy (Gramsci, 1971). Gramsci argued that this was the initial level at which the state and civil society (and its anatomy, the political economy) should be analyzed, and where the foundations of social hegemonies were built. This national focus predominates in Gramsci scholarship not only in Japan and Latin America, but also in Western Europe, as reflected in the work of the Birmingham University Centre for Contemporary Cultural Studies (e.g., Hall, 1982; Larrain, 1983), and in the ongoing debates in *New Left Review* and *Socialist Register* on the nature of culture, ideology, the state, civil society, and hegemony in capitalist society. There have also been many discussions in left-wing journals over the question of imperialism, although these have usually been couched in terms of theories of ultra- and superimperialism, rather than posed in Gramscian terms.

The movement toward the extension of Gramscian ideas to the study of international relations has been slow and relatively recent, and has involved relatively few ambitious studies concerned with defining the origins, development, and dynamics of the emerging global political economy. Nonetheless, impressive work has begun to discuss themes of the internationalization of state and civil society, the international aspects of social hegemony and supremacy, the transnational class and bloc formations and economic forces, the role of international organizations, and other issues that help to define the nature of global politics in the twentieth century (e.g., van der Pijl, 1984; Cox, 1987; Augelli and Murphy, 1988; Gill, 1990; Overbeek, 1990). Important here is the pioneering of Robert Cox, who published two important essays in *Millennium* in the early 1980s, the latter of which can be fruitfully read as an introduction to the application of Gramscian concepts at the international level (Cox, 1981, 1983).

Thus, although many social scientists are aware of the application of Gramscian ideas to analyze the role of politics, popular culture, and ideological and cultural hegemony at the national level, this is much less the case for IR and IPE. This may be partly because little of Gramsci's thinking focused on questions of political economy per se, mainly because he seems to have worked within classical Marxist assumptions about the political economy of capitalism and feudalism. As a result, authors working in this area have begun to invent their own conceptual apparatuses and ontology (e.g., van der Pijl, 1984; Cox, 1987) because no satisfactory apparatus existed to analyze the dynamics of the global political economy of the 1980s. In this light, it is clear that much needs to be done to develop Gramscian perspectives in ways that can have appeal to students of IPE and thus make a more general contribution to the development of the field.

Differences Between Gramscian and Positivist IPE

How then does the Gramscian approach differ from the major traditions and prevailing orthodoxy in these relatively new interdisciplinary fields? There are three main differences that can be outlined initially:

First, as I have suggested, like the studies mentioned above, in international studies the Gramscian approach is an epistemological and ontological critique of the empiricism and positivism that underpin, for example, the prevailing theorizations in the field of IPE, as well as the cruder forms of "mechanical Marxism." This is because the Gramscian approach is a specific form of nonstructuralist historicism. As Robert Cox (1987) has pointed out, the notion of structure in Gramsci is opposed to the structuralisms of Louis Althusser, or, from a different tradition, Kenneth Waltz. Nevertheless, Gramsci's approach is consistent with the idea of historical structures, which are partly constituted by the consciousness and action of individuals and groups. Thus Gramsci's approach stands in contrast to abstract "structuralisms" insofar as it has a human(ist) aspect: historical change is understood as, to a substantial degree, the consequence of collective human activity.

More specifically, Gramsci's historicism has three main components: (a) transience, (b) historical necessity, and (c) a dialectical variant of (philosophical) realism (Morera, 1990).

The first component, transience, implies that history and social change are cumulative, endless, yet nonrepetitive processes, with different rhythms and tempos, applying respectively to structural developments and to patterns of apparently discrete events. Thus the critique of political economy for Marx and Gramsci begins with the concept of the historicity, or historical specificity of the capitalist market system, rather than seeing it as natural or eternal.

The idea of historical necessity implies that social interaction and political change take place within what can be called the "limits of the possible"—limits that however, are not fixed and immutable, but exist within the dynamics of a given social structure (comprising the intersubjective aspect of ideas, ideologies and theories, social institutions, and a prevailing socioeconomic system and set of power relations). The dialectical aspect of this is that although social action is constrained by, and constituted within, prevailing social structures, those structures can themselves be transformed by collective action (for example through what Gramsci called "the war of position," involving either leading and/or subordinate groups in society). Thus the problem of historical necessity is understood in dynamic and dialectical terms in ways that challenge the subject/object dichotomy of positivist epistemology. In this sense, Gramscian historical materialism builds upon and extends aspects of the Marxian critique of classical political economy. Marx showed how, by abstracting from the social relations of production, Ricardo developed an ahistorical and therefore misleading conception of the freedom of the individual:

In money relationships in the developed exchange system . . .

individuals appear to be . . . independent, that is to collide with one
another freely and to barter within the limits of this freedom. They
appear to do so, however, only to someone who abstracts from the
conditions of existence in which individuals come into contact . . .
Close investigation to these external circumstances of conditions
shows, however, how impossible it is for individuals forming a part of a
class, etc., to surmount them en masse without abolishing them. (Marx,
1971: 83–84)

Gramsci's variant of philosophical realism identifies the intellectual
process as a creative, practical, yet open-ended and continuous engagement to
explain an intractable social reality. This process is, like the processes of
chance within a given necessity, a dialectical one, and is thus a part of the
historical process; it does not stand outside it. Indeed, Gramsci developed the
unique concept of the "organic intellectual" to show how the processes of
intellectual production were themselves in dialectical relation to the processes
of historical change. Intellectual work directed toward social explanation was
often directly or indirectly linked to political strategies, themselves developed
from different perspectives. Such perspectives exist in political time and
space. Thus by linking the theory of knowledge production to a theory of
identity and interests, Gramsci was able to show how, at least in this sense,
theory is always for someone and for some purpose (for an application of this
argument, with respect to the world order concepts associated with, among
other things, the perspective of transnational capital, see Gill, 1990; for
wider arguments see Cox, 1987; Gill and Law, 1988). This viewpoint then
can be contrasted with the positivist and technocratic assumptions that
inform the outlook of most professional economists in the West and Japan,
and those working in the major international economic organizations like the
International Monetary Fund and the World Bank. Thus the observation also
applies to those working within the neoclassical tradition, including
Keynesians, with their engineering assumption that the role of the
economist is to build a behaviorist apparatus enabling the fine tuning of the
economy.

Second, the Gramscian approach provides a general critique of
methodological individualism and methodological reductionism. The latter, of
course, is frequently found in some variants of Marxism as well as in other
traditions. Indeed, analytical Marxism seeks to synthesize methodological
individualism and methodological holism, for example, in developing a
theory of exploitation (Roemer, 1982; for an overview see Mayer, 1989). In
the Gramscian approach, history and political economy are not understood as
a sequence or series of discrete events or moments that when aggregated equal
a process of change with certain governing regularities. For Gramsci it is the
ensemble of social relations configured by social structure ("the situation")
that is the basic unit of analysis, rather than individual agents, be they
consumers, firms, or interest groups, interacting in a (potentially) rule-

governed way in the "political marketplace" at a given moment or conjuncture, as in modern public choice theory (Frey, 1984).

Third, the approach insists upon an ethical dimension to analysis, so that the questions of justice, legitimacy, and moral credibility are integrated sociologically into the whole and into many of its key concepts. This is reflected in Gramsci's dual conception of politics and the state. On the one hand there is a classical Marxist concern to analyze the state as a class-based apparatus of rule. On the other is the Aristotelian view of politics as the search to establish conditions for the good society, where the state is seen as at least potentially able to be transformed from an apparatus based upon social inequality into an ethical public sphere. Thus, unlike the prevailing orthodoxy with its priority given to political order and the pragmatic need for systems management, the normative goal of the Gramscian approach is to move toward the solution of the fundamental problem of political philosophy—the nature of the good society and thus, politically, the construction of an "ethical" state and a unitary society in which personal development, rational reflection, open debate, democratic empowerment, and economic and social liberation can become more widely available. It is important to emphasize here that this is a rather negative definition, concerning minimum conditions, of the "good society," and it offers no promises nor prescriptions for the form that such a society might take: historical structures can be changed by collective action in a "war of position," but there is no historical inevitability. The key contrast here would be with teleological Marxism, with its promise of possible utopia(s), or Francis Fukayama's much-publicized dystopia of the "end of history": the eventual unfolding of the logic and spirit of liberal democratic capitalism. In Gramscian terms, telos is "myth":

> From Sorel, [Gramsci] took the notion of social myth (e.g., the modern prince as a myth). Myth presupposes a psychic force, a compelling movement combined with a rejection of the prevailing norms (e.g., as hypocritical, demystified). It is a normative force but not a normative plan or set of normative criteria. It can generate movement but not predict outcome. Thus the normative element is crucial but not as teleology.[1]

To summarize, then, in contrast to the tendency in much of the U.S. literature on IPE to prioritize systemic order and management, from a vantage point associated with the ruling elements in the wealthy core of the global political economy, the historical materialist perspective looks at the system from the bottom upwards, as well as the top downwards, in a dialectical appraisal of a given historical situation.

In sum, the Gramscian approach highlights the limits of a narrow political economy approach to the analysis of IR. For Gramsci, a broad-based and more integrated perspective is achieved by the elaboration of a historicist version of the dialectical method developed from Hegel and Marx, and also influenced by Machiavelli. In the *Prison Notebooks*, this took the form of a critique of the German historicists and, more specifically, of the Italian idealist, Benedetto Croce (Gramsci, 1971).

The Critique of Political Economy: Four Arguments

Here I attempt to summarize the key theoretical and applied features of a historical materialist approach to social and historical explanation. A materialist theory of knowledge assumes that nothing—not God, the idea of liberty, nor providence, for example—exists outside and apart from nature and society. In my view, this also implies that no teleology or spirit exists as a guide to our purpose for that process. Nevertheless, metaphysics and idealist theorizing are a part of the social reality that is to be explained because they help constitute the social outlook and predispositions of individuals, and larger groups, within social formations. Following Ted Benton, Esteva Morera (1990: 122) argues that a materialist theory must meet four conditions:

1. Materialism acknowledges the existence of an object of knowledge, independent of the knowing subject, the process of knowledge production, and the system of knowledge itself.
2. The adequacy of the object of knowledge provides the ultimate standard by which the cognitive status of thought is to be assessed.
3. Thought and ideas are recognized as realities in their own right and thus are an object of knowledge.
4. Those realities are theorized as not *sui generis* but as the result of causal mechanisms.

I will now relate these points to four arguments informed by the thoughts of Gramsci and other historical materialist thinkers on these matters. Here I attempt to indicate that a creative historical materialist approach is able to transcend the limits set by these four conditions to produce a reflexive and dynamic form of political economy explanation.

As will be argued below, for example, the concept of mechanical causality (point 4, above) is inconsistent with historicism, since historicism is concerned with explanation, rather than causality. This entails the rejection of technological, economic, or indeed any form of reductionism. Explanation in this sense is founded in an approach that insists upon the centrality of the interrelationship between the "subjective" and "objective" in historical development, for example with its focus upon the social organization of production and class relations in the state, that is aspects of life where subjective and objective interpenetrate: the "second order reality" that Gunnell

(1968) identifies as the object of social science. This line of argument relates to the difference between what Gramsci called "historical economism" and "historical materialism."[2]

Beyond the Intransigence of "Social Reality"

We can accept that there is a certain intransigent "reality" to society and nature (which we can never fully know or explain because of its scale and complexity). Therefore, this reality is to a certain extent independent of the processes of knowledge production. Further, the "truth" of social reality is made more intractable because it involves the thoughts, motivations, and intersubjective meanings of individuals who have different forms of self-consciousness and awareness as to the social nature of their actions/inactions. Thus social reality has different dimensions, which cannot necessarily be understood or fully recorded, although abstractions concerning the structural components of such social reality can and must be intellectually produced.

However, following Hegel, we can argue that there can be no immediate knowledge because this would imply that we have no consciousness that mediates with such a reality. Consciousness, then, implies an explicit or implicit conceptual apparatus and language. As outlined in *Grundrisse*, Marx's (1971) adaption (or inversion) of the Hegelian method (further extended and elaborated by Gramsci) applies a particular materialist approach to society and continually extends, refines, and elaborates its conceptual apparatus, generating new concepts and discarding others. This occurs in the context of a dialectical process: our senses are theoreticians; what is or can be is produced conceptually and our conceptual frameworks are produced by the environment or society. Here we can refer to Marx's ideas concerning the "concrete-real" (which determines theory) and the "thought-concrete" (which is an understanding of the concrete, or the significance of social facts generated by the process of reflection and thought). Such a distinction implies that each conceptual framework produced its own version of the concrete-real and thought-concrete (Resnick and Wolff, 1987). For Marx, then, knowledge was the process of change in which the two concretes are interconnected and mutually transformed.

At this point we can locate a key issue that differentiates historical materialism from empiricism and positivism: a change in thinking is a change in the social totality and thus has an impact on other social processes; a change in the social totality will provoke change in the process of thought. Hence the process of thinking is part of a ceaseless dialectic of social being.

The Limits of Ontological Objectivity

Moving now toward the way that thought-concretes are developed and elaborated, by making an initial distinction between the appearance and essence of inner and outer manifestations of social reality, we can move to a better correspondence with such a reality theoretically (an argument that presupposes the possibility of a never complete, but a closer approximation of, ontological objectivity). By following Marx's method as outlined in *Grundrisse*, this is attempted through an ongoing and endless process of the generation of abstractions and concepts, which are reconstructed and refined as they encounter a mass of often undifferentiated data. This method, to use the metaphor of Engels, enables the theorist to approach a more comprehensive and consistent explanation of social reality, rather like the way an asymptote approximates a straight line.

This position seems to be superficially similar to that of John Stuart Mill and the skeptical empiricists who argue that the senses or their surrogates can never yield social knowledge that can truthfully approximate social reality. However, historical materialists take this argument one step further by arguing that society is a totality or system that is regulated or conditioned by structural relations and can thus never be understood through the method of empiricist atomism. Further, the process of development of thought-concretes is ongoing and thus is simply arrested and incomplete if it rests with, or is explained through, transhistorical abstractions or theories, such as those associated with the Cassandras of the rise and (inevitable) fall of U.S. hegemony. (For an elaboration of this literature, see Gill, 1986, 1988, 1990.) This argument was, of course, originally made by Marx when developing his critique of political economy—for example, his criticism of Ricardo and Malthus. This point is further developed below with regard to structuralism and Gramsci's critique of Bukharin.

Thus, whereas modern IR theory takes the rise and decline of hegemonies and balances of power in the interstate system as largely given, with its primordial anarchic form constitutive of the development possibilities in international relations since at least the time of Thucydides, historical materialists argue that this structure, insofar as its existence can be substantiated, is a particular configuration of states and social forces, corresponding to a particular epoch and having certain conditions of existence that are corporeal and transitory (for the archetypal realist statement see Gilpin, 1981: 11). In other words, Marxists stress the conditional and historical application of what for Gilpin seems to operate as something akin to a sociological abstraction.

Indeed, whereas empiricists move toward the understanding of social reality from the perspective of methodological individualism, historical materialists develop a theory based upon social structures as the fundamental unit of analysis. In this sense, although all social realities are theorized, some are more theorized than others. Thus, for Kenneth Waltz (1979) the interstate system is viewed in individualistic terms, with states as atomized actors interacting within the structure of anarchy; i.e., Waltz, Gilpin, and most U.S. international political economy operate within what Richard Ashley (1988) calls the anarchy problematique.

By contrast, Robert Cox (1987) suggests that there are different forms of state and world orders whose conditions of existence, constitutive principles, and norms vary over time. These conditions include different social modes of production and social structures of accumulation, with their own characteristic ethics and politics, which vary in political time and space. Thus no transhistorical essentialism or homeostasis is imputed to any given social system or world order. Moreover, as Cox is at pains to show, the state itself and the forms of state action are themselves differentially constituted in complex ways by blocs of social and political forces that operate within the limits of a given historical necessity.

To make some applications of this point clearer, and in a more substantive way, let us sketch some aspects of the postwar system from this perspective.

First, and most fundamental, is that it is assumed that any historical materialist approach to understanding and explaining a given world order system must analyze it as a whole. The particular ontology used is by no means self-evident and must, on one level, be a theorized one. Synthesizing insights of different writers from within this perspective influenced by Gramsci, then, our ontology must be founded upon the idea of global social formation constituted in part by the degree of integration/disintegration of basic social structures and social forces. This is the fundamental basis for understanding the "international": that is what is usually seen as a relatively autonomous interstate system articulated with related forces, mechanisms and institutions of production and exchange at the "domestic" and "international" levels.

In other words, our understanding of the dynamics of the political economy is founded upon certain sociological ideas concerning, for example, the degree of "embeddedness" of world orders in sociopolitical structures at the national or transnational levels (e.g., Polanyi, 1944). Thus, in the contemporary era (i.e., since 1945), we can call such a historically specific yet changing ensemble of social structures and social forces the "global political economy" (Gill and Law, 1988).

Thus since 1945, in the era of the *pax Americana*, a new world order structure emerged that was in some ways qualitatively different from its predecessors. However, this new system cannot be explained with regard solely to apparently unique features, for example, the existence of weapons of mass destruction or the long-term threats to the survival of the species through ecological catastrophe (previous weapons systems caused mass destruction and former civilizations were either displaced or eliminated partly because of adverse environmental and ecological changes). Hence the conventional focus of much IR theorizing, the interstate system, and the transition from a balance of power/hegemony (Westphalian) international political system toward a "post-Westphalian" system (Cox 1990) needs to be explained through the examination of the ways in which social forces and social structures are entering a period of transition so that, in classical Marxist terms, there is both a growing socialization (universalization) of aspects of social life, and a disintegration of previous forms of identity and interest, between, for example "internationalist" and "nationalist" groups of interest.

This transformation and struggle, among other things then, involves a dialectical interplay between forces that are relatively cosmopolitan, and others that are more territorially bounded, such as nationalist movements and ideologies, military-security structures, particular linguistic forms and patterns of identity.

In a more specific sense, the formal system of state sovereignty, which was in some ways reinforced and constituted by earlier forms of international economic activity (hence the term the "international" political economy) appears now to have been cumulatively undermined by more pervasive and deep-rooted economic integration and competition (including interstate competition to attract supplies of capital and investment from overseas, and to promote the competitiveness of "home" industries). This has created a new force-field of constraints, opportunities, and dangers, i.e., new conditions of existence for all states, groups, and classes in the system, as well as extending, albeit in still limited and contradictory ways, a growing structural power for internationally mobile transnational capital (Gill and Law, 1989).

To continue the Orwellian metaphor, some are more constrained than others in this world order system. Not only does this new order coincide with a decisive change in the productive powers and balance of social forces within and between the major states, but also state structures in the major capitalist countries have been transformed into different variants of the neoliberal form, more oriented to the integration of their economies into the emerging global system of production and exchange, in which knowledge, finance, and information play more decisive roles, when contrasted with the interwar period. This is what Cox (1987) means by the process of the internationalization of the state, involving coalitions, class alliances, and sociohistoric blocs of forces across as well as within countries.

At the same time, peripheral economies have become more tightly geared to the economic activity of the core, and their developmental rhythms have become partly subjected to the imperatives of Cold War politics and the growing integration of trade, investment, production, and finance, as the story of the 1980s attests—a period of arrested development potential, with the Third World debt crisis involving huge transfers of resources from the poorer countries to the richest. In the emerging post-Westphalian system, the cosmopolitanism of international economic forces has been accompanied by a disciplining of the Third World through a combination of market power and the discipline of the Bretton Woods international organizations under U.S.

leadership (Augelli and Murphy, 1988). This capitalist cosmopolitanism is also important in any explanation of the breakdown of the Cold War blocs structure between the United States, USSR, and in Europe. Here changes occurred in large part because of the intensification of technological innovation and military rivalry, especially between the United States and USSR. In the context of a deep crisis in the social structure of accumulation and thus of the productive power of the various nations of the Soviet-led bloc, the social myth of the communist utopia, which had reached its apogee in an earlier period of history, was vaporized almost completely. This hegemonic, organic crisis of "actually existing communism" proved to be especially severe in Poland, Romania, East Germany, and most important, the USSR. In the context of the brittle (and economistic) legitimacy of the communist states, with the relations between state and civil society coordinated by an authoritarian and paternalist structure of political power, the inability of the USSR to respond to the long-term challenges posed within the context of existing forms of post-Stalinist political economy led to its collapse as an alternative social myth (to capitalism).

In the world capitalist order, then, power appeared to be reconcentrated in the metropolitan countries, which were, however, also undergoing substantial transformation in what is, clearly, a global process of restructuring. The social forces and political arrangements associated with what John Ruggie (1982) called "embedded liberalism" were progressively undermined by the growing extension, resources, and power of internationally mobile forces, undermining the historic blocs of social forces that constituted, at the national level, the structural underpinnings of the postwar international political economy. In Gramscian terms, the ensemble of these blocs was politically synthesized within the context of the twin pillars of American hegemony (the Cold War structures and the liberalizing international economic order) into an *international historic bloc* initially in a transatlantic, then later Trilateral (i.e., including Japan) format. However, the recessions and restructuring of the 1970s and 1980s, allied to the cumulative internationalization of production, consumption, and exchange, and the integration of global economic forces, meant that the integral nature of these historic blocs was undermined, and an underdeveloped, yet clearly emergent *transnational historic bloc of forces* (associated with dominant interests in the metropolitan countries and elsewhere) began to emerge, particularly during the 1970s and 1980s. The contradictions of this development, which involves a crisis of the old hegemonic structures and forms of political consent, negotiated internationally, are now unravelling the former international historic bloc and are bound up with the new and emergent transnational bloc (Gill and Law, 1989; Gill, 1990).

Even here, however, the contradictions of the system may be intensifying. Developments in the metropolitan heartland of the system, with ripple effects in the Third World, for example as pointed out in Susan

Strange's book, *Casino Capitalism* (1986), may be leading to a situation in which production and exchange structures are becoming disarticulated in an era of shortening time-horizons and speculative capitalism (e.g., growing disparities between productive investment, international trade and capital, and exchange markets), so that, on one level, the ethical appeals of the social contracts of the era of embedded liberalism are rapidly being laid to waste. As Strange points out, the game of economic life comes to resemble a combination of snakes and ladders and (Russian) roulette.

How are we to begin to explain the nature of these changes? In the conventional literature in IPE, what has just been discussed is usually understood as the disjuncture between "domestic" and "international" forces in the international exchange system, along with an international diffusion of interstate power leading to a move away from the stability of the superpower duopoly toward a more complex plural system. The question then is how is order possible "after hegemony?" (Keohane, 1984). Theories have been developed to ascertain how the metropolitan capitalist nations at the center of the system can cooperate fruitfully in a post-hegemonic world characterized by slower growth and economic instability. Much debate centers on the problem of the highly imperfect coordination at the summit of the system, that is how to cope with the complexities of "two-level" or "multi-level" or "mixed" games between larger numbers of national actors, i.e., governments (the pioneer here is Axelrod, 1984). However, the question that continues to constitute, and has constituted the research agenda for orthodox IPE theory during the last decade is: How can cooperation be achieved under anarchy?

Another way of looking at this question, however, is to situate a discussion of interstate forums, international organizations, and informal councils like the Trilateral Commission, in the context of the development and application of hegemonic strategies on an increasingly transnational basis. Yet this level of analysis is still insufficient to explain adequately the emergence and salience of these strategies, and the political struggles that are entailed by them. The political gods at the summit of the system, and the various forums in which they interact, such as the Group of Seven summits, operate within the limits of the possible, limits situated within the context of the historical transformations discussed above, as well as the blocs of social forces with which they are associated at the domestic level in their own countries and elsewhere (Gill, 1990).

Given the historical complexity of these forces, the importance of, and interaction within, these elite forums cannot simply be explained with abstract formulations such as the Prisoner's Dilemma (which Axelrod claims can explain biological evolution and trench warfare in World War I equally well). Since such intergovernmental and transnational forums have existed for some time, their growing importance can only be explained historically. Apart from being concrete institutional responses to the crisis of transformation in the postwar world order system, corresponding to an uneven globalization of the political economy, they are also initiatives that are bound up with the birth and early development of an international political and civil society that is in some respects new and suggestive of a reconfiguration of the world order order in the late twentieth century.

From a world systems viewpoint the above developments would appear to correspond to a situation where power appears to have been reconcentrated in the "core" states, while realists, agreeing to a point, would lament the dissolving of the glue of bloc structures associated with the balance of terror and the decline of U.S. power and leadership. However, what may be the most important aspect of the current epoch is the fact that social relations and social structures are in a period of extended and deep-seated transformation or crisis on a global scale—a crisis which is in fact, a crisis of both the existing Cold War and inter- and intra-capitalist order.

Insofar as there are leading elements in this process, the principles of organization of this reconstructed and restructured world order system are increasingly those associated with liberal economic ideas and interests (e.g., transnational capital and the Bretton Woods institutions), which are engaged in a dialectical struggle vis-à-vis embedded mercantilist and statist perspectives (often associated with the public sector, the security complex, and protected industries that are noncompetitive internationally). This struggle and transformation involves not only the states in the capitalist core, but also configures the agenda of social transformation in Latin America, in central and eastern Europe, and in the Soviet Union.

A good recent example of the internationalization of political and civil society and of the internationalization of authority under these new conditions was the way in which the Bretton Woods institutions, the Organization for Economic Cooperation and Development (OECD), and metropolitan capitalist governments and interests rapidly came together to produce a radical and draconian package of reforms, to swiftly transform the Polish economy, in January 1990. This was, as the OECD put it at the time, the launching of an unprecedented strategy of social transformation from a communist, protected, and mercantilist society, into a market-based, capitalist society, a "great transformation" which took at least 70 years to accomplish in nineteenth-century England (Polanyi, 1944). The plan for Poland was itself based upon a learning process among capitalist elites in light of the experiences of the 1970s and 1980s, and the experiments with the use of IMF/World Bank conditionality. The new strategy applies Kornai's (1986) concept of macro/micro restructuring and the idea of hard budget constraints (on state expenditures and also on individual enterprises) in ways that will extend and deepen the structural power of capital. This strategy, which is by no means certain of success, is nonetheless not a pure market strategy: there is some political direction and internationalization of authority in order to prevent the mistakes of the 1970s (over debt recycling) and the 1980s (over the debt crisis) from being repeated. This strategy then, insofar as it has an internal logic, represents the use of direct political power in order to develop the structural power of capital (see Gill and Law, 1989, for an elaboration).

In this context the ultimate form of "conditionality" was reflected in the economic, monetary, and social unification of East Germany with the Federal Republic started on July 1, 1990. This was, of course, soon followed by full political unification on October 2, 1990, when the Volkskammer dissolved itself and a crowd estimated to be over a million people gathered in front of the Reichstag in the old Prussian capital of Berlin. Observers reported that the mood of the emotional crowd as a mixture of joy, bewilderment, anxiety, and catharsis. The West German political establishment gathered in the Schauspielhaus and its cocktails were made headier by the echoing song of the "Ode to Joy" from the Ninth Symphony. Not wishing to dampen their euphoria, the normally sober Bundesbank was denying the prospect of economic hopelessness in East Germany. As the Germans celebrated to the strains of Schiller and Beethoven, Mrs. Thatcher offered her congratulations after earlier ominous warnings about German dominance in Europe. The Soviet Union announced that unification was caused by the logic of the enlightened policy of perestrioka, and the European Commission said that it meant that the process of economic and political unification in Europe would be accelerated (see, for example, *Financial Times*, October 3, 1990).

The Structure of Necessity and Political Consciousness

The postwar transformations just described are not simply the result of impersonal cumulative structural transformations, although these changes— following Fernand Braudel (1979), those relating to the *longue durée*—have created the structure of necessity in which the *événements*, or events of history, occur. Yet social reality involves consciousness and thus encompasses philosophical, theoretical, ethical, and common-sense ideas. Beethoven, rather than Wagner, was chosen to symbolize the cathartic emotion of the united Germany for its present generation of political leaders. In the case of Gramsci this aspect is reflected in his interest in the questions of consciousness and politics, the role of the intellectuals and philosophy, and the substantive attention given to the superstructures, notably civil society, in his conceptions of hegemony and the constitution of society:

> Critical understanding of the self takes place therefore through a struggle of political "hegemonies" and of opposing directions, first in the ethical field and then in politics proper, in order to arrive at the working out at a higher level of one's conception of reality. Consciousness of being part of a particular hegemonic force (that is to say political consciousness) is the first stage towards progressive self-consciousness in which theory and practice will finally be one. Thus the unity of theory and practice is not just a matter of mechanical fact, but part of a historical process, whose elementary and primitive phase is to be found in the sense of being "different" and "apart," in an instinctive

feeling of independence, and which progresses to the level of real possession of a single and coherent conception of the world. This is why it must be stressed that the political development of the concept of hegemony represents a great philosophical advance as well as a politico-practical one. (Gramsci, 1971: 333)

Here then, Gramsci is arguing that critical understanding is not an automatic process: it involves reflection and effort within oneself as well as within the context of the wider struggle of ideas and political programs. "Progressive self-consciousness" is thus defined developmentally and politically, the awareness of self is reconstituted through an appreciation of prevailing thought-patterns and the nature and distribution of life chances. Thus the moment of self-awareness leads to a more complex and coherent understanding of the social world and is a form of historical change (and thus a change in the balance of social and political forces). Thus the achievement of self-consciousness is understood dialectically. Politics and the individual are thus central to the definition of structures and of change, and are not abstracted "falsely" out of a theory of history.

This argument does not imply that Gramsci is an idealist or that he subordinated economics to politics in his social theory, because society is conceived as in classical Marxism as a totality primarily constituted by a mode of production that can be analytically separated into ideas, institutions, and material forces but which in reality is a general, integrated, if contradictory, entity. Certain systems of thought such as religion or common sense (or "philosophy of everyday life" as Gramsci would have it) or social institutions, like the family, can outlive any given mode of production or social structure of accumulation, and thus there is no necessary congruence between "base" and "superstructure." The same would apply to systems of government and politics more generally: a capitalist mode of production can go with authoritarianism, dictatorship, or parliamentary democracy. What is crucial is to place each of these sets of ideas and social institutions in its proper sociohistorical context, because importance and meaning can change over time.

Likewise, if we take the case of the revolutions of 1989 in Eastern and Central Europe, the structural aspect of the explanations of this type of change was an implosion of economic performance and a deep-rooted and long-term crisis in the irrational and embedded social structure of accumulation of "actually existing socialism" (Kornai, 1986): a system which lost momentum since it could not reconcile its own contradictions.

For example, Kornai shows how, at least in the Hungarian case, the practice of politically allocated but largely open-ended subsidies allied to the system's overall centralization and the setting of abstract and unrealistic plan targets resulted in an inefficient system of allocation and incentives: there were no real market signals as exist in capitalism, and no financial or market constraints to punish the inefficient. The allocation of labor was distorted (massive underemployment, hoarding of labor and factors of production). The system simply did not provide the goods and services that people either wanted or needed. In Habermasian terms, this represented a deep rationality crisis of a social system premised upon, as it were, the perfect computation of social needs and economic activity.

This organic crisis was intensified, on the one hand, by the long-term economic challenges being posed by the advanced capitalist countries, and on the other, by the military and economic implications of the strategic challenge of Reaganism to the USSR. The lack of any substantive legitimacy under conditions of declining economic performance merely underlined the increasingly brittle legitimacy of the Stalinist antidemocratic system. This crudely materialist and antidemocratic form of legitimacy was of course made more fragile by the virtual elimination of any autonomous political activity and thus arrested the creation or rebirth of a civil society. Thus like a snowball gathering size as it rolls down a hill, when it reached its point of destination, the contradictions of the system had reached the scale of an avalanche.

Kees van der Pijl (1988) calls this phenomenon the organic crisis of the Hobbesian, repressive state form. At its worst, in Romania, this process (which was condoned if not welcomed during the 1970s and 1980s by Western leaders because of Ceausescu's opposition to Moscow and his ability to pay his bills to foreign bankers) involved the abuse of political and human rights of the population and the virtual starvation of the people to pay for, among other things, a grotesque marble palace. Here the key point is that a Gramscian analysis would have suggested that a Hobbesian state structure is inherently unstable for two reasons: it lacks ethical credibility and, because its political system is not embedded in "the fortress and earthworks" of a strong civil society. Like Ceausescu's palace, it could be toppled by an insurrectionary form of revolutionary spontaneity.

In van der Pijl's theorization, the strong hegemonic state-civil society complexes in the West are associated with the idea of the "Lockeian state," that is, one in which there is a vigorous and largely self-regulating civil society. This type of state-civil society complex is exemplified by the Anglo-Saxon countries, and to a certain extent by many of the member states of the European Community. The international counterpart to this type of hegemonic formation is the British Commonwealth, which is rooted in the history of British imperialism and colonialism, but represents, at the international level, the transformation of coercion into consent and informal regulation of interstate relations.

Here the contrast can be made with the usual idea of a strong state found in the bulk of IR theorizing, which is often associated with van der Pijl's contrasting Hobbesian state form—a strong state that dominates civil society from above, with the political capacity to centralize political power so as to develop and mobilize the national material resources. This type of state form, however, is generally nonhegemonic because it lacks firm foundations within the "fortress and earthworks" of a strong civil society, and by implication has fragile legitimacy.

Thus, instead of the tendency to reify the state and the interstate system, the Gramscian approach explains the nature of the state in terms of the complexity of state–civil society relations, and shows how the nature of state power is related to the strength of the synthesis between the key forces in the economy and society, operating politically on an inclusive basis. The synthesis between these forces creates what Gramsci called a historic bloc, which may at times have the potential to become hegemonic. For ethical hegemony to be possible, the state must necessarily be constituted by general legitimacy and active consent, which implies inclusion of the interests of the subordinate elements within the system. Thus, in the most fundamental and complete sense, the achievement of hegemony is concerned with the transcendence of narrowly based economistic or corporate perspectives, so that a genuinely universal position, synthesizing particular into general interests, could come to prevail.

We might also compare the revolutions in Eastern and Central Europe (which were largely peaceful, with the exception of Romania) with the crisis of legitimacy in China, was well as with the decay of state authoritarianism and military dictatorship in Latin America. As I have mentioned, van der Pijl suggests that in the last twenty years each of these variants of the Hobbesian state form had undergone or is undergoing a fundamental crisis. This crisis reflects not only the feeble legitimacy of Communist rule (e.g., the coming to power of Vaclav Havel as a symbol of the ethicopolitical rejection of the Communist order in Czechoslovakia) and the rejection of the long-term irrationality of the form of political economy associated with the post-Stalinist Communist development path involving mercantilism, planning, and widespread social protection and microinefficiency (e.g., the Polish adoption of an IMF-designed draconian macro- and micro-economic package of socioeconomic reconstruction in early 1990), but also the cumulative pressure of international forces operating on each of these countries.

By implication, at the international level, the movement toward a more liberal and integrated global political economy and the beginnings of social reconstruction in Eastern Europe and Latin America are two sides of the same coin of a profound restructuring of the international order. Not only the Hobbesian states, but also many others are moving in a more market-oriented direction and thus toward the internationalization of something resembling a Lockeian form of self-regulating civil society (although the German model of the social market economy is a key variant in the pan-European context). Despite the contradictions and conflicts involved in the transformation of Eastern and Central Europe, we may see this development, at the European level, sooner rather than later: the Cold War appears to have been eclipsed. On July 6, 1990, NATO finally announced that it no longer regarded the

Warsaw Pact as its enemy, and early in August 1990, British Prime Minister Thatcher was advocating a seat for Mikhail Gorbachev at the next summit of the Group of Seven in London in 1991.

What seems to characterize the nature of the world order system of the late twentieth century then, is a series of profound crises of identity, ethics, and socioeconomic restructuring at the domestic/international level encompassing all three categories of country we have discussed: in metropolitan capitalism, the communist/post-communist states, and in the Third World. These crises are linked together by the forces at work in the global political economy. From this vantage point, the outcome of these developments is likely to be determined mainly at the domestic level, that is within each of these countries. Nevertheless, the globalization of the political economy, and the transnationalization of social and political forces, means that new conditions prevail. These changes cannot be captured simply through a theorization of historical structures which is static, nondialectical and premised upon the separation of the "domestic" and the "international."

Historical Change and Counter-Hegemony

It is clear that the achievement of hegemony within a particular social formation is a complex and contradictory process because counterhegemonic forces will come to challenge the prevailing institutional and political arrangements. Hegemony is even more difficult to achieve (and therefore much rarer if not theoretically impossible) at the international level, where there is no single world state or a fully developed international civil society. It can be argued, however, that there is a substantial framework of international law, international organization (and thus a set of international norms, rules, and values), and an increasingly internationalized structure of production and exchange (and thus a complex web of private and informal linkages, some of which involve state agents). International hegemony, as normally defined in the literature, has been associated with the dominance and leadership of a powerful state within the system of international relations, achieving power over other states. However, for theorists influenced by Gramsci this is an unsatisfactory definition because it associates social forces with a territorial entity, whereas the global system needs to be conceived as a totality, and the social forces that operate within that system are not territorially bound or determined. Thus, as Robert Cox puts it:

> Hegemony is a structure of values and understandings about the nature of the order that permeates a whole system of states and non-state entities. In a hegemonic order these values and understandings are relatively stable and unquestioned. They appear to most actors as the natural order. Such a structure of meanings is underpinned by a structure of power, in which most probably one state is dominant, but that state's dominance is not sufficient to create hegemony. Hegemony derives from the

dominant social strata of the dominant states in so far as these ways of doing and thinking have acquired the acquiescence of the dominant social strata of other states. (Cox, 1990)

Giovanni Arrighi points to some of the reasons why the term "hegemonic" seems to apply to the leading strata and dominant social forces emanating from Great Britain during the nineteenth century as industrial and commercial capitalism began to internationalize. While keeping its domestic market relatively open, and with comparative advantage in trade in industrial goods, the United Kingdom had substantial control over the world market. It also had a general mastery of the global balance of power and a "close relationship of mutual instrumentality with *haute finance*" (and thus the ability to manage the international monetary system under the gold standard). This enabled the United Kingdom to govern the interstate system "as effectively as a world-empire," and thus helped to sustain the unprecedented 100 years' peace among the great powers (Arrighi 1989). Material power was not a sufficient condition for this to be possible. According to Arrighi, the key to British hegemony was:

> the *capacity to claim with credibility* that the expansion of the power of the United Kingdom served not just its national interest but a "universal interest" as well. Central to this hegemonic claim was a distinction between the power of the rulers and the "wealth of nations" subtly drawn in the liberal ideology propagated by the British intelligentsia . . . presented as the motor force of universal expansion. Free trade might undermine the sovereignty of rulers but it would at the same time expand the wealth of their subjects, or at least their propertied subjects. (Arrighi, 1989: 34, emphasis added)

Thus the combinations of material, coercive, and hegemonic capacities created the possibility for, and reality of, British supremacy, particularly in the middle decades of the nineteenth century. This enabled an extraordinary and generally legitimate (at least among the ruling elements in the most developed European countries) capacity to restructure the world to suit British national interests. However, this was not hegemony in a fundamentally Gramscian sense, although Arrighi's analysis shows how a "situation," that is the intersection and interaction of sets of social forces that produce a synthesis of interests, explains the *credibility* of British leadership in the international economy of the nineteenth century. What would strengthen this account is reference to the fact that the gold standard and its operation was constituted by, and depended heavily upon, the cooperation of other European states, and in this sense was a European system. The key element here is that insofar as Britain's rulers were hegemonic in the nineteenth century, they required the consent of other leading elements within metropolitan states. Moreover, in a global sense, the costs of adjustment under the gold standard tended to be borne most heavily by the poorer colonies under the control of each of the imperial, metropolitan European nations, and as such was by no means globally embedded nor consensual (Polanyi, 1944).

Thus, social change—and in the above case, international political stability—at any historical moment is the result of the interaction of structural, or relatively permanent, aspects of social reality and specific conjuncture of events; it is the product of synchronic and diachronic forces. Hegemony, in other words, can never be the simple product of the preponderance of a single state or grouping of states exercising power over other states. This is, of course, partly because human beings have consciousness and free will within the limits of the possible and thus any attempt to construct a hegemonic system of rule, over time, may generate, dialectically, a set of counterhegemonic forces, which may or may not be progressive. The corpse of *pax Britannica* was buried in the trenches of Ypres and the Somme. The theoretical point here is that the social world is qualitatively different from that explained by the natural sciences (which can be likened to a system of mechanical causation), and thus mechanical theories like the neorealist theory of hegemonic stability have limited scientific validity.

Thus no unilinear, pseudochronological concept of time can be applied to understand and explain constellations of social forces and historical conjunctures. Social structures and social events are partly constituted by processes that reflect different rhythms and historical tempos. Here Gramsci's analysis is similar to that of Braudel (1979) and the *Annals* historians. As Braudel argued, with respect to historical time, the first dimension changes very slowly, like the topological relationship between continental plates, between humankind and its geography (geographic time). The second dimension, with a faster rhythm than the first, is that of change in fundamental social structures, the *longue durée* (social time). The third rhythm, the most rapid, which focused on individuals, events, and specific conjunctures, was *l'histoire événementielle* (individual time). Any historical analysis (and by implication any study of the global political economy) should be sensitive to all three.

After Vulgar Marxism and the U.S. Orthodoxy

I have not yet addressed directly the problem of how to move beyond these epistemological questions and move in a more detailed way toward an ontology, social theory, and analytical method that avoids the lapse into arguments concerning the determinacy of either politics or economics, or some underlying or ultimate causality, although my position on this question is implicit in much of the above. Indeed, because of restrictions of space I cannot even begin to develop the points that are needed here. However, the work of both Cox (1987) and van der Pijl (1984) can be fruitfully consulted on this matter because each develops a rather sophisticated historical materialist ontology, and each applies his own unique method to what David Law and I (Gill and Law, 1988) call the global political economy—the fundamental concept of our ontology. The global political economy concept implies an integrated system of knowledge, production, and exchange, and includes the dialectical relations between capitalist systems and states—ecological, ethical, and other aspects of the whole. We have also outlined a preliminary research agenda that stems from this concept in a recent essay published in the journal of the International Studies Association, *International Studies Quarterly* (Gill and Law, 1989).

However we develop a given social ontology, it is crucial to remember the abstract, momentary, and necessarily incomplete nature of all thought processes and knowledge systems. Thus, we should heed Marx's warning in his admonition of the classical political economists:

> The vulgar mob [i.e., of classical economists] has therefore concluded that theoretical truths are abstractions which are at variance from reality, instead of seeing, on the contrary, that Ricardo does not carry true abstract thinking far enough and is therefore driven into false abstraction. (Marx, *Theories of Surplus Value*, vol. 2, cited in Resnick and Wolff, 1987: 58, note 44)

Here falseness is not simply equated with the approximation of an abstraction to some independent reality, as both Marx and Ricardo conceptualize the relations of thought to the "concrete-real" quite differently. At issue is how and why and with what consequences the classical economists and Marxists arrive at their different "thought-concretes." Two points seem relevant here. First, there is a relativity in each claim to truth. Second, social conditions interact with and influence the survival, "scientific" status, and consequences of rival social theories: knowledge is also a process of social struggle, again between hegemonic and counterhegemonic perspectives and principles.

Thus, from this point of view, the hegemonic perspectives within IPE can be criticized in not probing deeply enough into the complex role of ideas and consciousness and the interaction of knowledge systems with the rest of historical processes—an extreme example of what Marx calls "false abstraction," resulting in abstractions with no concrete grounding in history. Marxists also fall prey to this methodological error. For example, Gramsci shows how Nicolai Bukharin's *Theory of Historical Materialism: A Popular Manual of Marxist Sociology* eliminated the dialectical standpoint and introduced "metaphysical materialism" or "idealism upside down" (Gramsci, 1971: 437). The search for unitary, last-instance causes reduced the "philosophy of praxis" to something akin to the search for God, and the philosophical process to social mechanics:

> The philosophy implicit in the *Popular Manual* could be called a

positivist Aristoteleanism, and adaptation of formal logic to the methods of physical and natural science. The historical dialectic is replaced by the law of causality and the search for regularity, normality, and uniformity. . . . In mechanical terms, the effect can never transcend the cause or the system of causes, and therefore can have no development other than the flat vulgar development of economism. (Gramsci, 1971: 437)

Indeed, many similar and quite fundamental criticisms can be made of the explanatory usefulness of the prevailing positivist approaches to the study of IPE, for example, its ahistorical nature; its lack of a dynamic, dialectical quality; the narrowness and incompleteness of its abstractions, which are confined, almost tautologically, to the relations between theoretical abstractions (i.e., unitary rational actors called states); and the tendency to extreme parsimony in explanation relative to the infinite complexity of its object of analysis, the international system.[3] Given the preceding arguments and observations, the persistence of the prevailing U.S. approaches would appear to be surprising were we to live in a rational scientific world where, following the injunctions of Karl Popper, those theories that are internally inconsistent and/or are refuted by the evidence should be consigned to the intellectual scrapheap.

How then, do we explain the persistence of such a perspective? In my view, this can be explained in two ways. Despite its limitations it has a degree of *practical effectiveness* that partly stems from its parsimony and surface plausibility: it provides a framework for an instrumentalist social science to develop policy frameworks. And, to a degree, its use has corresponded with the rise of U.S. globalism, bound up with the tremendous dynamism of capitalist development in the United States. This is not to suggest that American policymakers accept uncritically either its framework or its policy recommendations. Senior figures in the U.S. political establishment are often more subtle and pragmatic. More important then is that particular policies and initiatives can be articulated and justified through the use of these ideas, insofar as they correspond to "common sense," and are reinforced by an appeal to "authority" (in the sense of learning, wisdom) and to "tradition" or the advocacy of a particular "way of life." There are at least two elements that help to explain this practical effectiveness.

First, the plausibility of this approach at the policy level corresponds to the predominance of positivist and behaviorist traditions in Anglo-Saxon academia. These traditions have served to constitute the bulk of American social science, and are rooted deeply. They go back a long way in the short history of the United States. The resonance of this perspective is amplified by the substantial scope and weight of the largest and best-funded academic community in the world. Of course, many academics from other countries receive graduate training in the United States, which has many of the world's leading research universities and think-tanks. The effect of this pattern of academic development is both to insulate the perspective from fundamental attack, especially within the United States itself, and to diffuse its impact on a global scale. This argument can be related to the social basis and funding of research in the United States, where there is widespread privatization of research initiatives and programs. This filters into public debates and policy formulation. This is not to imply, however, that there is any simple input-output linear programming of policy. The U.S. political system is one of the most complex in the world.

Second, as Augelli and Murphy (1988) illustrate, the abstract application of this discourse, with its substantive liberal and imperialist bias, gains strength from and sits well with deep-rooted elements in the U.S. Manichean political culture. Two aspects seem important here: (1) U.S. anti-intellectualism and pragmatism (and attraction to simple parsimonious theories and to detailed empirical work) and, perhaps more fundamentally, (2) the pervasive metaphysics of denominational religion, with its ideas concerning manifest destiny, evangelism, and crusaderism, which evokes a twin sense of mission and responsibility to save the rest of the world from itself. Moreover, the isolationist tradition, like its schizophrenic counterpart, messianic imperialism (both premised on the opposition between "us" and "them") parallels the radical separation of subject and object in positivist thought.

Thus, as in the pseudoreligion of Soviet Marxism, there is a tendency to protect a standard U.S. theorization (from which scores of doctoral theses, and thus many academic careers, have been built; consider the academic industries around regime theory and hegemonic stability theory). Thus the U.S. positivist paradigm is consolidated. A process of social and intellectual enclosure ensures that adherents and their theorizations are insulated from critical dialogue with those of contending perspective or paradigms. The dominant paradigm, for its adherents, assumes the mantle, as it were, of near, if not absolute, truth.

Notes

I would like to thank the editors for their invitation to contribute this essay, which can be read as developing the critique of the American orthodoxy as defined in Chapter 1. However, it can also be read as a general critique of positivist, mechanical, and economistic perspectives within Marxism and other traditions. I am also grateful to Frank Pearce and Robert Cox for helpful comments, the former for clarifying issues relating to Marxist structuralism, the latter for highlighting the importance of Gramsci's concept of myth.

1. Note from Robert Cox to the author, September 29, 1990.
2. I am grateful to Robert Cox for emphasizing this point.
3. See Chapter 1 for an amplification of these criticisms.

PART 2

NEW RESPONSES TO THE TRADITIONAL AGENDA

The second section of the book consists of three chapters by scholars who use new conceptual frameworks to capture the traditional issues of orthodox IPE. In Chapter 4, Diana Tussie confronts current concerns about "increasing protectionism" among the major trading countries. She argues that current concerns have been heightened by the orthodoxy's misreading of the history of the postwar, open trade system under U.S. dominance, which, in fact, always made room for protection. Tussie argues that, contrary to the orthodoxy, today's protectionist moves are less a trade issue than a consequence of the recent transformation of the postwar monetary and financial systems.

Richard Higgott's concern in Chapter 5 is with current attempts to maintain and extend the openness of the postwar trade regime. He argues that scholars and policymakers with more distance from the U.S. trade policy agenda are able to understand things about the regime, and opportunities for its progressive transformation, that would elude the orthodoxy. In particular, he suggests that extension of the liberalizing regime to trade in agricultural (the issue that U.S. policymakers declare is of greatest concern to them in the current round of GATT negotiations) is more likely to be a consequence of the agenda setting done by the Cairns Group, a north-south alliance of significant agricultural exporters, than a consequence of "hegemonic stability" provided by the United States.

Finally, in Chapter 6, economist Douglas Nelson provides a sympathetic critical review of the wide literature relevant to applying game theoretic models to trade policy. Game theory, Nelson argues, can provide a language for integrating insights about trade policy that come from many branches of the social sciences, not because models of strategic interaction among rational individuals can subsume insights from research programs that focus on the social construction of individuals, political agendas, values, and common knowledge, but because game theoretic explanations point to where such insights are demanded.

4

Trading in Fear? U.S. Hegemony and the Open World Economy in Perspective

Diana Tussie

Is the trading system really becoming more protectionist? The wave of concern about the resurgence of protection in industrial countries has sterilized academic thought since the end of the 1970s. The end of a well-oiled system of free trade under U.S. leadership, so we hear, is in sight. The drift into protectionism will become irresistible without self-restraint and some enlightened self-interest on the part of those countries whose actions shape the system. The world shall find it difficult, otherwise, to enjoy continued prosperity under the ensuing system of polarized trading blocs.

A major source of these fears lies in the perception that an entirely new feature of present trade relations is the overtly discriminatory nature of such rising protection managing to get around the accepted rules of international trade. To be sure, only in very few cases have fresh regulations taken the form of increased explicit tariffs. More often there have been informal agreements to restrict competition in the form of "voluntary export restraints" or an increasingly frequent and arbitrary application of discriminatory tariff surcharges in the form of antidumping and countervailing duties. By nature these duties discriminate among foreign suppliers by singling out those perceived—more often than not misperceived—to be subsidizing or dumping their goods. Such discrimination, it is widely supposed, is an entirely new feature of world trade. Part of the problem with this characterization is that the standards against which the past is measured have been greatly exaggerated.

A second and related cause of concern stems from a different set of rather simplified assumptions on the nature of the present trading system. It seems that the specter of the Great Depression and the panic of witnessing its repetition may be clouding our understanding of what is new in the current trading system, and not a mere resurrection of the past. This misperception has led to a situation in which most contemporary discussions on the prospects for world trade share a false dilemma—whether our trading system today has become more or less open vis-à-vis some recent golden age when nondiscrimination reigned and the United States ruled the waves unchallenged.

Setting a trend in current academic thought on the nature and roots of protection, Kindleberger (1973) argued that it will emerge when there is no country able or willing to take up a leading role to ensure order, stability, and free trade. In order to promote and sustain the openness of the system, a leader must be in the position to give the long-term needs of the system more weight than the short-term needs of its own people when it comes to formulating international trade policy. In the last chapter of his seminal *The World in Depression* (Kindleberger 1973), the argument was put forth that the crisis was so deep, lasted so long, and had such vast consequences because no leading country was able and willing to take up the role of a stabilizer. The 1930s were a period of transition from British to U.S. leadership, when the United Kingdom could no longer fulfill its duties as a leader and the United States remained reluctant to assume its new international role. Kindleberger held that a leader should be able to act counter-cyclically when needed; in case of crises or negative trends the leader ought to step forward as a stabilizer capable of avoiding the temptation of the *sauve-qui-peut* behavior that inspires most countries. The main responsibilities of the leading nation facing international economic disruption are to furnish an outlet for distressed goods, to maintain the flow of capital to would-be borrowers, and to serve as a lender of last resort in financial crises.

The basic contention that the promotion of an open international economic system is related to a hegemonic distribution of power has held formidable sway, and in a variety of versions it has dominated subsequent academic debate (Gilpin, 1975; Krasner, 1976). Under this conception, declining U.S. hegemony would result in the erosion of international economic liberalization; a decline of hegemony presages a decline in the openness of the system.

Trends in international economic liberalization throughout the 1980s have not been very consistent with such a world view. Despite some setbacks and a few difficulties, the world economy has remained relatively open. In fact, the trend toward continued liberalization has continued in important ways, as evidenced by the Uruguay Round.

The argument that the United States should still be regarded as a hegemon has been forcefully made by Bruce Russett (1985) and Susan Strange (1987). An empirical assessment of the economic power capabilities of the United States conducted by Webb and Krasner concluded that although "there is some ambiguity about how the United States should be classified," it is still more powerful than any of its competitors and is "far larger than Britain was at the peak of its power in the nineteenth century" (Webb and Krasner, 1989: 195).

An early alternative to the waning hegemony thesis to explain the resurgence of protection was offered by Strange and Tooze (1981). Slow growth and the existence of surplus capacity in major sectors of the world economy were held to be the principal sources of rising protectionism, regardless of the power or the attitude of the leading economic state. An implicit corollary to be drawn from the surplus capacity explanation was that the tide would turn against protection once economic activity began to pick up. The available evidence for the 1980s, however, indicates that with the exception of a few recessionary years, trade continued to grow and, even despite the high records attained at the end of the decade, the panoply of trade restrictions remains intact. Moreover, the program for a single European market and the regional trading arrangement between the United States and Canada have rekindled the debate on the possible fragmentation of the multilateral system.

A major theme of this chapter is that the crucial factors affecting the trade regime today are neither the decline of U.S. hegemonic power nor the depressed state of the world economy. The trading system is certainly undergoing profound structural change. Yet the roots of such changes are to be found, on the one hand, in the monetary and financial system, and on the other, in the trading system itself with the widespread loss of significance of tariffs as a result of the successful rounds of GATT negotiations. Both lower average growth rates and waning hegemony are secondary factors affecting the shift in trade policies. Excessive concentration on these variables has neglected the more fundamental forces at work sidestepping the discussion of the central issues.

Before focusing on the shape of trading arrangements as we approach the twenty-first century, I will take a step back in history to put the nature of U.S. leadership into perspective. This will prepare the way for the analysis of future developments. The contention that the attainment of a liberal multilateral trading system is hindered by declining hegemony presumes what it should first demonstrate: not too long ago there used to be a hypothetical trading system with a significant degree of certainty, transparency, and nondiscrimination—all guaranteed by U.S. supremacy. Yet this benevolent idea is not fully borne out by a more detailed or nuanced characterization of postwar trade history and U.S. attitudes. Agreed rules have been bent, if not constantly, then, at least quite consistently, and even at the peak of its power the United States was not a well-disposed outlet for distressed goods. Moreover, it has set precedents in seeking legitimacy from GATT for rule-breaking behavior in order to defend particular trade interests.

Protectionism, Recession, and U.S. Leadership[1]

U.S. trade policy was never devoid of mercantilist inspiration to the extent that Britain's was. At the point of assuming its leadership role, immediately after the war, the United States was reluctant to become a ready outlet for world exports. As the war drew to an end, the United States held a substantial trade surplus with the rest of the world, which warranted unilateral reductions of trade barriers so that with the opening up of the U.S. market, the gap between deficits and surpluses could be bridged. Professor Hubert D. Henderson, advising the British government, had argued that:

> The principle of reciprocal concessions comes very near to saying that tariff reductions, calculated to increase American imports, can only be made for tariff concessions by other countries, calculated to increase American exports by an equivalent amount. This, in turn, comes very near to making it a sine qua non of tariff reductions that they should do nothing to . . . readjust the balance of payments of the world. (Henderson, 1949: 611–612)

In order to secure a balanced international economy, Henderson had recommended that countries reduce their tariffs and encourage imports, not in proportion to the reciprocal concessions they were able to secure, but in proportion to the strength of their balance-of-payments position. The recommendation bore affinities to Keynes' International Clearing Union by which countries in surplus would be required to increase their imports to ease the adjustments of deficit countries. As Henderson himself acknowledged, this was far removed from "the reign of acceptability" to U.S. public opinion. Instead, a more mercantilist approach was enforced with the *quid pro quo* principle institutionalized in GATT. The uniqueness of the U.S. resource base and its variegated economy meant that strong producer interests could be found in favor both of protectionism and of free trade. The U.S. foreign trade policy had of necessity to balance out political pressures and counterpressures on the home front. Its adoption of a liberal trade policy was more ambiguous, less across the board than Britain's had ever been. As noted by Meyer (1978), the major difference between the trading order under the hegemony of the United Kingdom and that under the U.S. primacy was that Britain had reduced tariffs unilaterally and sustained not only a free export policy, but also a free import policy. In contrast, the United States offered to free its imports on a contractual basis, with an eye to reciprocal benefits at the conclusion of negotiations, regardless of handicaps at the starting line.

Moreover, the rise of nontariff barriers to trade is often somehow incorrectly associated with the rise of the new protectionism in the seventies. In fact, the roots of such a trend are to be found quite clearly in the GATT charter itself in the case of agricultural products and from the mid-1950s onward in the introduction of the first voluntary export restriction schemes affecting exports from Japan and developing countries of Asia. The United States, at the apex of its power, played a crucial role in initiating and legitimizing protectionist policies under GATT.

From the very start these policies were overtly discriminatory. Although the brunt of competition from Japan and the developing countries was felt equally in Great Britain and the United States, it was the then unchallenged hegemony that gave an unequivocal lead in breaking the so-called free trade consensus.

Indeed it was precisely because of its power over the world economy and within its managing institutions that the United States was able to take the initiative in justifying protection under the GATT, first in the early 1960s, when the cotton industry was in trouble, subsequently in the 1970s, when the problem had extended to man-made fiber, and lastly in the 1980s, when other natural fibers were brought under the regulatory framework created in GATT for such discriminatory restrictions. As the following paragraphs will show, there have been marginal differences—if any at all—in the U.S. policy process in times of undisputed primacy and in times of waning hegemony.

The first voluntary export quotas of postwar trade history were implemented by Japan in response to requests from the United States in December 1955. By January 1957, Japan had delineated a five-year plan of export restriction to satisfy U.S. pressure. Although the United States was not the sole country to feel the competition from lower-cost countries, it was the only one that could and did turn its own need for protection into a global regulatory framework to manage trade.

The United States was alone in the early 1950s in not discriminating against Japanese imports until 1956, when imports of cotton reached 1937 levels. Although this represented a mere 1.7 percent of domestic production, Japanese cotton textiles accounted for more than 60 percent of total imports. Such successful expansion put the industry onto the defensive. To compound the problem, a price support system for cotton growers was instated in 1955 (and it remained in force for ten years), and so the price of the industry's raw material rose relative to the world market. Faced with this situation, the industry approached the U.S. Tariff Commission with four petitions to apply safeguards under Article XIX of GATT. The petitions, however, were rejected; the administration was not willing to pay the costs that Article XIX involved. Indeed, invocation of Article XIX meant that a tariff increase on textiles would lead to tariff renegotiation with other GATT members. In any case it would not offer domestic industry a greater sense of security because Article XIX does not permit selective treatment against a specific source.

Furthermore, the United States had been pushing the Europeans to admit Japan to GATT from 1952 to 1955, and could hardly, as soon as it had been successful, apply an escape clause against its own godchild. Yet another powerful consideration stopped the Eisenhower administration from going to GATT:

> It had recently over-played the GATT's waiver provisions by asking for (and obtaining) a broadly-termed waiver to restrict agricultural products from entering the United States, without the customary time limits. It is no exaggeration to say that this incident had caused GATT's first major crisis and had resulted in a considerable loss of confidence in the United States as the leader and principal proponent of freer world trade. . . . It

> was therefore politically the worst possible moment for the United
> States to address itself once more to GATT (in the name of self-seeking
> protectionism) and ask permission from the Europeans (essentially) to
> restrict its imports from Japan. (Curzon and Curzon, 1976: 258)

Yet the administration was not unsympathetic to the claims of industry,
even though, as mentioned above, total imports constituted less than 2
percent of domestic production. The conflict between "self-seeking
protectionism" and free trade for other markets was resolved with "Japanese
goodwill." The petition for Article XIX safeguards, although unsuccessful,
had brought the problem home and had given the administration a
justification and a bargaining counter for approaching the Japanese bilaterally
with a five-year program of voluntary export quotas. The compromise reached
with Japan to satisfy the textile industry rendered possible a round of trade
liberalization. Congress extended the Reciprocal Trade Agreement Act and
hence gave President Eisenhower authority for initiating the Dillon Round of
Trade negotiations.

The conflict in U.S. trade interests was not, however, a new
phenomenon. Suffice it to recall that the International Trade Organization
(ITO) floundered on congressional approval, although the proposal had been
conceived by Department of State officials with a wider vision of U.S.
influence. When drafting the General Agreement, the United States had also
introduced a double standard: quantitative restrictions for industrial protection
were forbidden (Article XI), but they were permitted for the agricultural sector
at the request of the Department of Agriculture in order to allow the United
States to continue its price-support program. In 1960, Eric Wyndham White,
then executive secretary of GATT, conceded that Article XI had been "largely
tailor-made to U.S. requirements" (quoted in Dam, 1970: 260).

It was soon to be seen that the Japanese expedient was ephemeral.
Although Japan was effectively restrained (her share of cotton textile imports
to the United States declining from 63 percent in 1958 to 26 percent in
1960), the slack was swiftly taken up by Hong Kong, whose share of cotton
textiles imports rose from 14.0 to 27.5 percent (U.S., International Trade
Commission, 1978). The value of these exports leapt from $3.6 million in
1956, when Japan first began to regulate her exports, to $108 million in
1958, thus exposing a potential threat. The government of Hong Kong was
approached with a quota scheme but turned it down. Furthermore, Portugal,
Egypt, Taiwan, Spain, Pakistan, and India had also come into the world
textile market, somewhat aided by the U.S. farm program, which had raised
the price of cotton to domestic mills above those prices prevailing in the
world market.

Kennedy's presidential campaign in 1959 promised the industry more
effective rescue; Kennedy redeemed the pledge on May 2, 1961, issuing a
textile program that, among other measures, requested the Department of
State to "seek an international understanding which will provide a basis for

trade that will avoid undue disruption of established industries" (U.S., International Trade Commission, 1978: 7). Thus, the administration moved to get GATT to enforce first the interim Short-Term Agreement (STA) extended subsequently into the Long-Term Agreement (LTA) for a five-year period from 1962 to 1967. In essence, the STA and the LTA legalized the restrictions on Japan and authorized negotiations with reluctant suppliers.

The LTA "promised enough protection to cause a group of 75 interested Congressmen to thank President Kennedy" (*New York Times*, 16 February 1962). Once again, the appeasement of the textile industry served to pave the way to congressional approval of the Trade Expansion Act of 1962, which conferred on the president the authority to initiate the Kennedy Round of GATT trade negotiations.

This tug of war between two sectors of the U.S. economy—the one whose production was largely internationalized serving to spur the movement toward world trade liberalization versus another, more inward oriented, trying to stall the effects of foreign trade on the home market—was restaged under Nixon, and yet another compromise had to be reached. Again, Nixon's presidential campaign of 1968 pledged further import relief to the textile industry, which by now claimed protection over the whole range of textile products through all stages of production, from yarns to clothing and all types of fiber, both natural (cotton and wool) and artificial. This time, however, Japan was less forthcoming, and at one point Senate ratification for the return of the Okinawa base to Japanese jurisdiction seemed to be conditional on the conclusion of the textile agreement. Impasse on the textile front lasted until Nixon's new economic policy in 1971 (with devaluation of the dollar and a 10 percent surcharge on imports). Regardless of this all-too-obvious turning point in the capabilities of U.S. leadership, the Japanese conceded in October and signed a three-year agreement (1971–1974) covering their exports of wool, artificial, and cotton products, "a forced settlement squeezed out of the Japanese government" (Destler et al., 1979: 315). Further agreements were subsequently reached with Hong Kong, South Korea, and Taiwan. President Nixon's desire to secure reelection contributed to the timing.

Despite its declining power, the United States was still able to usher the issue into GATT yet again. In the course of 1973, when the LTA was due to expire, negotiations to further extending restrictions to wool and man-made fibers were initiated, and resumed in the Multi-Fibre Agreement (MFA). The initiative removed an important obstacle to congressional approval of the 1974 Trade Act, the statute that was to authorize executive participation in the Tokyo Round of multilateral trade negotiations.

Both the Carter and the Reagan administrations followed in the same footsteps. Although Reagan's initial stance was pro–free trade, it was the responsibility of his administration to extend the coverage of the MFA to natural fibers other than wool and cotton when the 1986 renegotiation took place prior to the launching of the Uruguay Round. History shows a policy of having to take one step backward to placate the protectionist lobby for every step forward required by sectors interested in foreign markets. The dualism of U.S. trade interests was reproduced in GATT as a natural development of U.S. economic prominence. As in other aspects, GATT could not but be "the international counterpart of U.S. tariff policy" (Meyer, 1978: 126).

It is difficult to reconcile this historical pattern with the cavalier picture of hegemonic functions that has become conventional wisdom. A close reading of history suggests that the United States has been instrumental in defining the shape, extension, and coverage of trade regulations. Equally, Strange and Tooze's argument about the resurgence of protectionism in relation to world economic recession depicts only part of the picture. As the previous discussion suggests, from their inception regulations took an overtly discriminatory form, singling out the most competitive countries. Protectionist measures were taken by the United States during times of both unchallenged hegemony and unparalleled world economic boom.

Since 1984, growth has picked up in the economies of the Organization for Economic Cooperation and Development; yet trade restraint agreements have not only not remained in place but have continued on the increase. In the period 1984–1987, when trade was growing healthily, the share of nonoil imports affected by selected NTBs (Non Tariff Barriers) increased by almost three percentage points (Table 4.1); this increase tripled the one corresponding to the period 1981–1984 when trade was sluggish.

World trade grew in 1988 by a spectacular 8.5 percent, yet total trade restraint arrangements increased between September 1987 and May 1988 by almost 100 percent (IMF, 1988). These figures rebuff hopeful forecasts on the waning of restrictions with the onset of economic recovery. For one thing, regardless of either growth records or the distribution of power among states, some of these regulations are becoming an integral part of the system. On the other hand, a contrapunctual set of regulations has merely acquired new brilliance as border measures receded with the staging of GATT rounds. This means that new areas had to be opened up for negotiation.

The Changed Trading System: A Stylized Perspective

The consensus that protectionism has been on the rise in major market economies has thrived unchallenged, overlooking the ascendency of other deep-rooted changes affecting the fabric of the world economy in another direction. It is necessary to assess these changes to comprehend the true impact of protection and the precise state of the trading system. The origin of such changes is double natured; taken together they act as important counterbalancing weights for gauging the overall openness of the system.

Table 4.1 Imports Affected by NTBs in Industrial Countries
(% of total imports)

	1981	1984	1987
Nonoil imports	18.7	19.9	22.6
food items	35.3	38.7	38.2
manufactures	18.1	18.3	21.5

Source: IMF (1988).
Note: NTBs includes certain paratariff measures, import deposits and surcharges, variable levies and quantitative restrictions, automatic licensing, price controls, antidumping and countervailing actions, and import surveillance.

On the one hand, there is a purely trade issue. Until not too long ago, when assessing the degree of protection offered to domestic industries, it was appropriate to focus on the level of tariffs and the extent of quantitative restrictions. Both of these measures, tariffs and quantitative restrictions, are border regulations applied by customs authorities at the point of entry. With the gradual removal of such purely commercial measures, the mantle presently covered by trade policy has broadened. A wider net has been cast.

On the other hand, there is a financial issue. Most trade analyses have not managed to escape from the thrall of neoclassical thought, holding that trade in goods and services determines foreign exchange rates. It is true that under the Bretton Woods system of fixed exchange rates, the tariff and the exchange rate were linked together as complements. Stable exchange rates not only allowed for rational calculation in foreign trade; there was as well the fact that the rules of the system restrained countries from pursuing policies that would result in large macroeconomic imbalances. Yet capital flows and exchange rates since the early 1970s have moved quite independently of foreign trade and indeed have run counter to it. To take the trade aspect first, we now face a significantly liberal system in terms of traditional instruments of trade policy. Tariffs have been lowered through several GATT negotiating rounds to a minimum among the main trading countries. When the full extent of the Tokyo Round tariff reduction became effective in 1987, import-weighted average tariff rates reached about 4.3 percent for the United States and 6 percent for the EEC of Nine. For Japan, which had brought forward the full implementation of its cuts by March 1983, the comparable figure is 2.9 percent (GATT, 1979). The tariff has thus lost much of its traditional significance as an effective means of protection, although there are, of course, important exceptions at the sectoral and product level. One of these exceptions is, as we have seen, the textile and apparel sector.

The GATT rounds led to increasing interpenetration and interdependence among the industrial countries; countries were left very much exposed to one another. This development was compounded by the difficulties in implementing legal safeguards under GATT. Safeguards procedures allow countries experiencing "unforeseen circumstances" (Article XIX) to backtrack on commitments made to trading partners. Yet once tariffs became bound in GATT they were rarely raised again. The reason lies in the interlocking nature of trade negotiations: the country withdrawing a concession is obliged to preserve the balance of trade advantages and so offer an equivalent concession or suffer retaliation.

Without going into too much legal detail, it is clear that the fear of unravelling the whole GATT edifice has deterred protection-needy countries from recourse to this legitimate safety valve in any significant way. Yet the dilemma for importing nations was that not to act meant risking the dislocation of domestic markets, whereas action under Article XIX (nondiscriminatory in principle) would disrupt the trade of third countries that were not seen to be the cause of the problem (Winham, 1986: 123). To get out of this dilemma, countries have avoided seeking protection on a legal basis and have devised bilateral agreements that aim to restrict the volume of imports from particular countries or to monitor the prices at which these imports are placed on the market. As shown in the previous section, the textile regulations inaugurated by the United States were a precedent.

In short, tariff dismantling coupled with the obstacles to the implementation of effective safeguards in the form of new tariffs have deprived countries of this conventional trade policy tool. Mechanisms were thus devised to handle import flows that had customarily been regulated through tariffs.

Accompanying the quiet and staged decline of tariffs, a second change was set in motion amid more fanfare with the collapse of the Bretton Woods system of fixed parities in the early 1970s. Its replacement by floating rates has had important (and to a great extent unexpected) repercussions for trade policies. The shift from fixed to floating exchange rates, which ironically was meant to stabilize currency speculation, has in fact invited it, leading to an overexposure of trade flows to the liberalization of money flows. Present exchange rate fluctuations bear scant relation to trade performance; therefore, currency downswings and upswings cannot easily be likened to the competitive devaluations that were rampant in the thirties. Nonetheless, changes in nominal and real exchange rates have been significant and have affected international competitiveness. In any case, the link between exchange rates and trade flows, a second traditional means of regulating trade, became unraveled.

Different reasons have diverted analysts from focusing on the financial and monetary problems affecting world trade. Generally narrowly defined trade-related measures have been pointed out as vicious protectionists tools leading to slow growth. Most analyses have tended to place the danger of major economic disruptions in new trade-restraining practices, disregarding the unprecedented monetary and financial openness (Strange, 1986) that has become the driving force of the world economy. As Peter Drucker has very cogently argued, a major change that has occurred is the emergence of "the symbol economy—capital movements, exchange rates and credit flows—as the flywheel of the world economy in place of the real economy—the flow of goods and services" (Drucker, 1986: 782).

In today's world economy, the "real" economy of goods and services and the "symbol" economy of capital, money, and credit are no longer bound tightly to each other. They are indeed moving farther and farther apart. World trade in goods and services amounts to around $3 trillion a year. But the London Eurodollar market alone has a yearly turnover of $75 trillion, a volume at least 25 times that of world trade. In addition, there are foreign exchange transactions in a host of other money centers. The result is that exchange rates no longer genuinely reflect real comparative advantage. The translation mechanism has broken down.

The peculiar economic policy of the Reagan administration added a further measure of uncertainty to the global system. Although Reagan managed to combine strong economic recovery with low inflation rates in the years following the recession of 1982, domestic success was achieved at a very high cost in terms of international economic stability. The addition of a tough monetary policy pushed the value of the dollar to a record high; the real effective exchange rate reached a record level of 145, based on a value of 100 for 1980.

The strength of the dollar was presented by the Reagan administration as a reflection of the robustness of the U.S. economy. In fact, this "macho policy" contributed to weakening the competitiveness of domestic sectors producing tradables, lowering the price of imports, and raising the relative costs of U.S. exports. An overvalued dollar fed the growing U.S. foreign trade deficit, which grew from $42.6 billion to almost $160.0 billion between 1982 and 1987.[2]

The deficit was financed by massive inflows of capital and dwindling net outflows, which made the United States a debtor nation in 1985 for the first time since World War I. Most importantly, for the first time in recent history the major debtor owed its foreign debt in its own currency. Herein lies the key to the disorder and uncertainty afflicting world trade conditions.

The U.S. trade deficit had a stimulating effect on world trade, especially after 1983; yet the high exchange rate also overexposed vulnerable sectors to foreign competition they could not possibly meet. The result was that price-fixing or market-sharing agreements had to be sought in order to put a brake of some kind on soaring imports. Such ad hoc under-the-table deals mushroomed during these years because of the obstacles to straightforward tariff increases, which might be perceived as more permanent and therefore more menacing in that they could trigger chain retaliations. A quota, moreover, has the added "attraction" that it fixes import volumes regardless of the vagaries of exchange rates. The rising number of quota agreements enforced in particular, but not only, by the United States since 1980 have had in this way a damage limitation purpose.

The causal association running from exchange-rate appreciation to increasing NTBs is not necessarily reversed once a currency begins to depreciate. Table 4.2 gives some indication of this: when the dollar took a plunge in 1985, NTBs in the United States did not recede; on the contrary, they continued to increase. One reason is that exchange-rate volatility and related macroeconomic distress brings uncertainty and therefore fans the pressures from domestic producers for increased insulation.

Exchange-rate instability is also another key factor explaining why new trade regulations take a nontariff format instead of the orthodox tariff increase. Indeed, even short-term movements in the exchange rate can nullify the effect of a tariff. A quota or a price-fixing deal, on the other hand, eliminates the uncertainty. Taken together, these factors have introduced a novel element in the international trade system. Because the volatility of exchange rates has had a greater impact on trade among industrial countries than on north-south trade, the new regulations have flourished mainly, if not exclusively, on flows among the industrialized nations (UNCTAD, 1989).

Herein lies a new feature of the new trading system. After the dismantling of the arsenal of restrictions that had mushroomed in the 1930s, trade among industrial countries remained relatively free of fresh quota restrictions. The bulk of quotas that evolved in the 1960s was aimed at competitive LDCs, as the MFA most poignantly illustrated. An indication of this nascent trend is offered by the growing share of U.S. imports from other industrial countries covered by quota restrictions of one form or another. According to World Bank estimates, in 1981 this share was equivalent to 9 percent; by 1986, as much as 15 percent of such imports were covered. Yet VERs (voluntary export restraints) are not the sole device used to put some sort of order on import growth. Other forms of trade regulations have emerged to accompany the declining incidence of tariffs and the impaired role of exchange rates.

New Forms of Trade Management

To face the twin pressures of reduced tariff protection and impaired exchange rates, industrial countries came to the point where they needed to widen their negotiating agenda in both issue areas. Attempts at regulating exchange rates were initiated with the Plaza Agreement in late 1985. In order to neutralize the worst effects of financial liberalization, major countries tried to coordinate maximum ranges for exchange rate fluctuation and the future value of their currencies; steps were also taken to slow down the self-defeating competition to capture international financial flows via interest rates. Although the question is far from being resolved, there is a growing awareness that major

Table 4.2 Extent of Protection Through NTBs
(1981=100)

	1982	1983	1984	1985	1986
United States	107	107	112	120	123
European Economic Community	107	110	114	121	118
Japan	100	99	99	99	99

Source: Bhagwati (1988).

countries are going to have to compromise to reach some workable arrangement, however short of ideal.

Just as new areas of negotiation have to be tackled in finance to counter the excessive freedom of financial flows from effective regulation, in the trading system itself new areas have of necessity to be opened up once tariff dismantling has increased the exposure of economies to one another. Two classes of nontariff measures have come to the fore as a result of this exposure. There are those that have been erected, both legally and illegally, with more or less ingenuity, as a counterbalance to liberalization; these have been dealt with in the preceding section. But there is another kind of NTB that stems from virgin areas, issues to be tackled as liberalization progresses.

With GATT rounds having shed a significant number of tariffs, a first "peel of protection" of major economies has been removed. Thus with border measures receding, nonborder measures applied by governments to assist, favor or outrightly protect their industries have by force become more visible. Measures that were traditionally seen to have only indirect links into trade policy are now found to have "trade-interfering effects." Thus the dividing line between trade and other policies has become increasingly artificial, the distinction between border and nonborder measures having been blurred.

The complexity and importance of this development is patently illustrated by the growing scope of GATT rounds. The Tokyo Round, for example, over and above the conventional tariff reductions concluded six codes on nontariff barriers (government procurement, import licensing, subsidies and countervailing duties, dumping, technical standards, and customs valuations). With the exception of the code on government purchases, these codes focused on measures applied at the border that were seen as capable of offsetting the effects of disappearing border measures. The mandate for the Uruguay Round is a further step in this direction, going much beyond border measures with the inclusion of intellectual property rights, investment measures, provision of services, and so on. Here the aim is not merely to prevent the left hand from undoing what is achieved with the right hand, but to broaden the scope of GATT's supervision. Thus the conventional concept of protection has become more ambitious; it has been widened to include a host of measures and policy tools that hitherto were out of the bounds of international concern. The accountability of governments for their trade and trade-related actions has increased with their shedding of the outer layer of protection.

An illustrative case showing the new realms that have been opened up is the dispute over the type of subsidies provided to the airliner jet industry between the United States and four EEC countries. The former alleged that the Airbus Industries consortium had been granted generous financial subsidies and thus the U.S. aviation industry had become a victim of unfair competition. The Europeans have replied that this sector in the United States is not precisely a model of perfect competition; in particular, the airline industry has not been immune to subsidies in albeit somewhat more nuanced ways. The'argument goes that the cream of the defense budget has provided the industry with a captive market, and large government contracts have served as actual subsidies to research and development costs. Thus a subject as usually unrelated to trade as the destination of the defense budget can turn into the bone of contention of an international trade dispute.

Similarly, in the EEC, the disparate treatment of inward foreign investment across countries has reached a turning point and jumped onto the trade agenda. As a result, the hitherto unquestioned practice of mutual recognition of rules of origin has come under fire. The Treaty of Rome did not establish the principle that all members had to apply the same rules of origin for goods counted as European and therefore entitled to zero tariff rates; rather, it was accepted that each country was free to set the rules that best served its interests with the proviso that they should be mutually recognized by other members. With the upsurge of tariff-jumping Japanese investment into the EEC and the different treatment accorded to it across countries, the principle of mutual recognition become a controversial issue. Taking an unprecedented course of action, in 1988 France refused to consider as "made in the EEC" automobiles exported from Britain but manufactured by Nissan. The refusal was based on the argument that Nissan cars lacked the minimum percentage of European content that the French consider acceptable, despite meeting the laxer British requirements. Thus, the treatment accorded to foreign investment and broader matters of industrial policies have become a subject of discussion at the bargaining table. The ever closer integration of economies turns such simple expediency as mutual recognition of rules of origin obsolete. It is natural that this should lead to an eventual drafting of a standard system for determining rules of origin. Inroads into harmonizing a host of rules such as these will be the task at hand into the twenty-first century.

In sum, as liberalization of trade proceeds, the range of government practices considered to have trade impact has broadened. The implication of this is that the conventional distinction between a country's domestic and foreign trade policy has been broken down, forcing governments to increasingly discuss a wider range of policies with their trading partners.

National authorities then must submit to a gradual erosion of their unfettered prerogative to supervise and regulate the national market. An alternative to such an erosion lies in the opening up of new areas of negotiation in order that a compromise is achieved with trading partners. This is the Uruguay Round track. Another such alternative may be found in country groupings within which the most sensitive economic policy issues that have laid dormant behind the "peel of protection" can be discussed and even harmonized.

Once tariffs are shed, it is only natural that new institutional arrangements should develop and untapped issue areas should be opened up. These are here to stay. Even if the high growth rates of the 1960s were sustainable throughout the 1990s, it would be unrealistic to pursue or even expect a revival of the 1960s' trading system. This is now obsolete because of the structural changes that have taken place since then.

These changes in the structure and the foundations of the world economy are the new realities under which trade now operates, and, although highly visible, such changes have not been fully incorporated into our understanding of the trading system. Yet these are precisely the factors that preclude a repetition of the *sauve-qui-peut* retrenchment; today the international economy has become more fully integrated.

Looking Forward

Nontariff barriers have indeed gained increasing salience throughout the 1980s, yet it is unwarranted to conclude from this alone that the continued openness and stability of the trading system is at stake. The precise effect of NTBs is not easy to interpret. The growing salience of such measures is concurrent with the freeing of exchange rates and the reduction of tariffs to the point that they no longer constitute significant impediments to trade among developed countries.

In the narrowly commercial sense, NTBs may have slowed down if not reversed the process of trade liberalization. We cannot be too sure about the precise incidence of these measures because cross-country data are available only from the beginning of the 1980s. Hence the overall level of protection imposed by present NTBs cannot be directly compared to the level of protection that had been guaranteed by more stable exchange rates and by the tandem of tariffs and NTBs throughout the 1960s and 1970s. In an ever more closely integrated world economy, the choice seems to lie between managed exchange rates and managed trade or some pragmatic combination of both.

The rise of protectionist measures in the 1980s can no longer be related to slow growth. Between 1981 and 1984—slow growth and even recessionary years—the share of imports affected by selective nontariff measures grew a mere one percentage point from 18.7 percent to 19.9 percent; whereas from

1984 to 1987, when world trade may not have been booming but was certainly growing, this share went up from 19.9 percent to 22.6 percent, jumping almost three percentage points (UNCTAD, 1989). Further, in 1988 and 1989, when trade growth achieved surprisingly robust figures, trade regulations continued on the increase.

Neither can this so-called new protectionism be too closely or solely related to the decline of U.S. hegemony. The United States is still a leading economy, even though its hegemony may not be as paramount. It may not be the postwar colossus that it used to be, but it still is a first among equals. It is therefore pertinent to question where the United States is leading the international trading system.

Despite its rhetoric and much conventional wisdom, the United States never abandoned a tradition of discrimination. Its trade policy never fully lost its appetite for mercantilist expedients and, when necessary, had few scruples to use its power to enforce discrimination. New forms of regulation may be on the increase, yet it does not seem that the United States will lead into a system of retrenchment within blocs unraveling what has been achieved. The constant alarms over a return to the trading conditions of the 1930s are not warranted. Such interpretations unduly underrate the strength of liberalizing forces at work.

Yet the trading system is no doubt undergoing a process of structural transformation. Its new forms of regulation are not passing phenomena; they are here to stay because they respond to the shedding of the peel of protection that cushioned major economies, and thus to the resultant fundamental changes in the economic environment. For one thing, we have seen that many nontrade issues have come to the fore as internationally negotiable propositions. The format, range, and incidence of foreign investment and tax rules and industrial and regional development policies are bound to become a central issue of future negotiations.

Increased visibility is not the only consequence of the removal of the peel of protection. In many cases governments have indeed stepped up their assistance to industries precisely to make up for the increased exposure to foreign competition. In short, government intervention at the submacro level has become more intense. The puzzle in which the removal of one kind of protection appears only to have opened the way for another kind can be explained by adapting for our purposes an argument put forth, to be subsequently debunked, by Bhagwati:

> The evidence of increased non-tariff barriers and administered protection just as tariffs had been reduced to new lows suggests the intriguing possibility that there may be a Law Constant Protection: If you reduce one kind of protection, another variety simply pops up elsewhere. You then have a Displacement Effect, not evidence of any increase in protectionist pressure. (Bhagwati, 1988: 53)

New regulatory devices have been instated, but the reason for these is not necessarily the intention to dispose of what has been obtained by way of tariff reductions via GATT. There are both discriminating and liberalizing trends at work in the trading system today. As was suggested above, a growing number of policies that used to be unrelated to trade have become an integral part of trade negotiations. Further progress in this direction requires that growing portions of state sovereignty be surrendered, as illustrated by the process of building a truly single market in Europe. Given that most countries will be extremely reluctant to cede sovereignty to a global multilateral organization, the most significant steps to further trade liberalization will tend to be selective. These initiatives will take the shape of new free-trade agreements within which existing NTBs and trade-related policies can be either harmonized or even dismantled altogether. These are the sorts of issues with which Canada the United States, and Europe are now trying to cope.

The impact of exchange rate volatility and related nontariff regulation is now greater in the north-north direction than in the north-south direction. Thus here lies the locus of attempts to form new free-trade areas.

Unfettered trade, the free flow of capital, stable exchange rates, and full national sovereignty such as we know it today cannot go together. Something has to be surrendered; and if national regulatory regimes are to be put on the table, the multilateral option is not altogether feasible. The first step to further liberalization in these circumstances cannot but be restricted to a limited number of "like-minded countries" at a time. The GATT option will receive renewed impetus at the end of the road when this business is finished, much in the same way that bilateral Anglo-American negotiations preceded and culminated in Bretton Woods.

Notes

1. This draws from Tussie (1986), especially chapter 4.
2. Other explaining factors are, on the one hand, the slowed reaction of the European economies to the pull of the U.S. recovery compared with historical experience (Brittan, 1984), and on the other hand, the creditor-imposed deflationary adjustment in the debtor countries of Latin America after 1982.

5

Toward a Nonhegemonic IPE: An Antipodean Perspective

Richard Higgott

It need not be stated that the concept of hegemony has been the most used and abused in the lexicon of international relations at the level of both policy and scholarship over the last decade. In part, the purpose of this chapter is to continue that process of abuse in order to dilute further the utility of the concept for the scholar and the practitioner of international relations in the pursuit of their craft in the 1990s. Indeed, the title of this chapter is deliberately ambiguous. International political economy is used to connote that body of scholarship that has been a principal site of intellectual inquiry throughout the 1980s (see Tooze, 1990) within the discipline of international relations, and also as a way of describing the global order in the post–World War II era. In this second sense, the international political economy in this period is the site of U.S. hegemony for much of that period and the site of change that is taking place in the global order in what we might, for want of a better expression, call an "era of waning hegemony." International political economy is also a hosting metaphor (Apter, 1987) that allows us to acknowledge the continued importance of the classical focus in international relations on the world of states while at the same time taking account of the growth of the economic dimension in international relations in the post–World War II era.

It is within this twofold context that the purpose of the chapter is located. Its aim is to assist in the codification and production of a nonhegemonic international political economy. There are a variety of ways in which to approach such a topic (see, for example, Ashley's [1989] deconstruction of the notion of hegemony); the approach adopted here is both simple and more traditional in that it is clearly what we would call "state centric." Its purpose is (1) to provide a critique of the concept of hegemony as the driving force of much international political economy scholarship—especially in its North American variant—and (2) to look at some of the ways in which the international political economy in the 1990s will continue a process of nonhegemonic evolution. The perspective adopted is what I call antipodean—not just a euphemism for "Australian" but also a representation of what we might call a view of hegemony "from below." The argument presented suggests that an examination of international political economy through, for example, only Australian lenses provides a useful contribution to correcting the hegemonic perspective that has for too long predominated in both policy and scholarship. It is not suggested that such a form of analysis is unique, but simply that it is an alternative. Other scholars are already making similar contributions (Varynyen et al., 1988).

This chapter is an attempt to contribute to both theory and practice in international relations. At the theoretical level, it joins the debates of the last decade over the shape, form, and consequences of the supposed shift from hegemony to an as yet indeterminate future for the global order. At a practical level, the chapter poses the broader question of the appropriate options and responses for a smaller player to the changes in train in a contemporary global order driven not only by the issue of hegemonic decline and what it portends for the declining hegemon and the other major actors, but also where scholarship is equally driven by the interests and concerns of an academic community operating principally with a similarly conceived hegemonic intellectual baggage. To the extent that the chapter is concerned with looking at some of the key issues in the management of the contemporary global order from the perspective of a small, albeit not insignificant, actor in that order, it is also an attempt to provide a nonhegemonic contribution to international political economy as an analytic enterprise for the 1990s.

To be blunt, the chapter is intended to stand in sharp contrast to that growing body of United States–centered literature—the exemplar text of which is clearly Joseph Nye Jr.'s recent work *Bound To Lead* (Nye, 1990)— and that has the concerns and interests of the United States as its principal focus. Rather, the chapter is concerned with what international political economy, as both theory and practice, might look like in the 1990s for other states. The chapter finds many of Nye's assertions about the diffusion of power, the growth of global interdependence, and the "eroded hierarchy" (Nye, 1990: 237) unexceptionable. Analysis and prescription for coping with such change, however, are argued to represent a different enterprise from a non–United States–centered perspective than is invariably assumed to be the case in the mainstream of the international relations fraternity. Given that most scholars of international relations practice their craft in the United States, this should come as no surprise. The central assumptions that underwrite much of this literature are not always appropriate on their own terms; they are certainly not always appropriate underpinnings for analysis of and prescription for other states.

Lest this be seen as a misleading representation, consider briefly the essence of a recent round table discussion of the issue of hegemony and hegemonic stability theory at the 1990 meeting of the American Political Science Association (August 30–September 2, San Francisco). Four of the

United States' leading international relations scholars (Robert Gilpin, Robert Keohane, Stephen Krasner, and Joseph Nye) debated the status of hegemonic stability theory. The discussion was balanced and lucid, and the audience was treated to a variety of persuasive arguments as to why the concept's utility was theoretically problematic and should be constrained in its use.

Yet the discussion provided a range of mixed messages. On the one hand, the packed room of scholars could have been forgiven for pondering the degree of influence the notion of hegemonic stability had had over the theory and practice of international relations in the preceding years. This was especially the case when Keohane suggested that his notion of purgatory was an interminable debate about hegemonic stability theory. Gilpin went one stage further. It was not purgatory but hell he suggested. Nye, picking up the theme, created that hell in the room for one member of the audience by reading from his book one of the more excessive statements that dealt extensively with the implications of the rise and decline of hegemony.

On the other hand, and notwithstanding the large number of non-Americans in the audience and Keohane's lost attempt to suggest the importance of a plurality of ideas and actors in structuring the contemporary international political economy, the discussion was obsessively Americo-centric. Stephen Krasner, all too typically unfortunately, captured the essence of the present state of theorizing about international relations in the United States: "Sure people in Luxemburg have good ideas," he said, ". . . but who gives a damn? Luxemburg ain't hegemonic." It is the aspiration of this chapter to move beyond this position. To do so it considers the more pressing problems inherent in contemporary international political economy and suggests some of the ways in which a non-hegemonic international political economy would treat some of the "givens" of mainstream scholarship in a more problematic manner.

The Nature of Hegemonic IPE and the Basis of a Nonhegemonic Critique

The period of the late 1980s and early 1990s has been, and is, clearly an era of profound change in the global order that has, in turn, led to a process of contestation in, and rethinking of, the intellectual identity of the discipline of international relations as well. International political economy as an area of intellectual enterprise has been at the center of concern and contestation over the last decade. The nature of contestation has, of course, been varied and complex. At the risk of oversimplification, however, one question can be seen as central to much of our endeavor. This concern has been to unpack the nature of stability and change in the global economic order using (1) the notion of hegemonic stability; (2) the question of and implications of its decline or otherwise, as the case may be; and (3) the prospects for securing cooperation after hegemony as our organizing framework. Not surprisingly, the preponderant analyses of these broad questions have been transmitted through the lenses of the major actors in general and the designated hegemon in the post–World War II era—the United States—in particular. Prior to an attempt to ask what these issues might look like when viewed through the lenses of a "third party," the central elements of the contemporary debate on hegemony are set out below.

At its simplest, and at the risk of caricature, hegemonic stability theory (HST) asserts that the functioning of an orderly international economic order is possible due to the presence of a hegemonic state that establishes and underwrites the principle of order as a public good. The characteristics of the hegemon are "an unrivalled position of economic and military superiority among core states" (Goldstein, 1988: 5). The corollary of the thesis is that the absence of a hegemon creates a vacuum in the management of the international economic order with ensuing suboptimal results for all. In more policy-related terms, HST throughout the 1980s has been about the role of the United States as a declining hegemon—or not, as the case may be—in the international system. Those scholars in the North American and European communities not concerned with upholding the theory have been bent on challenging it (for example, see Strange, 1987).

The debate has been subject to considerable abuse, and the United States is frequently portrayed simply as a passé, jaded superpower going the route of previous hegemons. Such a view is a distortion of the works of the hegemonic stability theorists. None are saying that the United States is no longer the world's major economic power, nor that it is inevitably destined to go the way of the United Kingdom in the nineteenth century, nor that it is to be passed by the Soviet Union as a military power at the end of the twentieth century. Despite having lost its lead in some industrial sectors, it remains strong in all, and predominant in most, of the sectors of technology characteristic of postindustrial societies. Despite its declining share of nationally circumscribed indicators such as industrial production and exports as shares of world production and world trade, respectively, the United States still has an informal, nonterritorial empire based on the components of what Susan Strange has called "structural power" (Strange, 1988; see also Nye, 1990).

Yet within all those contesting positions, one common element remains: the vast majority of scholarship in international political economy since it became increasingly fashionable over the last decade has been focused, in one way or another, on the question of U.S. politicoeconomic hegemony in the global order.

In addition, underpinning this form of inquiry has been the intellectual hegemony of an almost unchallenged faith in rationality. Although it cannot be discussed in any detail here, it is not my intention, of course, to suggest that major critiques of rationality as the intellectual driving force of mainstream international relations in the United States and Europe do not exist. The last few years have seen a wide range of such critiques emerge.[1] Rather, I am making a statement about the degree to which such critiques have failed to make other than passing impressions on the vast majority of scholarship in international political economy in particular or, indeed, international relations in general. Even the most philosophically sensitive of mainstream scholars, while stressing the need to take account of the "reflective critique" (based on human subjectivity), insists on the need to focus full square on "substantive rationality," if we are to avoid "diversionary philosophical construction" (Keohane, 1988: 382).

Both hegemonies—HST and an unbounded faith in rationality—have been taken too much at face value, despite the existence of telling critiques that should, in many circumstances, have caused us to undergo fundamental rethinking of what constitutes knowledge and power in international relations. Again, I am not suggesting that the essence of such a rethinking does not exist, but that such critique has yet to be molded into a corpus of structured knowledge that would allow us to move more closely toward what I would call a nonhegemonic international political economy. In the remainder of this section, I offer a few introductory thoughts on and address a few of the general propositions about the nature of what *might* constitute the essence of a non-, or counter-, if you will, hegemonic international political economy.

The dominant hegemonic perspective in international political economy emanating from the United States, and to a much lesser extent the United Kingdom, has permeated other nationally based international relations disciplines around the globe in large part, of course, because it has in effect been invited to. Peripheral intellectual communities for so long—and indeed too long—have been willing to remain unquestioningly associated with an intellectual sphere of influence at the center. This need no longer be the case, however. I am not suggesting the swapping of an intellectual parochialism for a regional one, but rather that it is possible to see emerging a variety of different points of challenge to long accepted orthodoxies. It will be argued that peripheral intellectual cultures can, should, and do mediate and reform disciplinary innovations as well as simply reproduce them. Nonhegemonic international political economy can be a catalyst for intellectual reform and should find a home and support in the intellectual communities of smaller countries in a nonhegemonic era such as the one we have entered. At a practical level, too, it would seem not unreasonable to suggest that the practice of international relations, driven by notions of consensus-induced cooperation rather than the political realism of the superpower, might better serve the interests of smaller countries.

The fortunes and behavior of smaller state actors in the global order can no longer be adequately explained, if in fact they ever were, from within the confines of a state-centric discourse utilizing a relational power politics realism. The discussion of Australia will demonstrate the importance of a more structurally grounded conception of power in which the international political economy constrains the actions and autonomy of governments in a manner that was for too long unacknowledged by our focus on the activities of the United States. Actors, other than the erstwhile or putative hegemons, depending on a combination of will and contingency, are capable of either confronting or supporting the interests of the hegemonic state. They can, for example, provide regional resources and support and afford legitimacy to the hegemon's exercise of power. The converse can also be the case. In addition, in the appropriate circumstances, smaller states can play the role of innovator and initiator in the processes of global management and cooperation.

None of this is, of course, very novel. It is, however, an important starting point for analytical approach that wishes, in the words of Stanley Hoffmann (1977: 59), to take the study of international relations "born and raised in America . . . away from the fire" to which it has become too close.

From this obvious starting point, several other general methodological implications seem to arise. A nonhegemonic international political economy, for example, would have a much more complicated theory of the state and sovereignty than has prevailed to date. It is not one that would reject the centrality of either in the theory and practice of international relations. Rather, it is one that would attempt, as Ashley (1989: 255) recently suggested, to "reconcile the simultaneous essential contestedness and 'essential identity' of . . . the sovereign state." Indeed, a single or parsimonious conception of the state—especially the "state-as-actor"—must be considered of little or no utility for an understanding of theory in international relations. Three supposedly self-evident points in support of such a contention may be made here: (1) States are not, and have never been, the only major units of identification and interest in global politics. Other competing and cross-cutting loyalties exist, and—be they religious, ethnic, class based, or whatever—they limit the utility of the notion of government acting in a discrete and uncontested national interest. (2) States do not act. People—individually or collectively and by the continual transgression of territorial borders—act. (3) Sovereignty as a normative and legal concept may circumscribe a territorially defined legitimacy, but has only limited utility for an understanding of the nature and practice of world politics in the 1980s and 1990s. Sovereignty, or sovereign activity, as a category of governmental policy or practice is, for all states, a matter of degree and contingency. It has been the traditionally undifferentiated, seemingly homogenous theory of the state in international relations that has seen statecraft, as a system of behavior, treated in not dissimilar fashion to rational economic man in microeconomic theory.

A more sophisticated approach to theorizing the state would extend the sovereignty problematic to include the competing claims of international state practices located in a social as well as a geospatial environment. Consequently, it would need to combine traditional "state-centered" approaches to interstate relations with the work of a wide range of theorists of interdependence. In addition, a more complex theoretical approach to the state in international relations would take account of the recent work concerning state-society relations and agent-structure relations by sociologists, such as Anthony Giddens (1985, 1987), Michael Mann (1986), and Peter Evans et al. (1985). The aim of such work is not to deny the centrality of the state in international relations rather than to recognize the way in which historical and social practices constitute and reconstitute sovereignty in multiple locations and functions.

Central to their discussions, and germane to this chapter, is a recognition that there is a duality of influences at work in the ordering of international relations rather than just an independent variable plus an accompanying set of dependent variables. Agents and structures combine in historically specific circumstances to establish state interests and capabilities that transcend traditional domestic/international and economics/politics dichotomies and pose severe challenges to the centrality of rational state actor models, which remain the hard core of contemporary neorealist international political economy. Such an approach to theorizing is, of course, decidedly lacking in parsimony and is not readily amenable to the applications of a positivist social science. This, of itself, may be by no means a bad thing. As Albert Hirschmann (1985) has suggested, there may be other things more important in the process of understanding than the search for parsimony. Failure to accept the need for theory grounded in both agents and structures has resulted in flawed theory in the past and will remain so in the future (Wendt, 1987: 365). A more complex approach to codification (rather than theorizing) might at least allow us to move to the provision of what Keohane (1986a: 162) has called "thick description"—and which, he argues, much previous theorizing has not allowed us to do.

A further manner in which a nonhegemonic international political economy would be lacking in parsimony would be in the way it treated the concept of rationality as decidedly problematic. To be more specific, I am not suggesting that rationality, methodological individualism and the notion of actors in international relations operating under the strong influence of utility maximization should not be a central focus of our concerns. Rather, I am suggesting that the hegemony of rationality would not invariably prevail in a nonhegemonic research program. International political economy, as has been forcefully pointed out by Susan Strange (1985), has in many ways succumbed to the methodological imperialism of economics in a less than healthy manner for intellectual inquiry.

By a variety of different counts, utility maximizing is not axiomatically optimal behavior. For example, the notion of the state as a rational actor, as Rosenau (1986: 862–863) has argued, is little more than an "ideal type." Further, it is the agents, acting on the behalf of states—or nonstate institutions, as the case may be—that have interests. In this regard, they are driven not only by rational calculation but also by their own definition of given historical circumstances. In such circumstances information (knowledge), or frequently the lack of it, is a vital currency and form of power. Consequently, psychological and organizational criteria can be as important as allocative/productive (economic) criteria. To date, however, the study of international political economy has paid scant attention to the cognitive critique of rationality, which emphasizes not only sins of making commission on the part of rationality-driven theory—for example, error-induced decisionmaking arising from a distortion in the information upon which decisionmaking is based—but also sins of omission. The ground is sufficiently well trodden for the simple support for this assertion to suffice here. Assuming the primacy of rationality in exchange relations, for example, denies a role to other dimensions that might be of equal significance. As Robert Jervis has persuasively argued, Prisoner's Dilemma games—the exemplar of rationality-driven theorizing—invariably ignore the fact that a sense of obligation may in fact exist between the parties to a given relationship:

> Such a sense of obligation—if shared—may well have great practical value. . . . Individuals in society cooperate much more than the Prisoner's Dilemma would lead us to expect. Only economists behave as the theory says they should; others are likely to contribute to public goods, especially when fairness calls for them to do so. (Jervis, 1988: 347–348)

To dismiss Jervis's proposition as naive, "idealist," or antirationalist would be a mistake. Rather, his proposition recognizes that other forms of identification, shared values, or morally constituted norms provide an important (indeed maybe overriding at times) complement or counter to rationally bounded activity. Rationally ordained, egoistic behavior may, for example, be a major inducement to various forms of international economic cooperation, but it is not the only one.

It is not a little ironic that rationality has become stronger at the center of a burgeoning international political economy at the same time as its paradigmatic status in security studies is undergoing a process of questioning (see Jervis, 1989). But rationality is at the center of both international political economy and security studies. It is in their explanations of behavior inconsistent with rationalist assumptions that they differ. Security studies, with intellectual roots in diplomatic history and emphases on stress-induced crises, tend to privilege individualistic, psychological, and organizational explanations. International political economy, with its roots in political science, economics, and economic history, tends more to stress societal and structural explanations. A greater sensitivity to nonrationalist-based explanatory variables is an important component of a nonhegemonic international political economy.

In essence, what I am calling for is a greater degree of intellectual pluralism in the study of international political economy in the 1990s that would permit and expect a process of "contest among subordinate subjects [rather than] some privileged focus and register of unambiguous and universal truth" (Ashley, 1989: 265). As it has developed in the hegemonic center, international political economy has been, in Ashley's terms, a quintessentially "unicentric" form of politics. It has been one that has constructed a view of the United States as possessing, in the post–World War II era, both a will and capability to construct a global order, of and for its own purpose perhaps, but uncontestably as a wider contribution to the public good. A nonhegemonic international political economy as a scholarly enterprise would treat such an intellectual framework with considerable skepticism. One hegemonic center of power formalizing the norms and practices of sovereignty, production, and exchange in the global order is too tall an order. No single entity, even a so-called hegemonic state, represents the total embodiment at any given time of accepted practices and norms in international relations.

It must be noted, however, that my critique of neorealist international political economy is not underwritten by an assumption that everything is contextual or relative—as might appear to be the case in even some of the more thoughtful recent attempts to widen debate in international relations theorizing (George, 1989). Rather, it is guided by the not unexceptional proposition that the status of theorizing in a given environment cannot be underwritten, or explained, by one set of political and social norms alone. Hegemonic theory can be challenged not only because of the demonstrable empirical evidence of relative, if not absolute, U.S. decline, but also because, as Ashley puts it, the notion of hegemony, as it has largely prevailed in the study of international relations, is seeing its "rituals of enframing . . . losing their power of self-evidence" (Ashley, 1989: 280) and, we might add, at both the core and periphery of its reach.

In summary, this section of the chapter has suggested that a number of the major working assumptions that have guided the development of the study of international political economy in its intellectual heartland of North America over the last couple of decades need to be treated in much more problematic fashion than has been the case during this process of development. In short, three specific claims have been made:

1. There is a normative bias inherent in the assumption of HST that the United States has been the provider of the "public good" of order in the post–World War II era. Not only is this a self-serving and selective view of the role of the United States in the post–World War II international political economy, it is a view that would not meet with automatic acceptance in substantial sections of the world outside of the United States. Unfortunately, much scholarship and diplomatic practice has acquiesced in this interpretation

for much of the postwar period, and certainly for far too long after many U.S. policymakers had released hold of such a conception of obligation. In a powerful critique of this position, Richard Leaver, in a yet to be published piece, makes the point that U.S. "leadership" of the post–World War II global economy from the period of Bretton Woods until the early 1970s was in fact crucial "in turning what would otherwise have been sources of domestic weakness into sources of international strength" in the United States (Leaver, 1990b: 34; see also Block, 1977).

Even if we were to accept the orthodox interpretation of U.S. leadership in the building of the post–World War II regimes, such an approach currently finds little contemporary support as a way of coping with management problems in the global economic order in the 1990s. At a practical level, a nonhegemonic international political economy needs to give considerable attention to the building of economic cooperation in a posthegemonic era—a point well argued at a theoretical level by Robert Keohane (1984) in *After Hegemony* and, pleasingly I think, by Joseph Nye (1990: 253–259) in his blueprint for U.S. foreign policy in the 1990s, *Bound To Lead*. Both, however, pay little or no attention to the role, at either a theoretical or practical level, that other smaller actors might play in the processes of cooperation and institution building in the international political economy. The last section of this chapter provides a case study of the manner in which smaller players in the global economic order might contribute to the process of cooperation building in the absence of so-called hegemonic leadership.

2. "State-centrism" is an area of contestation in the pursuit of international political economy to date. To reiterate, it has not been suggested that somehow the state has been surpassed as the central unit of analysis in international relations. Such a suggestion has often been raised as a straw argument to undermine scholarship operating within a broadly defined interdependence paradigm. Yet, not even the gauchest of interdependence literature has ever suggested that the age of the nation-state is behind us. Rather, we need a more complex conception of the state and state action. Asking a range of questions taking into account agents and structures in different temporal and spatial domains (especially through the lenses of scholars and practitioners of international relations in smaller states) makes nonsense, for example, of Gilpin's (1987) assertion of the enhanced authority of the state in recent times. Scholarship less obsessed with the view from the center and more interested in the view from nonhegemonic domains would have recognized this long before the recent interest in the penetration of the United States by exogenous actors became fashionable.

3. The largely unchallenged faith in a positivist methodological approach and especially an unbridled commitment to rationality as an unshakable independent variable is problematic. Again, lest this assertion be misunderstood, I have not suggested that rationality is unimportant, but rather that it needs, in a variety of circumstances and times, to be

complemented or countered by other variables be they driven by, for example, morality, power culture, psychology, or whatever.

A Nonhegemonic IPE—The Antipodean Perspective

Although Australian study of IR emanated principally from British more than U.S. influences, it is, in its contemporary variant, what Raimo Varynyen might call an "interface peripheral intellectual culture", (Varynyen et al., 1988), with both U.S. as well as British influences current. In essence, for much of the twentieth century two themes dominated international relations, in both theory and practice: (1) the historically privileged role of "power politics realism" as an intellectual force and (2) the concomitant identification of a series of "threats" to Australia in the twentieth century, which have necessitated the need to align with appropriate "protectors."[2]

Of late, however, substantial change has occurred in Australian thinking about the nature of threat in international relations. The essence of this change has been a growing concern with the economic, as opposed to the politicostrategic, vulnerability of Australia as it has undergone a process of "marginalization" (see Higgott, 1987a and 1987b, for a discussion) in what is perceived by Australian policy makers and scholars alike (compare Harris, 1990) to be an increasingly unpredictable and predatory international economic order. The saliency of the economic dimension of Australia's international relations is now deemed of comparable importance—*at least*—to the politico-strategic dimension as Australia's vulnerability to the vicissitudes of a global economic order in transition from hegemony become more apparent.

To identify this process of change is not, I should add, the same as subscribing to hegemonic theory. Rather it is to recognize that major processes of change are in train. While declining superpower tensions may have ushered in a new era of strategic détente, difficulties in the international economic domain, especially economic competition between the major actors (United States, Japan, and the EC in any combination), and question marks over the future of manageable regimes for trade and finance that give impetus to regionalist, bilateralist, and unilateralist tendencies, raise questions for the smaller, third parties to these processes not easily accommodated in the prevailing theoretical approaches emanating from the main centers of international relations scholarship.

These demonstrable processes of change have theoretical implications. The study of international political economy is no longer governed by a belief in a set of broadly accepted institutional practices emanating from a U.S.-driven hegemony—if indeed it ever really was. Such an analytical interpretation denies an autonomy of interest or intent to the smaller participants in the U.S. hegemonic experience. To say that the post–World

War II economic order was primarily an institutionalized expression of U.S. military, financial, and industrial power is not the same as saying that it was constructed without the active participation of other states, be they allies, informal partners, or coopted clients. Australian policy and behavior in the post–World War II period are interesting illustrations of this process, and they highlight the importance of the duality of the roles of agent and structure and the complex nature of hegemony.

In the aftermath of World War II, Australia was a willing participant in the creation of the institutional structures and regimes that served to uphold the U.S. hegemonic enterprise. To argue as such is not, however—despite the recognition of certain constraints and vulnerabilities on the part of Australian policymakers—to suggest that Australia was merely a client of U.S. hegemony. Although history records that various Australian governments were unable (despite a desire to do so) to resist the policies of reconstruction that the United States laid out for Japan in the aftermath of the war, they were, nevertheless, able to exploit Cold War sentiments to gain substantial concessions in the realm of foreign policy from the United States, which were successfully translated into many years of domestic political legitimacy for the Menzies governments of the 1960s. A simple patron-client interpretation of Australian-U.S. relations misreads the degree to which occupants of executive office in the Australian federal system were consciously contributing to the establishment, consolidation, and reproduction of the institutional practices of U.S. hegemony in a manner that drew on an acknowledged congruence of interest of Australian and U.S. agency. Similarly, scholarship in international relations in Australia reflected the canons of the "realist" tradition, albeit strongly mediated by British influences (see George, 1988, for a discussion), that predominated in the United States and out of which the hegemonic persuasion emerged. This brief example is meant merely to establish what should be a well-accepted notion—that smaller players in the global order are agents, as well as subjects, of history, albeit with different capacities and interests to the hegemonic state. Australia was not merely a passive actor in either the British colonial experience or the more recent U.S. military experience in the Asia Pacific region in the post–World War II era.

Further, the contemporary international order is no mere extrapolation of the hegemonic moment. Both intellectual and "real" arrangements are undergoing a process of change. At the risk of stating the obvious, how we come to know and understand international relations conditions how we come to practice it. It is in this domain that peripheral intellectual communities and smaller states can and should mediate the dominant voices in the discourses of international relations. They have their own interests and histories and have a role to play in shaping wider discourse and process. In the hegemonic era, the standard view of both ideas and interests emanating from smaller communities has invariably been pejorative. At best they are passive actors, at worst free riders taking the public goods provided by the hegemon—be it liberal international orders or liberal ideas. However, as I have attempted to suggest, a nonhegemonic perspective in international political economy would recognize that smaller players are agents as well as subjects of history.

Although there is still a strong tendency in the international arena to package hegemonic ideas and hegemonic practice as being in the wider general interest, there is a growing inclination to attempt to implement policy that, in an increasing number of circumstances, is discordant with the interest of the hegemon. In the Australian case, I will argue that the close congruence between U.S. and Australian interests in the global political economy that prevailed for much of the post–World War II era is now less immediately recognized in both policymaking and intellectual communities in the smaller partner to the relationship than at any time in the postwar history of the relationship.

Although exogenous influences over the intellectual and policymaking communities in Australia from the northwestern quadrant of the globe remain strong, and ANZUS currently receives governmental support as strong as at any time in its history, the longer term historical tendency toward a derivative or parasitic relationship on its British parent, or self-selected foster parent of the United States, would appear to be on the wane. There is a growing recognition that the needs of a smaller country such as Australia are not axiomatically well served by a staunch adherence to theoretical and analytical categories that have evolved from superpower categories.

Two brief case studies are provided to illustrate the argument. The first looks generally at the theory and practice of international trade in an environment in which the United States is no longer able or willing to adhere to either the theory or practice of hegemonic stability—that is, to play the provider of the public good of an open liberal international trading system. The second study is related, but more specific. Following from a recognition on the part of Australia as a "third party" to changing theory in international trade and the manner in which it is practiced by the major actors, a brief examination is provided of its attempts, within the context of the current Uruguay Round of multilateral trade negotiations, to secure reform in the international regime in agricultural trade.

A Smaller State Perspective
on the New Mercantilist Era

The increasing tensions between, and recourse to illiberal practices by, the major players in the international trading system throughout the 1980s is one of the most discussed issues in international political economy. Central to this discussion has been the emergence of several new "truths" about the nature of free trade, and comparative advantage as the theoretical cornerstone of free trade. The essence of the argument emanating from some theoreticians and many politicians in the United States is that that country has lost its competitive edge and accumulated massive deficits on its trade balance because its principal partners (notably Japan, the European Community, and the other Asia Pacific newly industrializing economies) have engaged in unfair trade practices called variously, confusingly, and occasionally contradictorily the new protectionism, new trade theory, strategic trade policy, industry policy and so on.[3] Whatever the nomenclature, it has led to the development of what U.S. policymakers see as an "unlevel playing field" in the international trading system. Such a description is, of course, a caricature but it has had broad-ranging policy implications.

The consequent and appropriate U.S. response to counter its deteriorating position in the global economic order, it is argued, is to fight back. The United States has, throughout the 1980s, seen the growth of its own economic nationalists supporting the recourse to interventionist policies to promote competitiveness, spurred on by a belief that free trade may be more appropriate to 1890 than 1990. Believing that governments can help manufacture a comparative advantage in an era of oligopolization and imperfectly competitive markets, it becomes appropriate to pursue an activist tit-for-tat trade policy characterized by a fusion of trade and foreign policy. In times of increasing economic stringency, trade policy becomes a legitimate weapon in the search for national economic welfare in the international political economy similar to the role of defense policy in the pursuit of national security. For the United States, strategic trade policy becomes increasingly attractive (Cohen and Zysman, 1987).

There are, of course, those in the economic community who question both the theoretical and empirical validity of the new trade theory,[4] but such criticism misses the major point that makes this theory so politically popular, especially in the United States. Rightly or wrongly, it is seen as a way of fighting back against the increasingly competitive trade partners of the United States.

Importantly for the revisionist critique outlined in this chapter, the whole debate over the nature of the new trade theory has been conducted, almost exclusively to date, in the discourse of the major players in the global economy and the impact that it has on their industries and their competitiveness vis-à-vis each other. Looked at from a third party perspective, it takes on a different hue. None of the literature deals with the implications for smaller states of the foreign economic policies of major actors driven by the assumptions of what I would call "economic realism." Its implications are, however, as—if not more—profound for the smaller third parties to this process. Looking though Australian lenses, some of these implications can be spelled out.

A first comment that might be made relates to the theoretical underpinnings of strategic trade policy. It is clearly available only to major players in the global economic order. Contrary to the expressed anticipation of some members of the Australian manufacturing community, for example, it is not about throwing a life belt around inefficient industries. Rather, strategic trade policy is geared to promoting dynamic and innovative industries capable of generating a return well in excess of subsidy. The number of participants in the industry would be small, profits above the norm, and production predicated on a large domestic market in which the industry would gain experience prior to facing major international competition, in a manner similar to the processes in Japan after World War II. Strategic trade policy is also predicated on an advanced technology and a high research and development component that make the barriers to entry prohibitive to all but the largest and best supported of corporations—clearly not industries indigenous to most of the smaller to medium-size states in the global economy.

The second comment concerns the manner in which the adoption of unilateral approaches to *specific*—as opposed to *diffuse*—reciprocity (Keohane, 1986b) by a major actor is invariably of less damage to it than to smaller third parties that might be involved in relationships with that actor or the target state of the major actor's initiatives. The third party is most often the victim of any trade diversion that subsequently ensues (Higgott, 1989a). The details of any impact resulting from trade diversion are perhaps less interesting for the purposes of this chapter than a theoretical analysis of its implications for third parties to major actor economic disputes, which, perhaps not surprisingly, receive little or no attention in the literature emanating from the intellectual center of the international political community in the United States.

If we assume the United States to be a weakening hegemon attempting to bolster its position in a more competitive international economic climate, then policy to date has been geared to redressing the imbalance by the pursuit of two-person games with its major trading partners. The ramifications of these games may well, however, have greater impact on indirect participants than on the targeted second player. For example, Australia's major trading partners are the United States, Japan, and the European Community. Australia is a state with a relatively small market (population 16 million), high cost structures, and low productivity in those increasingly competitive industries that provide value added. Its major sources of export earnings are still to be found in the domain of primary products and raw material, and it relies for its high technology goods and manufactures to a greater extent than most developed countries on the international marketplace. It is a "free trade free rider," taking the benefits of the public good of an open international system provided by U.S. hegemonic leadership for a large part of the post–World War II era (Lake, 1988: 48).

Certainly an open international economic system is important for

Australian economic welfare. The pejorative nature of the terminology of hegemonic stability theory, however, needs to be resisted by Australia and many other smaller participants to the international trading system. Free riding does exist, both consciously and unconsciously, but not all small player behavior in all circumstances is, in fact, free riding. Small players can and do "pay their dues" to keep the system open in a variety of circumstances, cognizance of which is all too often lost in the process of hegemonic theorizing and mythologizing about the degree of openness, or otherwise, of the international economy. Historical evidence exists (to give but one example germane to this chapter) to demonstrate the degree to which Australia, along with several other states in the 1970s, waived a series of price provisions and agreed to compete a little less aggressively in the agricultural market place in order to allow other nations to maintain a reasonable market share, continue cooperation, and preserve the International Grains Agreement. Yet, to the extent that smaller states are not of their own volition given the structural limitations on their influence, nor are they in a position to maintain an open trading system, they are riding along with the major players, although often only after buying a ticket. Reliance on the provision of hegemonic leadership in the international economic order does, however, pose quite distressing questions that smaller players and a nonhegemonic international political economy need to address.

Given the constraints of a structural nature on smaller players such as Australia, it is traditionally assumed—in the game-theoretic terms of international trade theory—that a cooperative strategy is the best strategy in all cases. Even if this is so, it may not always be in the best interests of larger actors in the international economic system—especially in their dealings with smaller players—to cooperate. Problems for a state such as Australia emerge when it—like many others, it must be added—is a third party to a conflictual game between larger players with which it has important but asymmetrical relationships. It is in this context unfortunate, to say the least, that Australia's principal economic partners are those major states, or group of states, among which the greatest economic tensions have existed throughout the latter part of the 1980s and are continuing into the 1990s.

Although the economic strength of the United States, Japan, and the European Community may lead to mutual restraint that would minimize the prospect of all-out trade wars in the 1990s, it does not preclude these actors, as recent history tells us, from engaging in bouts of supposedly cooperation-inducing, tit-for-tat retaliatory trade strategies. Such strategies are not, of course, inevitably destined to succeed, and small players are often "sideswiped" in a wider tit-for-tat exercise. Further, as Conybeare has persuasively demonstrated, "free trade" is not "from an economically rationalist position" always a public good, and hegemons may "maximise their national incomes by optimal tariffs, not by free trade [but] by imposing trade taxes on smaller countries" (Conybeare, 1987: 72). Two important questions follow: Why would a hegemon underwrite a liberal trading system if it is not in its interest so to do? What are the implications of any answer to such a question for smaller players acculturated to believe their best interests lie in the existence of a hegemonic order providing a variety of public goods?

Several comments are germane here. First, the cost to the hegemon of providing the public good of economic order is deemed acceptable for the support it gives to the hegemon's wider ideological and political aspirations in a given historical period. U.S. economic hegemony allowed it to pursue its most ambitious of foreign policy goals in the post–World War II period (Block, 1977). Second, the rent-seeking activities of domestic interest groups within the United States drove, and still continue to drive, policy to take on a hegemonic role—or at least presently an economically nationalist role—be it for either sectoral or class-based advantage in the domestic economy. Rent-seeking groups in the United States in the present period, especially the agricultural sector in search of subsidy and the advanced industrial sectors in search of the kind of support envisaged by strategic trade theory, feel their interests to be better served by the reality of an increased governmental role (of the appropriate supportive, but nonregulatory, variety, of course) in the closing years of the twentieth century, rather than the "myth"-driven canons of free trade.

Viewed in this light, the implications of recent trade theorizing and practice for states such as Australia in particular—but the global economy in general—become much clearer. Historically, U.S. policymakers have been aware of the optimal position of keeping tariffs high while systematically securing lower access costs in other countries. In a time when the political advantages of hegemony are less readily apparent, nor as easily secured as in its heyday, the temptations of pursuing more self-consciously nationalist foreign economic policy is proving difficult to resist. Such policies severely limit the range of options open to small countries unable to engage in unilateral retaliatory action of their own.

Thus, by a combination of microeconomic theory and good deductive reasoning we can explain continued interest in the pursuit of economically irrational activity. Notwithstanding that rent-seeking activities may be detrimental to the maximization of national income in an aggregate sense, the interests of producer groups, given their readily identifiable harmony of interest, all too often hold sway over consumer groups. Such generalizations hold in all communities, but the implications of the world are considerable and adverse. The defense of third-party interests in such circumstances poses a considerable conundrum to which more attention in international political economy needs to be given—at both the general and the sectoral level.

The fact that discussion has focused principally on the United States is not to suggest that it is the only state engaged in such activities. Indeed it is not, as any close inspection of policy in the European Community will testify. Yet despite its relative decline, the United States is still the world's major economic actor, and the erstwhile hegemon that purports to keep the system open and liberal. As such, heavy-handed bilateral activities on its part place a much greater strain on the preservation of an open trading system than on those of other states. This situation is unlikely to change as long as there is a conviction in substantial influential centers of the U.S. policymaking community that it is possible for the United States, in part at least, to mitigate some of the pain of economic adjustment by exporting that adjustment to others through the initiation of aggressive reciprocity provisions and other nontariff barriers and by offering domestic support at home through subsidy program or strategic trade initiatives.

In the content of the new protectionism it is worth noting the manner in which Australia is attempting to demonstrate the degree to which the major actors are deviating from the norms of free trade. Major reports have been prepared by the Australian Bureau of Agricultural and Resource Economics on the trade distorting and inefficient nature of the Common Agricultural Policy, Japanese restriction on food imports, and the protection of the U.S. grain industries (see Australian Bureau of Agricultural and Resource Economics, 1985, 1988, and 1989, respectively). The first two of these were translated into French and Japanese, respectively, and all were distributed widely within their targeted areas. Such activity is in part explained by the fact that Australia is one of the world's most efficient agricultural producers, with a very low level of subsidy, although other sectors of its economy, it needs to be said, are less than clean. Nevertheless, policies such as Australian initiatives in the Uruguay Round, its decision not to seek a bilateral free trade agreement with the United States similar to that of Canada (Snape, 1989), and its attempts to foster not trade-restricting but trade-*inducing* cooperative arrangements in the Asia Pacific region (Harris, 1989; McGuiness, 1990), are a clear recognition by Australian policymakers that: (1) there is a lack of hegemonic leadership and commitment to multilateralism in the global economic order, which, we might add, they would have been willing to accept had it been forthcoming throughout the 1980s; (2) HST (Hegemonic Stability Theory) expresses a U.S. worldview and legitimizes the structural privileges that have accrued to the United States in the post–World War II era by virtue of its purported leadership role; (3) the United States has abused that role (as even scholars such as Robert Gilpin [1987: 345] concede); and (4) awaiting the return of U.S. leadership in the global economic order is not the best strategy for smaller states, and indeed attempts to secure a return to what was, after all, an idealized state may well inhibit other, more egalitarian approaches to problem solving, coordination, and cooperation in the global economic order.

The rules of a posthegemonic, multipolar system of economic management are yet to be established. The prospects of achieving such an end-state are not good and not even sought in all quarters. Yet, although structural constraints of size, power, geostrategic location, and so on will obviously condition the nature and scope of the role that a small state may play in the process, the way is open for innovation and initiative. Indeed, as part of a nonhegemonic perspective, the very notion of leadership should be treated in the 1990s with a good deal more circumspection and, in any case, in a much wider sense than in the past. As with the concept of hegemonic stability, leadership and other historically located concepts do not emerge from the pure world of ideas but from a combination of the "mythical," the philosophical, and the political. To hang on to such concepts in their presently unrefined hegemonic form as a key element in any renewed process of management for the global economy for the 1990s would be inadvisable indeed. As I suggest, a principal characteristic of the practice of international economic relations in the 1990s will be the emergence of a more complex understanding of what we might mean by the term "leadership."

The 1990s will be an era in which new, nonhegemonic rules of multipolar management may, or indeed may not, be created. As the title of Robert Keohane's (1984) major work on regime and institution building implies, there is the prospect of cooperation *After Hegemony*. Although some see it as fad (Strange, 1982), and others as ideological subterfuge to paper over and bolster the declining position of the United States, regime theory may well continue to grow in theoretical importance. At the very least it will continue in its evolution from the initial definitional status granted to it by Krasner as the provision of a set of "principles, norms, rules and decision making procedures around which actor expectations converge in a given area of international relations" (Krasner, 1983: 2). Perhaps the major theoretical option that remains available at the present time is to analyze and institutionalize cooperation (Keohane, 1988). In addition, and unlike hegemonic stability theory, it has the potential to be liberating in the provision of more egalitarian, cooperative, and nonhegemon-driven approaches to problem solving in the international order. In an area in which problems—of an environmental variety, for example—transcend traditional spatial demarcations of state sovereignty with impunity, such cooperative endeavors must surely take on both greater analytical and policy-related salience than in previous decades (Tuchman-Mathews, 1990).

A Nonhegemonic IPE II—Regime Reform and Agriculture in the Uruguay Round

The changes in the global order that are in place at the beginning of the 1990s, especially the continuing drift toward multipolarity and the diminished preeminence of both politicostrategic superpowers over their allies, suggests that the alliance structures of the 1990s will have to be cooperation driven rather than hegemon driven. Calls for junior partners to alliances to play a greater role in burden sharing will, somewhat inevitably, be met by a commensurate growth in calls for greater power sharing and consensus building within and between extant alliance structures. The provision of a similar diffusion of power and the continuing growth of economic interdependence will dictate a similar need for reform of the structures of the international economic system. To make a contribution to any process of reform should be a principal aim of a nonhegemonic international political economy. From the perspective of smaller actors in the global order, the environment of the late 1980s and early 1990s is, in this regard, one of considerable challenge and also opportunity. As Stanley Hoffmann recently noted, major and minor actors alike will need to engage in processes of dealing and convincing. "Games of skill must replace tests of will" (Hoffmann, 1989: 91). In such a context, innovative forms of leadership will become especially important. In the discussion that follows I outline briefly one attempt by smaller states to make a major contribution to the process of reform in the global economic order. The case discussed is the Cairns Group of Fair Trading Nations that has attempted to foster reform in global agricultural trade within the current Uruguay Round of multilateral trade negotiations.

Definitions of regime theory of the type extracted from Krasner above originated along with hegemonic stability theory. Such definitions clearly present problems of representation for smaller players in any process of regime formation at the levels of both recognition and acceptance. Regime theory, as James Keeley (1989: 84) recently argued, is underwritten by assumptions of both benevolence and voluntarism. For smaller participants to regimes and regime behavior, these assumptions can, and at times may, hold good. That they will hold good under all circumstances should not be assumed as a matter of course. As Keeley goes on to note, even the most liberal of regime theory can be "a form of special pleading by and for the powerful and the satisfied" (Keeley, 1989: 84). As regime theory and regime behavior have developed under U.S. hegemony, the agendas for consideration have tended to exclude the items of interest to the nonmajor players unless they have dovetailed with those of the major players (Strange, 1982). This is not an analysis I would at all wish to dispute in the international trade regime prior to the Uruguay Round. However, precisely because it would appear to have established a pattern of behavior different from the norm outlined by Strange, the role of the Cairns Group in the Uruguay Round of negotiations is both practically interesting and theoretically worthy of analysis. In this regard, the existence and activity of the group is theoretically more important for this chapter than the eventual outcome of the current negotiating round.

I have argued elsewhere (Higgott and Cooper, 1990) that the Cairns Group has succeeded in establishing itself, along with the United States and Europe, as the third force (a point acknowledged, it should be noted, by

GATT Secretary General Arthur Dunkel in the U.S. *Journal of Commerce*, 27 May 1987: 10A, and others) and as a major actor in both an "agenda setting" and "proposal making coalition" (Hamilton and Whalley, 1989) in the negotiation processes on agricultural reform in the Uruguay Round. Such an assertion is, of course, contentious. After all, at the time of writing, the round is still in train, no major agreement to dispense with the trade distorting-measures in agricultural trade has been secured, and general hopes for a successful outcome to the negotiations overall are not positive.

Anyway, the very idea of a coalition of small states exercising major influence in a round of GATT negotiations is both historically unprecedented and—if we are to be guided by regime theory and such analyses of the Uruguay Round that have merged to date (Winham, 1989; Nau, 1989), which pay little or no attention to the Cairns Group—theoretically improbable. Further, the literature to date abounds with case studies of coalitions of the weak that set out with high hopes only to be dashed in the last instance by the inexorable realities of power politics (see, for example, Rothstein, 1977, 1979, 1984; Krasner, 1985). Why, therefore, would I be pushing such a seemingly rash proposition? In essence, I would argue that even if the efforts of the Cairns Group to secure a breakthrough on agricultural trade were to come to nought, the role that the group has played in the negotiations between 1986 and 1990 represents for students of international political economy a unique exercise in what I might call the practice of nonhegemonic economic diplomacy. There are two major themes pursued in the larger study by Higgott and Cooper (1990) and reviewed briefly here: the first is contextual, the second is both organizational and intellectual.

The Contextual Theme

The Uruguay Round, in many ways, represents a microcosm of the general malaise that infected the global economic order in the closing decades of the twentieth century. Further, although agriculture had always been treated as something of an exception to international trading rules by the major players, it has come to exhibit all the worst elements of the new protectionism. Government policy in most countries—developed, developing, market oriented, "command" economies, major powers, minor powers—has been geared to defending the national agriculture sector. In addition, the manner in which it has fostered animosity and strain in the trading relationships of the major economic actors is well understood. Above all, the ability of the major actors—notably the United States—to set the agenda and direct trade negotiations has diminished in the face of changing configurations of power in the global political economy in general and the increasing institutional complexities of the international trading regime in particular. Although this process may have begun in the Tokyo Round (Krasner, 1979; Winham, 1986), it has reached unprecedented levels in the current round of negotiations. Traditionally, as Winham has observed, a "pyramidal structure" of decisionmaking has prevailed in which the superpowers established the negotiating agenda and in which "once a trade-off was established the negotiations process was progressively expanded to include other countries. In this way, cooperation between the United States and the EC served to direct the negotiations" (Winham, 1989: 290). Thus the essence of the prenegotiation, and by extension actual negotiation, process for Winham was the power and leadership of the major actors in the complex and uncertain context of multilateral negotiations.

Observation of the activity of the Cairns Group in the Uruguay Round calls for a revision to this heretofore prevailing mode. In part, a pyramidal model still pertains, but the consensus agreement for a new round of negotiations, and the notable inclusion of agriculture in that agreement— which emanated from the 1986 meeting in Punte del Este and the progression of the round to date, especially beyond the difficult Mid-Term Review in Montreal in late 1988—cannot be explained simply in terms of the brute power of the two major actors alone. Progress in both agenda setting and the negotiating process has been significantly facilitated by the activities of the Cairns Group as confidence builder, consensus seeker, and rich source of technical and political ideas for the eradication of trade-distorting practices in international agricultural trade. In short, it has provided much-needed leadership. As such, the activities of the group provide an insight into how smaller states can help foster reform in single issue areas important to them in particular and the global political economy in general, but which are increasingly characterized by a fragmented and complex process of decisionmaking and also in which the major actors need both support and coercion in moving toward cooperative outcomes in a nonhegemonic environment.

The Organizational/Intellectual Theme

Four principal factors can be identified: (1) aggregate strength of the group in international agricultural trade; (2) tightly defined group goals; (3) tight group discipline, notwithstanding the heterogeneity of group membership; (4) strong Australian technical and entrepreneurial leadership. Item (1) need not be discussed here, except to reemphasize the group's strategic significance in global agricultural markets. However, several general points can be made about the three other strengths exhibited by the group in the Uruguay Round.

By keeping its aims sharply focused on agriculture at all times, the Cairns Group has avoided ideological conflict and the dissipation of its energies in pursuit of wider nontangible goals. Similarly, in the course of the negotiations the group has not overplayed its hand or attempted to push the parties to the negotiations beyond what their own domestic political constraints or actions might permit. It has also recognized the degree to which reform in agriculture is not simply technical, or market specific, but also highly political; as such, the group has employed greater recourse to the ministerial decisionmaking process as a way of overcoming bureaucratic inertia in the breaking of technical deadlocks in the negotiating process than has historically been the case in GATT negotiations. As individual states, members would have had no role in this process. As a group, they have been the third force in decisionmaking on agricultural issues.

Also of importance has been the preparation and research that has underpinned the Cairn Group's negotiating position at all stages. Particularly, the group has had at its disposal the technical support of the Australian trade and agricultural bureaucracy, which has been extremely innovative in its refinement of the analytic capabilities of states to identify and measure illiberality in agricultural trade. More general is the manner in which many of its ideas have been successfully introduced into the negotiating process. It was this factor that cemented the strategically significant position that the group was able to secure for itself, not only as an "agenda moving coalition" (Gallagher, 1988; Higgott, 1988a) but also as a "proposal making coalition." Cairns Group initiatives have, to date, done two things. First, they have provided a "middle way" between the two major protagonists in the round without it simply being an exercise in "difference splitting." Specifically, in this regard they have recognized the degree to which procedure is a central factor in the success of any reform process. Second, the group's ideas have represented a substantive contribution to the debate over agricultural reform in both its technical and political guises. It has offered major proposals for securing not only immediate short-term relief but also suggestions for longer term goals that would provide, if adopted, for rational and significant reform in international trade in agriculture.[5]

Technical competence in the most technical of negotiations has been an important ingredient in establishing the group's credibility as a major voice in the round. In this regard, the success of the group to date (and I acknowledge the danger of writing about the round before it has completed its deliberations) has stemmed less from the fact that it was bargaining away concessions than from the fact that it was providing a middle ground upon which the majors could meet. The significance of the group is less that it impels the major protagonists to accept its positions by force of its collective economic weight or rational argument—strong as both might be— but rather that it has attempted to build confidence and provide a middle way for the major players to move beyond positions of intransigence. As such, the activities of the group are an important contribution to an as yet underdeveloped avenue of investigations in international political economy— the creation of "confidence-building measures" in the resolution of international economic conflict.

I use the phrase here not to mean reform per se—be it arms reduction or market liberalization—but (borrowing from the study of international security) to mean the regulation of the negotiating environment designed to improve communication and understanding, and to provide reassurance about the intentions of the participants to the negotiations in such a way as to reduce the prospect of conflict. As such, confidence-building measures are intended to generate predictability and monitor deviations from the norm in state behavior.[6] A major problem throughout the Uruguay Round, and indeed, the years of waning faith in the functioning of the GATT system, has stemmed precisely from the lack of confidence of the major actors in the intentions of their partners on the one hand, and their own abilities to compete successfully in the absence of protectionist support mechanisms on the other.

The dearth of study of confidence building in the international economy is not altogether surprising. It is a definitionally illusive concept and often not an explicitly articulated activity by those engaged in its practice. In a similar vein, the psychology of international economic relations has not been subjected to the same sophisticated scrutiny as has the psychology of international security by scholars such as Jervis et al. (1986). Yet, it must be apparent to all who monitor economic relations between the major actors, especially the United States in its relations with the European Community and Japan, that perceptions of mistrust and misunderstanding are every bit as significant in their potential for generating conflict between states as the reality of fiercer economic competition in a more globally interdependent era. In its attempts to bridge gaps in the relationships between the major players, create innovative processes of verification (transparency, self-regulation, and "tariffication"), and thus rebuild confidence in the GATT system in the current round of trade negotiations, the Cairns Group represents a concerted response by smaller, but collectively not insignificant, players to their individual inability to influence large-scale multilateral economic negotiations.

Yet Australian leadership has been important at not only the technical level. Its acceptability as a political spokesperson for a group comprising a variety of competing ideological and regional interests has also been important. This important point is made not, as some might suspect, as an exercise in antipodean self-gratification, but because it is not without wider analytic insight for more general efforts to secure global economic reform in a nonhegemonic manner. As Oran Young noted in a recent analysis of regime formation, leadership is not simply a function of hegemony. It is also a question of entrepreneurship involving "a combination of imagination in inventing institutional options and skill in brokering the interests of numerous actors to line up support for such options" (Young, 1989: 355). In providing support for Young's assertion, Australian behavior in the Cairns Group, and Cairns Group approaches to the current Uruguay Round, offer an important illustration of one option open to smaller states with a vested interest in regime change and that are not prepared simply to accept their assigned roles as free riders awaiting the hegemon-driven provision of whatever public good might be at stake in a given circumstance.

It also, I would argue, goes some way toward providing the foundations for a general and less hegemon-driven theory of leadership more appropriate and useful for the changing global political and economic environment of the 1990s. Leadership under hegemony was conceived of in fairly singular terms. Its strength was primarily of a structural nature, in which power was used "to overcome the collective action problems that impeded efforts to reach agreement on the terms of constitutional contracts in social settings of the sort exemplified by international security" (Young, 1990: 1). It is this type of leadership that the United States supposedly used to establish the post–World War II Bretton Woods and GATT systems. Structural power (correctly so in my view) occupies a position of theoretical centrality in contemporary international political economy across its intellectual spectrum.[7] However, a theory of power and leadership that is solely structurally driven is far too determinist and leaves little or no room for decisive policy intervention derived from technical innovation and political creativity, or what Young calls intellectual leadership and entrepreneurial leadership. On the other hand, a theory of leadership that has these two added dimensions offers the prospect of considerable room for development of what I have termed a nonhegemonic international political economy. It has been the central assumption of those policymakers driving the Cairns Group initiative that the quality of the decisionmaking processes is important and that they can help alter outcomes.

My argument, it should be noted, is not particularly radical. At this juncture it is essentially state-centric. Australia and the other members of the Cairns Group are, after all, egoistic actors engaged in rational utility maximizing. They are among the world's most efficient food-exporting nations attempting to secure a freer, more open international agricultural regime, the existence of which would be of major benefit to them. Further, they are also engaged, to a degree at least, in power maximizing by the exhibition of, if not the utilization of, their aggregate group strength in the major agricultural markets. But their behavior goes beyond a realist power politics approach. The Group's principal weapons have been educative and persuasive rather than the assertion of its potential and considerable brute market strength as a collective entity.

In short, the group has been engaged in an exercise in leadership that has accentuated its intellectual and entrepreneurial—as opposed to its structural—attributes. Its behavior represents a marked break with the more normal pattern of multilateral trade negotiations to date. It should be of considerable theoretical interest for the student of contemporary international political economy. I am not suggesting that the group is not interested in the use of leverage and reciprocity—the traditional stuff of GATT negotiations that its aggregate market position might give it, especially its potential to prevent an agreement on services and intellectual property in the round if a meaningful agreement on agriculture appears unlikely. Bargaining and reciprocity is still at the heart of all trade negotiating. Rather, I am suggesting that the group has recognized dangers that such an approach might hold for it and the prospect that other avenues of persuasion may prove more fruitful.

If the argument extended throughout this chapter has any substance, then the activities of the group tell us something about how power in regimes may be reformed in different temporal, spatial, and issue-specific dimensions. At the very least, the problematic of regime formation that prevailed under hegemony needs to be reformulated to take account of the changing configurations of power as we enter the 1990s. I am not, of course, saying that regime theory does not recognize the asymmetrical nature of power capabilities of individual regime members. What I am saying is that to date it has tended to take the asymmetries for granted in assuming how membership in a given regime is "voluntary" and thus, by their membership, smaller players are granting consent to its principles, norms, and rules. A nonhegemonic international political economy (as scholarship) would assume no such consent. Rather, it would start from a recognition of a need to analyze the degree to which major actor preferences are accepted by, or forced upon, smaller players and the manner in which smaller players might respond. In this regard, one final general point about regime theory must be made.

Regime theory in the 1990s should take much more seriously the prospects of, and need for, more innovative processes of coalition building than we may have been used to under hegemony. Although the decline of interest in coalition building in the 1980s, and in the wake of failed developing country attempts to bring about reform in the international order, may have been understandable, there can be no excuse for it, at both the theoretical and policy level, in the changing international circumstances of the 1990s. The Cairns Group is not the only example of innovative coalition building of late. Other issue areas, beyond the purview of this paper, have seen a renewed interest in the building of "middle power" (Pratt, 1990), "like-minded" (Hampson, 1990) and "north-south" (Wood, 1990) coalitions. In highlighting these issues, the Cairns Group's activities in the Uruguay Round have been an important laboratory for our understanding of the potential of coalitions in regime building and reform in the 1990s. A concerted effort is needed to ensure that the specific insights gained are put to wider theoretical use in the continuing modification of regime theory in the 1990s.

The specific role of Australia in this process also has something to offer the student of a would-be nonhegemonic international political economy. That the analysis here has been principally state-centric should not be a major problem. Discussion has been predicated upon the need to recognize both the strengths and constraints of such an approach. Similarly, because enough documentation has been provided to suggest that a detailed study would highlight for us perfectly the intricacies and juxtapositions at play in the agent-structure duality, as well as the combination of exogenous constraints and domestic imperatives, such themes need not be expanded upon here. One point that should be noted for its relevance to the earlier general discussion in this chapter, however, is that a nonhegemonic international political economy would also cause us to extend and look beyond (although not jettison, I hasten to add) rational actor models. It was argued in the first half of the chapter that economic utility-maximizing models are not sufficient to explain commitment to regimes in general or, illustratively, Australia's role in the Cairns Group. Normative and prescriptive accounts that consider notions of obligation, for example, were also argued to be salient.

Without overly developing the theme here, I would want to argue that one significant component in an explanation of Australian behavior in the whole Cairns exercise, as well as several other components of its contemporary foreign policy, is the need to be seen fulfilling the role, in the words of its current foreign minister, of a "good international citizen" (Evans, 1989a, 1989b). One could choose to dismiss such proclamations as simple rhetoric or a process of self-aggrandizement on the part of Australia's foreign policymakers. And although such elements may certainly be present, it would be a mistake to dismiss the degree to which there is a deep-seated commitment to multilateralism in contemporary Australian foreign policy, plus perhaps a strongly felt psychological need to be a "player" in international relations as part of a process of consolidating the "Australian Identity." Such intangible aspirations and deeply held commitments can, of course, be found in the foreign policies of other states. Without them, and notwithstanding the power of rational utility-maximizing models of regime formation, regimes would be unlikely to exist. A nonhegemonic international political economy would recognize the importance of the good citizen as well as the interest of the free rider in its theorizing.

The important general point to note, and of which the activity of the Cairns Group is an excellent example, has been well articulated by James Keeley when he suggested that our choice in regime theory is not simply between hegemon-driven or major power–driven regimes on the one hand, or the abandonment of "community" to the mercies of realism in international relations on the other (Keeley, 1989: 90). There is an alternative—indeed, there may be several—that emanates from a competing set of perspectives, ideas, and contests. I have outlined in this chapter just one issue that has arisen in the context of the current Uruguay Round in which smaller states are resisting major power initiatives, or more correctly, attempting to persuade the major players to commit to a series of initiatives that would bring about reform in the international agricultural regimes but which, for a variety of reasons to do with perceived domestic political and economic imperatives, the major actors are unable and/or unwilling to introduce of their own volition. To the extent that smaller players occupy a significant role in this process, then they represent an important modification to a realist explanation of cooperation in international trade reform.

Two brief discussions of this proposition must suffice here. (1) Realist theory has long argued, persuasively it should be added, that the smaller the number of players the more manageable the negotiating processes. Conversely, the larger the number of players the greater the potential for misunderstanding and multiple, potentially irresolvable, conflicts. While Hampson, in looking at regime creation in response to climate change, has demonstrated that such factors are much more serious in regime creation than in regime maintenance or reform—where at least some standardized forms of behavior have been established—the basic point remains that the smaller the group engaged in the negotiation the less is the likelihood of information breakdown. In this regard, the cipher-like activity of the kind exhibited by the Cairns Group not only creates a more manageable negotiation, it also acts as a conduit for information to followers in the negotiations in a manner that minimizes the danger of misunderstanding. As the Cairns Group and Hampson's study of regime building in response to environmental issues show, small group behavior can be an important substitute in the absence of hegemony. This can be either as a means "to get the regime off the ground" (Hampson, 1990: 60) or to set the agenda for reform. (2) Joseph Greico (1990), in his recent assertion of the superior explanatory power of realism over Keohane's (1988; 1989: 1–21) liberal institution as a means to understanding the outcomes of negotiations over nontariff barriers in the Tokyo Round, argues that the major actors (especially the European Community) saw absolute welfare gains as a secondary consideration to ensuring that competitors (especially the United States) did not take positional advantage or make relative gains out of the negotiating process. In short, positive gains for all partners were not sufficient to secure cooperation among the major players, according to Greico. If he is correct—and he presents a powerfully documented defense of his hypothesis—then the role of smaller players in cooperation building may offer a potential restraint on this tendency in a number of ways. Greico's analysis is founded upon a two-person game theoretic base. There would appear to be little room in it for other players. Yet, even were this the case in the Tokyo Round, it does not, I have tried to argue, pertain in the Uruguay Round. Other actors are of significance and, as smaller players and in contrast to the major players, they may be less concerned about the relative gains question and more interested in absolute welfare gains for all. This is not to say that smaller players will never be concerned over the question of the relative gains vis-à-vis other larger actors, as Greico, in fact, shows (Greico, 1990: 209–214). But in contrast to Greico's description of the European Community's posture on the nontariff negotiations in the Tokyo Round, smaller states in the Uruguay Round negotiations on agriculture, for example, have not shown themselves to date to be "defensive positionalists" (Greico, 1990: 169).

Nevertheless, the identification of the relative gains problem is one of the most innovative developments in realist thought in a long time. As Greico (1990: 232) notes, it pinpoints a range of important questions that need to be examined in our wider understanding of the achievement of international cooperation. However, it seems to me that it does not take seriously the potential effect on institutions of evolution over time—or at least not in the way that Robert Keohane (1989: 14) would exhort us to do. Its assumptions are what Rosenau (1986) refers to as habit driven, whereas a central component of a reformist international political economy would assume a process of significant learning on the part of all players—not just the major ones. The very existence of the Cairns Group in the Uruguay Round, for example, let alone its behavior, represents a quantum leap in learning from the Tokyo Round, I would argue. Following Keeley's (1989: 92) mode of analysis, the group would appear to have accepted the discipline and public space set by GATT as a realm for action but also, in this instance, chosen not to accept the managerial baggage that has accompanied it for much of GATT's existence—namely the necessity of U.S. hegemonic leadership. Although recognizing the role of the United States (and to a lesser extent the European Community) as the major player in the international trading regime, without whom no meaningful agreement can be achieved, the group has actively engaged in the reformulation of the regime's practices in what I would like to call a *nonhegemonic* manner. The argument has been developed only briefly in this section of the chapter. It clearly awaits fuller empirical explication in the aftermath of the Uruguay Round and theoretical explication in both abstract and empirical fashion in other domains. My point has been simply to demonstrate that in one specific issue area— agriculture—and even within the simple confines of a state-centric discourse, modification to the prevailing orthodoxy in international political economy is possible.

Conclusions

The aims of this chapter have been twofold. First, the chapter provides a brief account of the manner in which theory and practice in international political economy, as it has developed within the heartland of international relations in the United States over the last decade, need to undergo an international process of reform. Such reform would be sensitive to a set of emerging perspectives that treat many of international political economy's underlying assumptions in a more problematic fashion than has previously been the case. Three assumptions in particular were singled out for scrutiny: (1) the paradigmatic status of rational theory, (2) the illusion of a parsimonious theory of that state, and (3) the bias of American universalism.[8] The upshot of the critique provided here has been the call for a more consciously nonhegemonic perspective in international political economy than has emerged to date in North America.

Second, using Australian examples as a case study—but by no means proposing another bout of "exceptionalism" in theorizing, the second half of this chapter has attempted to suggest what nonhegemonic scholarship in international political economy might look like. In so doing, the emergence of the new mercantilism in international economic relations and recent attempts to secure reform in one area of the current GATT negotiations were addressed through the eyes of smaller parties to these processes.

At first reading there may be appear to be a disjuncture, or tension, between the two parts of the chapter. The first half exhorts us to widen our traditional approaches to the state and sovereignty that have prevailed in international relations for much of its modern existence in favor of an extended approach that theorizes these concepts in a social and historical context as well as a geospatial one. Yet the second half of the chapter focuses quite specifically on state action and, seemingly, state-defined interests. The tension is, however, more apparent than real. What I have tried to do is to treat the state, and agent-led state behavior, seriously, rather than reify it. I have assumed that the interests of state and nonstate agents alike—be they foreign policy bureaucrats, interest groups, or classes—do at various times, either separately or jointly, occupy different levels of importance in the decisionmaking process and have different levels of interest in the outcomes of any one process.

In the current multilateral trade negotiations, for example, reforms in various areas that might be greeted with widespread approval in one sector of a given society may be at considerable cost to other members of that society or to members of the same producer or consumer group in another society. Agricultural producers in the European Community do not have the same interests in agricultural reform as do producers in Australia and other Cairns Group members. On the other hand, producers of services in the European Community, as indeed elsewhere, have a vested interest in reform in the service negotiations, the success of which will stand or fall on the acceptability of the agricultural reform package to other GATT members. Further, domestic groups with interests in international regime reform are reliant on agreements being reached in negotiations conducted on a *state-to-state* basis—be they in the agricultural sector, or the service industries such as finance and banking, or whatever. State negotiators are being asked to secure access to regimes for private actors with interests that may transcend their home base. The interests and initiatives for reform that serve a given interest may lie elsewhere, but the process of building cooperation in the international political economy is still very much a government-based activity. In the current Uruguay Round, agreement will—or will not—be reached by bureaucrats and politicians representing states. The important general points to note are the continual interplay of agent structure relations in the international political economy in the contemporary period and the multifaceted nature of the notion of "agent."

The strength of international political economy as a field of study in the 1990s will depend on the degree to which it becomes increasingly sensitized to this interplay. Having allowed us to add the dimension of structural power to the relational understanding of power central to the realist discourse in international relations, and thereby rescuing the state from reification, international political economy must not make the mistake of reducing the state to the status of a residual category. Policymaking functions and leadership capabilities of foreign-policymaking agents will be of the utmost importance in international politics in the 1990s. Leadership is seen in the threefold sense outlined earlier: structural, intellectual, and entrepreneurial. Although structural, power-derived leadership in general, and U.S. structural power in particular, will continue to remain central, it has been argued that other sources of power and leadership will play a greater role in the process of inducing cooperation in international political economy in the foreseeable future.

Two points should be brought out, lest I be misunderstood. First, I do not see the post–World War II changes in U.S. relational power vis-à-vis the other major players as having been accompanied by a commensurate decline in its structural power, although the U.S. influence is more complex and diffuse in the 1980s and 1990s than it was in the heyday of the so-called Liberal International Economic Order. Rather, I have suggested the 1980s have been something of an "interregnum" in which an old order is passing away, but in which a new one has yet to be defined. As Stephen Gill has noted in a somewhat similar vein, following the processes of intellectual deconstruction of the 1980s we may witness a process "of intellectual construction in the coming decades" (Gill, 1990: 210). If, following Gill's line of argument, the analysis presented in this chapter holds true, then the 1990s will be an era in which the structural power of the United States—in both practice and theory—will remain central but not hegemonic. Second, but from the other side of the glass, I am equally not naive enough to suggest that good intentions of smaller players are sufficient factors on their own to guarantee enhanced cooperation. In keeping with much of the more conservative literature of international political economy, I recognize that regimes are easier to maintain and patch up than to create anew. My basic point is that the 1990s will see games of skill involving more players in more complex games than in the days when tests of will were much more one-sided.[9]

Political, economic, and intellectual influences emanating from other centers of power, especially in Europe and Japan, will evidently have a mitigating influence on the role of the United States. Such a situation is, I think, fairly self-evident. Less evident, however, is the assumption that smaller states, individually or collectively, may be sources of leadership and innovation. The aim of this chapter has been to suggest a number of ways in which such a consideration might become more apparent. Its aims have been more modest than the tone of its presentation might, at times, have suggested. This is invariably the lot of work that tilts at orthodoxy. Constraint and opportunity in the international political economy of the 1990s may not be as politically voluntarist as some scholars of the avowedly neoclassical persuasion might have us believe, but neither will it be determinist as those of the more structuralist persuasion would suggest.

Notes

1. See, for example and variously, the work of some of the following authors: Ashley, (1983, 1984), Tooze (1988), Jervis (1988, 1989), Der Derian and Shapiro (1989), Kratochwil (1989), and *Millennium* (1988).

2. For a fuller discussion of these themes, see Higgott and George, 1990.

3. Krugman (1986, 1990) provides the most balanced discussion of this material to date.

4. See Richardson (1989) and Grossmann (1986).

5. See, especially, Cairns Group (1986, 1987, 1988, 1989).

6. On arms control, for example, see Byers et al. (1987).

7. See Strange (1988), Gill and Law (1989), and Nye (1990).

8. Packenham (1973) still provides the best critique of this.

9. For an interesting illustration of this increased complexity in a Northeast Asian context, see Leaver (1990a).

6

Trade Policy Games

Douglas Nelson

Game theory seeks to build a theory of action from a particularly simple set of first principles. Theories of action attempt to treat both individual choice and social structure seriously in a single theoretical framework. Weber's (1922) classic, *Economy and Society*, still provides the clearest programmatic statement.

The relationship of economics to the action theoretic program has always been ambiguous. Although choice has been at the center of economics, it has always been a peculiarly asocial type of choice. Not only are the social foundations of production and exchange rarely examined, but individuals interact with one another only indirectly. In many ways this is not surprising; after all, the most profound social structural attribute of capitalism is the constitution of the economy as a domain that is normatively distinct from the rest of the social structure. Furthermore, it is a domain in which individual agency often appears to be particularly significant (i.e., behavior often appears to be minimally socialized). In this context, it is not unreasonable to focus on individual choice as simple constrained optimization. The game theoretic program, especially as outlined by von Neumann and Morgenstern (1944), is an attempt to do more to resocialize the analysis of rationality in economic environments. That is, it forces us to focus directly on the interdependencies among persons from which societies are constituted.

Oddly, although some of the language and results of game theory have received extensive use by leading proponents of IPE (Axelrod and Keohane, 1985; Keohane, 1986b; Putnam, 1988; Snidal, 1985), the action-theoretic foundations are generally less explicit than is common in the economics literature.

Game theory attempts to characterize and analyze individual rational choice in strategic situations, where a strategic situation is defined in terms of three major social structures: the payoff structure, the game structure, and the information structure. This chapter discusses individual rationality, and these three social structures in turn, in order to assess the role of game theory in the unification and clarification of research on the political economy of international trade. I conclude that game theory may play such a role, but that input from economics and social sciences is essential to the solution of some otherwise intractable problems in the theory of games. The attempt to build a theory of action relevant to IPE might center on game theory, but it cannot rest there.

Individual Rationality: Who Plays the Game

The problem of characterizing rationality, although nontrivial in some of its theoretical and empirical details, is, as we will see, far less difficult than the problem of identifying the individual presumed to be playing the international trade game. By "rational" we mean that the individual can compare the relevant alternatives and rank them in terms of (weak) preference. Under conditions characterized by risk/uncertainty we assume that the individual either knows the probabilities associated with each of the relevant states of the world and maximizes expected utility, or does not know the probabilities and updates them in a Bayesian fashion, engaging in subjective expected utility maximization.[1] In a strategic situation, rationality also implies that individuals explicitly take into account the behavior of the other relevant individuals by assuming that they are strategically rational (i.e., that everyone understands the strategic situation in the same way).[2]

Rationality of the sort just described is an attribute of human individuals.[3] The meaning of rationality with reference to collective entities (such as firms, governments, or countries), however, is far from clear. We need to be clear that when we assert the rationality of a collective entity, we assume considerably more about that entity than is generally realized. Thus, one of the virtues of explicitly adopting game theory as our language for thinking about the political economy of international trade is that it forces us to face up to this additional content. Drawing on the body of research that has grown from Arrow's (1963, 1983) fundamental contributions to the theory of social choice, we know that this sort of rationality is generally possible only under conditions of either dictatorship or some set of institutionalized social rules/norms. Leaving aside for now the issue of social norms, let us briefly consider dictatorship.

A dictator, in the social choice context, is a player whose individual ranking of social states (in this case taken to be outcomes in a trade policy game) necessarily determines social choices over the relevant domain. Now, if we believe that trade policy reflects rationality of the sort described above, it seems interesting to ask if some form of dictatorship is in operation. Alternatively, we might ask under what conditions dictatorship over trade is possible. In either case, there are two general types of answer: structural explanations that make dictatorship causally necessary and conjunctural explanations that make it contingent on some set of (unique) exogenous forces.

As a general rule, social scientists prefer explanations that make dictatorship a structural attribute of the system in question.[4] The reason for this preference is obvious: structural dictatorship allows us to treat this aspect as constant, which allows us to ignore it in our analysis. One begins by positing the domination of a particular group or class and proceeds to derive conclusions on the basis of that assumption. One version of this is found in Marxist political theory of the instrumentalist type. Such analyses presume that the government is dominated by the "ruling class," and much of the analytical effort is spent in an attempt to construct a description of observed outcomes such that the observed outcome is that preferred by the ruling class.[5] In contrast, the Chicago School's instrumentalism does not assert that a single interest dominates the state as a whole, only that single interests dominate decision arenas. Without some additional structure, this assumption would generate little in the way of useful hypotheses, but the Chicago School appends the additional (rather doubtful) assumption that the political game is always about the creation and division of economic rents. This structure permits politicoeconomic analysis to move from the outcome to the identification of the interest that dominated a particular decision.[6]

Assumptions of this sort doubtless render politicoeconomic analysis more tractable, but we need to be alert to their highly problematic nature. Even if we accept the notion of some form of dictatorship over trade policy, it is not at all obvious what the dictator's objective function should be presumed to contain. At a minimum, we might suspect that most governments are concerned with some mix of three classes of goals in their decisionmaking: efficiency goals, equity goals, and order goals. To assert the *general* predominance of one or another of these classes of goals is to make a (probably meaningless) normative statement. Furthermore, to the extent that we can identify a ranking in the actual behavior of most governments, we would have to conclude that efficiency goals are almost always ranked no higher than the other two, and usually lower.

More importantly, unless we can come up with a definition of either "government" or "state" that permits the attribution of unitary rationality over time, we should find the assumption of a structural dictator an excessively weak foundation from which to construct a positive analysis of the political economy of trade policy. The obvious benefit of focusing on governments is that they are made up of real people, with real preferences over policy. Unfortunately, even if we ignore intragovernmental conflicts, it is a definitional attribute of governments that they change, and that preferences over policy change with them. States, on the other hand, are presumed to be stable entities across time, but cannot be treated as rational entities.[7]

This leads us to the notion of conjunctural dictatorship. That is, even though governments may change, it is quite possible that (for historic reasons) there may be quite stable preferences over some specific policy area. For example, over the period 1934–1984 the assumption of a unitary rationality at the level of the state with the greatest influence on trade policy within the state is not unreasonable.

As a result of a unique combination of domestic and international conditions, the executive branch of the U.S. government was able to seize control of trade policy from Congress throughout this period (Nelson, 1989a). While the dating of the onset of the period of executive dominance is conveniently marked by the Reciprocal Trade Agreements Act of 1934, the terminal date is merely conjectural. The making of trade policy has always been accompanied by considerable political friction. Nonetheless, by the second Reagan term it seems clear that Congress had decided to attempt to regain some of its lost control over trade policy. This is perhaps best indicated by the explosion of interest in general trade policy outside the precincts of the House Ways and Means and Senate Finance committees, and the emergence of trade policy as a high-visibility campaign issue for the first time in nearly half a century.

Within the executive branch, throughout the period 1934–1984, the general direction of trade policy was determined primarily by trade specialists (economists and lawyers). Given the relatively high degree of agreement among such specialists, it is not surprising that U.S. trade policy has been characterized by considerable stability until very recently. Furthermore, given its dominant position in the period immediately following World War II, the U.S. government was able to institutionalize its vision of the global trading order, not only in GATT but in other countries through their participation in GATT.

Of course, even if history allows us to accept the assumption of unitary rationality, we still need to specify in considerably more detail the strategic problem to which this unitary rationality is applied, which leads us to the questions of payoff structure, game structure, and information structure. These formal structures are logically (and socially) prior to individual choice and not generally reducible to individual choice (except trivially).[8] Just as history can give us reasonable grounds for the assumption of individual rationality, anthropology, sociology, and political science, whose stock-in-trade is social structure, can provide grounds for reasonable assumptions about these structures as they influence trade policy. In addition, other branches of economics can give us some clear ideas about their effects.

The Payoff Structure: What the Game Is About

Of the various elements that describe a game, the most important is the payoff structure. Not only do payoffs tell us why the players are interested in playing, they tell us *what* they are playing. Given this importance, it is somewhat surprising to note that in most applications of game theory to specific strategic situations like trade policy, payoffs are (often implicitly) assumed as "given." In an applied context, however, we must ask (1) what is the game about? and (2) where do the payoffs come from?

Neither of these questions is particularly problematic in a purely theoretical context. The answer to the first question lies in the assumptions relating to the topological properties of the outcome space and the mapping from outcomes to utilities. The second question has no meaning at all in purely theoretical terms. Unfortunately, if we hope to build a rigorously (methodologically) individualistic theory of (rational) social interaction using game theory, this kind of purely theoretical account will not do.[9] If our game theoretic account of the political economy of trade policy is to be at all compelling, we need to be considerably more concrete about the structure of the political space in which the game is played, the nature of outcomes in that space, and the mappings from political to economic outcomes and from economic outcomes to utilities.

From Political to Economic Outcomes

It may seem like common sense to assume that there is some kind of trade policy space. There are, however, a number of problems with this formulation. The most obvious difficulty is that the construction of the space is itself a strategic act. First, to the extent that we can think of reasonably stable generic issues (such as international trade), it is often not clear what generic issue a specific event belongs to. In the case of trade policy, there are a variety of what might be called economic adjustment problems that may or may not have any link to trade that end up getting treated as trade problems. We identify an event as part of the trade issue area if it is treated under the trade-policy label, but the process of linking the event to the issue area may be strategically more important than its resolution within the issue area. Furthermore, it is rare that an issue is sufficiently separable from other issues to consider it in isolation. Also, the nature of the linkages between issues changes constantly. Thus, even at a fairly high level of generality, U.S. trade policy has been linked to national security policy, industrial (i.e., macroeconomic) policy, balance-of-payments policy, and agricultural policy.

Now let us suppose that we can identify a trade-policy issue area, separable from other issues, whose content is reasonably stable over time. Points in this space are the possible outcomes of the political process. Assuming, however, that (like other economic issues) action on trade policy is motivated by a concern with the effect of the outcome on the economy, we still need to be able to map political outcomes into the values of economically relevant variables—the economic outcome space. If we can assume that the politically relevant outcomes from a trade-policy action are (at least proximately) economic, the theoretical link between political and economic outcomes can be constructed reasonably easily. There is a substantial body of theoretical and empirical research on trade policy that studies precisely this mapping.[10]

The most relevant, nonmacroeconomic, domestic effects of trade policy can be sorted into those relating to the productive efficiency of the economy as a whole, details of the production structure, and income distribution.[11] We should also bear in mind that trade policy will generally have an effect on the active country's trading partners that should also be considered explicitly. The nature of these (domestic and international) economic effects will depend on the details of the underlying relations that define the economy. Let us briefly consider each of the classes of effect and the degree to which each has been and can be investigated using the standard tools of economics.

Effects on Productive Efficiency and National Wealth

Following the standard practice in the economics literature on trade and trade policy, let us take as our baseline case a small economy characterized by complete and perfectly competitive markets for goods and factors of production, and peopled by rational and well-informed economic actors (i.e., firms and households). A standard result from welfare economics is that, under these conditions, producers will produce a bundle of goods valued at least as highly as any other bundle of goods (given the available productive resources and technologies). The assumptions of the model guarantee that prices accurately convey the (private and social) opportunity costs of goods and factors of production, and that actors are unable to gain from strategic behavior. Under these conditions, trade-policy intervention will have the effect of decreasing productive efficiency. That is, intervention will cause resources to be allocated among industries so as to produce a bundle of goods valued less than some alternative bundle.[12]

Deviations from the model that generates this result are surely the norm; the trick is to specify the nature of the relevant deviations, and it is in this regard that the basic competitive model provides a convenient baseline for analytical purposes. A large class of such deviations can be conveniently handled within the standard trade-theoretic framework. The fundamental work of Harry Johnson and Jagdish Bhagwati, conveniently summarized in Bhagwati (1971), demonstrates that (at least in nonstrategic environments) most deviations can be identified with one of four archetypal distortions. Furthermore, policy interventions in otherwise undistorted environments can be categorized within the same scheme. In developing this scheme, Bhagwati presents a clear characterization of the effects of various types of intervention on production and consumption.

As we have noted, the Bhagwati-Johnson theory of economic policy relies on the assumptions that economic actors (firms and households) behave nonstrategically. As long as the domestic monopolist does not behave strategically, this framework yields the required information on the production effects of the monopoly and the effects of policy intervention. That is, it provides a characterization of the mapping from the space of political outcomes to the space of economic outcomes. The situation changes fairly dramatically when the market is characterized by strategic interaction among firms. The analysis of this case is one of the most dynamic areas of research by international economists. Unfortunately, the results in this field are difficult to characterize simply. This should not be a surprise; different market structures and different strategic situations within industries yield different effects from policy intervention.

Structure of Production

Although the great majority of economics research on trade policy has been concerned with productive efficiency (the theory of economic policy) or national wealth (rent shifting in oligopolistic markets), the political discourse has tended to concentrate directly on production structure and income distribution. With regard to production structure, the most prominent issues have related to either the "noneconomic" attributes of particular sectors or some form of positive externality.

The notion that there are sectors of the economy that are intimately bound up with a nation's sense of itself is an old and politically potent one. For example, we hear it argued in the United States today that we should not become a service-based economy because, in some sense, these sectors lack the dignity of other (especially manufacturing) sectors. That is, it is part of our vision of the United States as a nation that we are an industrial nation. Economists refer to policy goals related to such preferences as noneconomic because they do not emerge from a breakdown in the efficient functioning of the economy. Because goals of this kind do not imply any market imperfection, the economy in this case is easily represented as perfectly competitive. Thus, the mapping from political outcomes (e.g., tariffs, taxes, subsidies) to economic outcomes (i.e., expansion or contraction of manufacturing) is quite straightforward.[13]

A more significant argument for industrial policy is that certain sectors generate positive externalities that, because they cannot be captured by private economic actors without policy activism, will result in underinvestment.[14] It is well known that a wide variety of models can produce inefficient equilibria without some form of intervention. This suggests the fundamental importance of explicitly modeling the relevant relations. That is, explicit modeling forces us to face the empirical significance of our assumptions and the consistency of our logic. Perhaps more importantly, in the context of political economy modeling, we are enabled to ask whether the points in the space of political outcomes that will be generated by the political process are the same points that will result in welfare improvement.

Income Distribution

A change in income distribution is the effect of a change in trade policy with the most obvious political content. It is fairly common in both academic and practical discourses on trade policy to assert the importance of one or another distributional effect to trade-policy outcomes. Whether they are taken to motivate organized political action by those affected or to induce un–self-interested response by state actors, these effects are most often asserted ad hoc, not derived from an underlying model of the economy. The analytical informality of this approach is, perhaps, most surprising when the asserted effects are taken to define the payoffs to some explicitly modeled game-theoretic analysis. Furthermore, we can easily develop a more explicit link between policy change and income distribution by taking advantage of well-established results from the economic research on trade policy.

For example, under the standard assumptions of the Heckscher-Ohlin-Samuelson (HOS) model,[15] it can be easily demonstrated that an increase in the price of one of the goods will raise the return to the factor used intensively in the production of that good and lower the return to the other factor, relative to all other prices.[16] Thus, under the HOS assumption structure, this result explicitly links changes in policy (say, the introduction or removal of a tariff) to changes in income distribution. One particularly important extension of this result relates to the assumption of perfect factor mobility. Differential capacity to adjust to changes in the politicoeconomic environment would seem to be a fundamental characteristic of citizen-agents. The easiest way to represent such differential mobility is to assume that one type of factor (e.g., capital) is immobile between sectors whereas the other continues to be perfectly mobile. If we drop the factor-mobility assumption, we find that the effect of a policy change that raises the returns to an industry will unambiguously raise the returns to the immobile factors employed in that sector while unambiguously lowering the returns to the other specific factor.[17]

International Response

To this point we have implicitly assumed, in constructing the mapping from the space of political outcomes to the space of economic outcomes, that the only international adjustments to the policy choice are strictly economic and reflect re-equilibration of the economic system. Although this is a useful and convenient place to begin one's analysis, it should be especially clear in the context of an explicitly strategic analysis that this can be only a resting point on the way to a more complete analysis.

Like citizen-agents, foreign governments will have preferences over the domestic policy space, and we can assume, with considerably less confidence than in the case of domestic politics, that these preferences derive from the effect of domestic policy on foreign economic magnitudes. That is, we assume that the relevant mapping is from the space of domestic policy outcomes to foreign economic outcomes. Thus, the introduction of international relations does not add any special complexity in the analysis of payoffs. The foreign government is simply one more actor with preferences over policy. Further difficulties arise only when the game structure is considered.

From Economic Outcomes to Utilities

The final step in deriving the payoffs from playing a political-economic game is characterizing the link between economic outcomes and utilities. As long as we assume that individuals are risk neutral, strictly concerned with economic well-being, and selfish, the task is particularly easy. Under these assumptions, and the other assumptions that underlie the standard neoclassical model of the economy, we need keep track only of the effect of policy on factor prices (which determine individual income) and commodity prices (on which the income is spent). That is, all that really matters in this context is the effect of policy on the relevant individual's (expected) real income. Once we permit individuals to be risk averse, concerned with the welfare of others, or concerned with noneconomic aspects of their own or others' welfare, we need to be much more explicit about how changes in the politicoeconomic environment affect welfare. These are obviously empirical issues and present a clear opportunity for a more explicit integration of social scientific research with game theoretic research.

The Game Structure: How the Game Is Played

Where the payoff structure characterizes the players' goals, the game structure characterizes what they can do in pursuit of those goals. The game structure includes two major elements: the set of actions available to the players and the rules regulating the use of the actions. These are the basic elements (along with the details about what players are assumed to know) from which the players construct the strategies that determine where, in the outcome space, the game ends up (if anywhere).

In pure game theory the action set of each player (A_i) is often described simply in terms of that set's topological properties (e.g., it is a compact, convex subset of a dimensional real space). Each point in that space, a_i, is then a set of actions that constitutes player i's strategy. For simple games we can specify the strategies in more detail. In the Prisoners Dilemma game, for example, each of the players has an action set with two actions: $A_i =$

{cooperate, defect}. In the simple Cournot market game, each firm's action set consists of its technologically feasible output levels.

The introduction of time, even in extremely simple ways, requires the introduction of more structure and more rules. With regard to structure, it becomes necessary to specify the way in which time is taken to pass (i.e., how long are the time periods, where zero gives the continuous time case). Perhaps more importantly, the rules must now specify how moves are to be distributed across time. For example, will there be a set of simultaneous moves in each period or will there be sequences of alternating moves? In the latter case, there must be rules to specify the order of moves. In any event, with the action sets and rules specified, each of the players is assumed to adopt the strategy that, taking into account the strategies of the other players, yields the highest utility.

These are precisely the sorts of consideration that have long interested political scientists. Thus, game theory does not so much provide new questions or new theoretical accounts as it can provide a new language for integrating research in political science with that in economics. At the same time, input from the social sciences can provide more concrete contexts for dealing with game theory's most difficult problems.

Consider a simple voting model in which the only issue is trade policy and the only policy instrument is a uniform tariff. Each citizen will have a preferred level of the uniform tariff determined by the effect of the tariff on prices of consumption goods and the return to their factor portfolio. If each citizen's only available action is a vote on the level of the uniform tariff, we know that there will be a unique equilibrium at the preferred point of the median voter.[18] The existence of a unique equilibrium in this case rests on a set of assumptions that kept the game strictly one-dimensional. Once we permit the dimensionality to rise, we generally lose the unique equilibria.

Game theorists have responded to this general class of problems (problems of nonuniqueness) in three ways: the study of equilibrium refinements, ad hoc introduction of social structural elements, and evolutionary arguments.[19] The first of these is more closely related to attempts to deepen our understanding of strategic rationality, which is the subject of the next section of this chapter. The role of structure is immediately relevant.

It has long been known to game theorists that once we specify the structure of the game in more detail, the nonuniqueness problem may be eliminated. We know, for example, that agenda-setting power, exclusionary rules, and rules regulating order of participation can determine the outcome of a game. This sort of consideration is a staple of political science research, but game theory provides a convenient framework for linking the findings of political science research to the economics research reviewed in the first part of this chapter.

Division of Political Labor

One of the most dynamic areas of current political science research relates to the effect of institutionalized agendas and agenda-setting power on final outcomes of the legislative process. For example, as Shepsle (1979) has effectively argued, the existence of a division of legislative labor among a set of committees with clear jurisdiction over the issue domain and power to control floor action allows us to identify determinate equilibria. The brilliance of Shepsle's insight in the context of the nonuniqueness problem in voting games was the recognition that institutions matter. That is, once we surrender the (almost certainly vain) attempt to derive unique equilibria strictly on the basis of preferences, we can use the results of research on political structure to help us account for stable political outcomes.

In U.S. trade policy, the House Committee on Ways and Means played this sort of fundamental role with regard to trade policy management from the late 1950s until the late 1980s.[20] With the reforms of the early 1970s, however, the institutional framework for trade-policy management began to come undone: as Ways and Means lost its ability to maintain its jurisdiction, the politics of trade policy became much more open and unpredictable. There was no longer a structure to induce equilibrium.

Order of Participation

A very closely related aspect of game structure relates to the order in which players are allowed to move. First-movers, in a loose sense, have agenda-setting power. For example, the primary mechanism for effecting a marginal increase in protection in the United States is the administered protection law (i.e., antidumping duties, countervailing duties, escape clause cases, and unfair trade practice cases). There is no administrative mechanism for protection relief. This means that protection seekers have the first move with respect to a fairly complex action set that includes filing cases in one or more of the administered protection mechanisms as well as direct pressure on Congress and the presidency. Nelson (1989b) presents an extended illustration of the advantages of this bias for the case of automobiles in the late 1970s and early 1980s.

Standing

Rules of standing define which actors are allowed to play a given game. Excluded actors effectively have empty action sets. Formal standing rules are easily identified, but informal rules may be just as important. In the case of the legislative politics of trade policy, for example, it appears to be the case that substantial and direct trade impact is a necessary condition for standing on trade policy questions. If this is the case, it has the effect of excluding the preferences of the majority of the population from consideration on trade-policy questions. The result is legislation that represents the interests of the strongest proliberalization and proprotection interests, but not the interests of the majority.

In sum, just as political historians and economists can provide some, but far from all, the answers to questions of what the trade game is about, political scientists looking at domestic policies can help provide some of the answers to the question of how the game is played.

Information Structure: Common Knowledge and Values

No one will be surprised by the idea that we need to assume that game players know what their preferences are, what the structure of the game is, and what the payoffs from playing the game are. This, after all, is to assume that they know what they are doing. Without an assumption of this sort, the assumption of rationality would not have much analytical power. Furthermore, interviews, diaries, and memoirs indicate that people do, in fact, have clear ideas about the games they are playing. Many of us who are not adept at game theory, however, are surprised that this kind of knowledge is insufficient for game theoretic modelling.

The fundamental difference between game theory and decision theory is that in game theory the decisionmakers are assumed to condition their choices on what they expect other decisionmakers to do. Game theory is a theory of strategic rationality. This obviously implies that each player must have knowledge about the other players. Specifically, each player needs to know that the other players are rational and that they know the game structure and its relationship to payoffs, and needs to know their relevant beliefs about chance elements in the game. Without this knowledge it would be impossible to engage in strategic rationality. But even this is not enough. Each player must know that all the other players know these same facts about all the other players, because they must know how the other players are evaluating their plans. And so on, ad infinitum. This is what game theorists mean when they say that there is "common knowledge" of rationality, payoffs and beliefs, and of the game's structure.

The farther down this chain of common knowledge one goes, the more insistently does the question of its origins impress itself upon us. Except in strategic environments so trivial that the issue does not emerge, common knowledge implies quite intimate knowledge. Anthropologists debate whether this kind of knowledge is even possible across cultures, but there is no debate as to whether this kind of knowledge is casually available. It is not. One might even characterize the degree of community by which a group of people are related by reference to the level of such common knowledge. Thus, while game theory offers a powerful language for integrating the findings of ethnography and sociology with those of economics and political science, it is clear that the social sciences are sources of fundamental insights necessary for further development of the notions of common knowledge.

A similar argument could be made about the creation of community, a problem that game theorists would appear to be studying when they ask: can we agree to disagree? In simple terms, the issue is whether, after a suitable number of iterations, game players can arrive at common knowledge.[21] Such issues are obviously of considerable importance in the creation of an international regime for trade management. A substantial part of the business of regime creation is certainly the attempt to create a set of common expectations about the game of trade-policy management. Just as game theory has much to offer in the development of a theory of international system building (beyond facile references to the folk theorem that repeated Prisoners' Dilemmas can yield cooperation), concrete historical, social research on international system building has much to offer to game theory.

Consider the case of trade bargaining between the United States and Japan. It should be quite evident that trade relations between these two countries offer a wide range of mutually beneficial outcomes. Nonetheless, the political process of bargaining over trade issues seems to generate more conflict and to offer more potential for ending up with mutually damaging outcomes than those between the United States and any of its other trade partners. Even the most casual reading of the current Western literature on the politics, economics, and political economy of Japanese trade and industrial policy will reveal the importance of the "foreignness" of Japan to the problem of creating a political regime for managing trade relations between the United States and Japan.[22] The implication of foreignness is precisely that if the common knowledge assumption cannot be taken to hold, neither party can go very far down the chain of "we know that they know," and so on.

The importance of the failure of common knowledge in international strategic relations is particularly well illustrated by Ruth Benedict's (1946) observation that the "differentness" of the Japanese "made the war in the Pacific more than a series of landings on island beaches, more than an unsurpassed problem of logistics. It made it a major problem in the nature of the enemy. We had to understand their behavior in order to cope with it." That is, even at the limit of Wolfers's (1962) pole of power, the common knowledge assumption cannot be assumed to hold. Today, the result, as the international politics of the trade show all too clearly, is (given nonuniqueness) the incapacity of the United States and Japan to find a mutually beneficial equilibrium.

This would seem to be an excellent example of the type of problem in IPE where game theoretic reasoning could help integrate findings from economics, political science, anthropology, and sociology. At the same time, it also provides an opportunity for game theory to develop a more empirically grounded understanding of the structure and dynamics of common knowledge.

Summary and Conclusions

Throughout this chapter, I have argued that game theory's contributions to IPE, and in particular to an understanding of trade policy, can be quite significant, especially if the game theoretic research program is understood for what it is—an attempt to build a rigorous theory of action. Moreover, I have agreed with Ken Binmore (1987, 1988) that the further development of game theory itself requires an "algorithmic" approach. That is, we need to focus on the structures and processes by which "real" games are played. Trade policy provides an ideal laboratory for analysis of this sort, and the more explicit and complex understanding of society provided by history and the social sciences not only helps us define the conditions under which game-theoretic models of trade policy are the most pertinent, it also contributes to solutions to otherwise intractable problems in the theory of games.

We have seen that a concern with political history can help us identify situations in which game theory's seemingly unrealistic assumption of unitary rationality on the part of the players in the international trade policy game may, in fact, be realistic. Economics, including some branches of economics that are relatively unfamiliar to many IPE scholars, can contribute a much clearer understanding of what the trade-policy game is really about. The study of domestic politics can help us understand how trade-policy games are actually played. And the social sciences that provide insight into the normative and common knowledge boundaries of communities can help us when these assumptions of game theory are and are not met. All of this suggests a somewhat broader agenda for interdisciplinary collaboration and integration than that advanced by most orthodox IPE scholars, including those who advocate the development of game theoretic approaches.

When we are asked, as social scientists, to justify the current organization of the social sciences (i.e., economics, political science, sociology, and so on), our response is usually in terms of the virtues of a "division of labor." That is, we recognize that social reality is an organic unity, but we hope that by dividing the study of that unity into parts we will more quickly and effectively advance our knowledge. This hope, however, rests on the expectation that, somewhere along the line, the parts are being reintegrated into a composite picture of the whole that (increasingly) approaches a single picture of the totality.

There have been two (broadly construed) approaches to the problem of integration: interdisciplinary studies of narrowly defined problems and totalizing attempts to reform the social sciences. The first, with fields like public policy and even IPE as examples, have had considerable success at actual integration but have rarely extended the success beyond the particular cases they study. The problem, I believe, is that these approaches tend to be undertheorized (and sometimes antitheoretical), stressing the importance of detailed knowledge of cases to the exclusion of generalization or else working with confining, yet less-than-fully-explicit conceptual frameworks. Without sustained theoretical development, however, there is no cumulation and, thus, no sustained integration.

The second approach, with general systems theory and "economics imperialism" as exemplars, has precisely the opposite problem.[23] The proponents of these totalizing approaches consistently reveal an almost complete lack of interest in the concerns that motivate the discourses of the root disciplines they seek to reorganize. The result, certainly in the cases of general systems theory and economics imperialism, is that the totalizing approaches are not taken seriously by the root disciplines and end up becoming (usually fairly marginal) subfields within one or more of the root disciplines.

Game theory could easily become another case of totalizing reform, constituting itself as another high priesthood concerned primarily with tools. In this case, it would not save IPE from its confining and inadequate conceptualizations. This would be a tragedy. Game theory is not the master form of a future unified social science, but it could be the language that permits sustained integration of substantial parts of the current division of academic labor. If we accept this view about the place of game theory in the social sciences, however, it would seem to have clear implications for future research on the theory of games. Most importantly, game theory cannot constitute itself as a separate discipline attempting to reorganize other discourses on its own terms. Certainly game theorists in IPE should not attempt to do so. Instead, game theorists must become part of the other discourses. The failure to do this will not only result in its marginalization with respect to the other social sciences (as has been the case with the self-identified economics imperialism), and its failure to play the integrating role, but it also will lose the input from the social sciences that is so necessary in resolving many of its own unanswered questions.

Notes

I have been bothering friends and colleagues with the ideas presented in this chapter for some time now. To list them all would be as gratuitous as it is impossible. It would, however, be unfair not to mention Gary Miller, who tolerated considerably more bothering and contributed considerably more insight than can be easily conveyed in a brief mention like this. Thus, although he deserves credit for much that is good in this chapter, only I can be held responsible for any errors in fact, judgment, or taste.

1. Arrow (1971) and Harsanyi (1977) are excellent sources for demonstrations of the existence of expected utility and subjective expected utility functions.

2. Myerson (1986) refers to this assumption as "intelligence." This assumption is not the common knowledge assumption, which will be discussed later. Intelligence simply means that all players assume all other players are

strategically rational when evaluating strategies. Effectively, this eliminates "wishful thinking" from the strategic calculus. It might be noted that although intelligence is easy enough to describe informally, there are substantial problems in developing a precise characterization (Bernheim, 1986; Binmore, 1987, 1988).

3. This statement should not be taken to imply that the strict form of rationality described above is ever actually found in humans. Even less is it intended to imply an evolutionary argument of the "as if" sort. Rather, it seems to be a convenient characterization of what we take to be a fundamental attribute of persons: rationality.

4. This is less of a problem for normative analysis. That is, we simply assert some goal in terms of which we can order social outcomes as primary (e.g., efficiency, equity, order). We may want to make some argument about the positive primacy of this goal, but this should not distract us from the fact that the social choice problem is resolved dictatorially.

5. Jessop (1982) provides a careful, sympathetic account of Marxist theories of the state. It should be noted that, even within the instrumentalist tradition, these theories can become quite subtle. One not uncommon formulation of the Marxist theory of the capitalist state suggests that the state effectively functions to resolve collective action problems within the capitalist (i.e., ruling) class. Thus, it is only because state actors are not members of any part of the ruling class that they are able to act in the interests of the class as a whole. This permits the capitalist state to act against the demands of the capitalist class (in part or as a whole) on any given issue. Analyses of this sort have their roots in Gramsci, but contemporary versions of this sort of analysis can be found in Miliband (1969) or Block (1987). Similar sorts of formulations can be found in the non-Marxist literature on the state, such as Nordlinger (1981), Skocpol and Finegold (1982), and Skocpol and Ikenberry (1983).

6. The clearest statement of this position can be found in Stigler (1975):

> The theory tells us to look, as precisely and carefully as we can, at who gains and who loses, and how much, when we seek to explain a regulatory policy. . . . The announced goals of a policy are sometimes unrelated or perversely related to its actual effects, and the *truly intended effects should be deduced from the actual effects.* (p. 140)

Stigler's work constitutes a particularly pure form of this type of instrumentalism. Just as with instrumentalist Marxism, this general approach can be used with impressive subtlety. The Rochester/Caltech school of political economy has generated a body of work that is individualist and instrumentalist, while reflecting an impressive appreciation for the institutional arrangements that affect outcomes (McCubbins and Sullivan, 1987; especially the papers in parts 2 and 4).

7. I argue this point at some length in Nelson (1987). The basic point is that "state" refers to a set of structural relationships, not to an entity capable of choice. Although it is true that the nature of the state, and the way it is embedded in the overall social structure, may act as a systemic constraint on the choices of governments, it cannot be reduced in any meaningful way to individual choice behavior.

8. We can always reduce the social to a series of behaviors by biologically discrete individuals. The point is that such a reduction may not constitute a coherent account of the phenomenon in question, and almost certainly cannot

constitute a complete account of it. We can construct *rationalizations* of any given social structure in terms of rational choice. There are, however, several problems with such accounts. First, with regard to some institutionalized patterns of behavior, it is difficult to construct compelling rational choice-based accounts of any kind. Second, if we look at a set of structures (even if they are all rationalizable in choice-theoretic terms) it is unlikely that the rationalizations are consistent. See Elster (1989) for a nice presentation of these arguments with particular reference to social norms. Finally, and perhaps most importantly, we need to bear in mind that such rationalizations do no more than show that a structure is consistent with rational choice. To carry the argument into the realm of necessity requires the attribution of a functional logic to the effect that structures seek rationality.

9. This should not be taken to mean that pure theory has no place in social scientific discourse. Quite the contrary, pure theory creates and refines the intellectual tools that are indispenable to social science. The point is merely that without empirical content the discourse remains philosophical and not social scientific.

10. The story of the effects of trade-policy actions is one of the oldest in all of economics. An excellent historical survey can be found in Viner (1937). Corden (1974) remains the most accessible introduction to the modern theory of trade policy. The only major body of work not covered by Corden is the new work on strategic trade policy; that has received an excellent unified presentation in Helpman and Krugman (1989). Perhaps the best introduction to this literature is the set of nontechnical papers by the leading scholars in the field collected in Krugman (1986).

11. This list quite obviously exhausts neither the theoretically possible nor the politically relevant economic effects of trade intervention.

12. The literature on the effect of trade policy on production in an otherwise undistorted economy is quite standard. A convenient presentation is Bhagwati and Srinivasan (1983, chapter 13).

13. For detailed discussions of the mapping from political to economic space, see Johnson (1960), Bhagwati and Srinivasan (1969), Tan (1971), and Vandendorpe (1974). Economic policy in support of national defense objectives is a particularly important case of noneconomic objectives (see Srinivasan, 1987).

14. See Cohen and Zysman (1987) for a particularly strong representation of this position.

15. The HOS model assumes that there are two industries that produce their outputs by applying capital and labor in the quantities determined by their technology and the conditions in product and factor markets. The production technologies are assumed to be completely characterized by production functions that are linear, homogeneous, twice differentiable, and strictly quasiconcave; both factors are assumed to be in fixed supply and to be costlessly and instantaneously mobile between industries; and all markets are assumed to be perfectly competitive. Finally, one of the two industries is assumed to use a greater proportion of capital to labor at all factor prices; that industry is referred to as the capital-intensive sector.

16. Virtually any international economics textbook will present this theorem. See Caves and Jones (1985: 116, 510–511). For a particularly clear analytical presentation of the basic model and its major comparative static results, see Jones (1965).

17. For an excellent presentation of this model, see Jones (1971). Also see Hill and Mendez (1983) for a useful generalization of this model to varying

degrees of mobility for both factors, and Takayama (1982) for a useful survey of major results in both the HOS and specific-factors models.

18. Mayer (1982) presents this model in detail.

19. See Maynard Smith (1982) for an excellent introduction to evolutionary game theory.

20. There were several relevant aspects of the trade-policy management system in the U.S. Congress. First, the Democrat party controlled Ways and Means for most of the relevant period. Second, Democrats interested in assignment to the committee needed to be "right on trade" (i.e., in support of the trade liberalization program). This meant that the preferences of the Ways and Means Committee were consistently more liberal than those of the House of Representatives as a whole. Third, Ways and Means had clear jurisdiction over the core of the trade issue, which meant that it proposed legislation to the floor. This meant that its action set included setting the agenda while the floor's action set involved only voting on the legislation and (depending on the rule under which the bill was reported to the floor) amending.

21. See the essay by Binmore and Brandenburger (1990) for a useful survey and discussion of this issue. By way of comparison, a game theorist might want to look at some of the classic work on symbolic interactionism, e.g., Goffman (1967, 1974).

22. For examples of analyses that stress the "differentness" of Japan, see Johnson (1982), Prestowitz (1988), and Fallows (1989).

23. See von Bertalanffy (1968) for a programmatic statement of general systems theory, and Hirschleifer (1985) for a short, but strong, programmatic statement of "economics imperialism."

PART 3

BEYOND THE TRADITIONAL AGENDA

The final section of the book is intended to build upon the arguments presented so far by illustrating how IPE can move beyond the traditional agenda. It has been a central part of our argument that we are not advocating any "new" synthesis to replace the orthodoxy. Our conception is one of the opening up of the universe of IPE, without the narrow privileging of subjects and issues that is an inherent part of such an orthodoxy. The three chapters in this section are examples of this opening. They do not represent in any sense the totality of such examples in contemporary IPE scholarship. They are, however, important not only in what each chapter presents individually, but also in what they represent in the context of the book as a whole.

Deborah Johnston, in Chapter 7, considers the construction of the periphery in world politics. Developing and extending discourse analysis, she then applies this to an understanding of the way in which the Third World and political development have become constructed in Western thought. Hers is one of the first explicit applications of a postmodernist perspective to issues of international political economy. As such it provides both an introduction and a model for other scholars.

In Chapter 8, Ofuatey-Kodjoe is also concerned with issues of development, or, to be more accurate, with the IPE agenda of African scholars and policymakers. The heterodox voices that he summarizes and critiques represent a second generation of scholars attempting to understand neocolonialism, the specific historical formation of the contemporary African state, and the interconnected African crises of the 1980s (environmental degradation, food shortages, increasing external indebtedness, and political decay). The new IPE developing in Africa, like the new Latin American IPE represented by Tussie, rejects the orthodox interpretation of the genesis of the current world political economy. Furthermore, in Africa, more than in Latin America, the issues privileged by the orthodoxy are clearly of secondary or tertiary importance.

In the final chapter, Ann Tickner offers a feminist critique of IPE. Part of a larger work on a feminist critique of international relations, this chapter opens up the orthodoxy to questions of gender and begins to link IPE into the broader social and political project that questions of gender demand. It provides an appropriate conclusion to the volume, discussing the widest range of human experience excluded by the implicit claims of orthodox IPE. And it illustrates the breadth of the emerging alternatives.

7

Constructing the Periphery in Modern Global Politics

Deborah S. Johnston

Politics begins with the recognition of the "other." This is perhaps most apparent in global politics with its focus upon the actions of so-called sovereign states. But even if we gaze into the past, beyond the modern state system, we find a similar correspondence between politics and otherness. The Greeks, for example, recognized themselves as civilized—that is, as citizens of the city-state—and foreigners as barbaric or "other." A similar arrangement is also found in medieval Europe. Here we find Christians, those who belonged to the true faith and those who did not. Two things become apparent in both the classical Greek and medieval configurations. The first is that the "other" is viewed as something impure and dangerous. It is something that would contaminate the pure essence of that which is viewed as good, whole, virtuous, and clean. For example, the heathen was viewed as someone who would pollute the sanctity of the church, which was perceived as God's representative on Earth; thus, all heretics must be excommunicated. They must be isolated from that which is considered pure of form—the church. Second, we find that the "other" is really a negation, manifestation, or complication of that which is viewed as pure, that which is whole. The heathen is, simply put, a non-Christian. Whereas the church constitutes itself as the earthly *presence* of God—that which is true and real, natural and necessary to the interpretation of history—it creates something called the heathen in terms of the *absence* of God. Heathens, as "others," cannot exist outside of their relation to both God and the church. They have no presence of their own, but are merely corrupt aberrations in the medieval configuration of forces, in which God is viewed as the center around which history is organized.

A similar discourse of the "other" can be found in modern global politics. Whereas the classical Greeks relied upon the citizen/barbarian distinction and medieval Christians upon the Christian/heathen distinction, modern global politics relies upon a distinction between core and periphery, developed and underdeveloped countries, and/or the First and Third Worlds. Within these latter dichotomies,[1] we find that the second term is an aberration of the first. Just as the heathen defiles the church, which is God's representative, the Third World is cast in suspicious terms, as some alien form that, if left unchecked, could disrupt the harmonious expansion of the industrialized First World. The underdeveloped Third World is constructed as "other" to the developed First World. The First World is viewed as the natural unfolding of history, necessary to the progress of man. The Third World is merely some deviation—but mind you, a dangerous deviation—that must be managed and controlled lest it corrupt the pure form of the developed First World.

In this chapter I want to look at the construction of the Third World, or more generally, the periphery (see note 1) in modern global politics. I would like to consider how it became possible in early postwar discourse to conceive of this entity we call the Third World as underdeveloped— economically, culturally, and politically. In other words, how is it that both academics and policymakers have come to think of the Third World as underdeveloped as opposed to anything else they could have conceived of it is as being? How is it that the Third World has become problematized as "other" to the so-called developed First World? Now, asking these types of questions is not an easy task. Coming up with possible answers is even more difficult, for it necessitates a questioning of the very boundaries we often take for granted—boundaries that over the years we have neutralized, depoliticized, and naturalized. We are forced to critically confront these boundaries, asking ourselves how it has become possible to erect them and by what means they are maintained. In other words, we need to critically address the developed/underdeveloped dichotomy, a dichotomy that assumes two distinct identities, logically opposed to one another. What we must do is consider how it became possible to construct these identities, how they are maintained, and how they are resisted.

The relevance of Michel Foucault's work on genealogy and disciplinary power for this project is most apparent. Foucault, in *Discipline and Punish* (1977) and *The History of Sexuality* (1980) adopts what he calls a genealogical approach to the study of power in modern society. In Foucault's analyses, genealogy focuses upon how human beings come to think of themselves as subjects and objects in history. It is concerned with the social practices (both discursive and nondiscursive) that have constituted (that is, produced) human beings as sexual, healthful, moral, and disciplined subjects (and objects). Genealogy attempts to locate traces of the present in the past. To this extent it opposes itself to conventional historical method, which seeks to identify origins, discover underlying laws, and trace the march toward progress. What the genealogist does is write effective history— everything in historical motion, dissolving the comfortable illusion of identity, formness, and solidity (Dreyfus and Rabinow, 1982: 110). In doing this, the genealogist studies the emergence of a "battle," which defines and clears a space, a field. This space is both the result of long-term practices and the field in which those practices operate. It is both the space in which subjects are constructed in history, and in which they play out their roles.

In *Discipline and Punish*, Foucault shows how the disciplined subject—the delinquent—emerges within such a field, and how the practices associated with penal knowledge gave rise to an autonomous, knowing being—the delinquent. Here Foucault distinguishes traditional modes of domination dependent upon public space and authority—the majestic mark of the sovereign—from modern modes of domination, which are directed at the soul, the mind, and finally the will of the subject. As the horrific violence associated with public execution began to disappear, it was replaced by a more complex and ever subtle form of therapeutic correction and rehabilitation, the object of which was to constitute offenders as autonomous knowing beings, subjects who would eventually, it was argued, discipline themselves. Thus, through this complex web of power and knowledge, the delinquent emerged as the ordered, analyzable, useful, and docile subject of penal practice. Disciplinary power, through its surveillance, hierarchization, categorization, and normalization has given rise to the modern subject—the disciplined subject.

The relevance of the genealogical approach and disciplinary power to the present concern with Third World development is to be found in the connection between development practices (e.g., investment, aid, foreign missions, technical assistance, and increasingly debt negotiation) and the emergence of the underdeveloped state as the subject and object of those practices. Rather than taking this entity called Third World for granted, rather than naturalizing its existence, the genealogical approach allows us to explore its historical construction. We are able to map the divergent practices associated with "development," showing how it was possible to construct through disciplinary power the underdeveloped state in early postwar discourse.

In the remainder of this chapter, I would like to explore in general terms this very question: How is it that the Third World has been problematized as underdeveloped in early postwar discourse? To do this we will need, in the broadest of terms,[2] to outline a "genealogy of development." I will not attempt a genealogy itself; to do so would require more time and space than I have here. But I would like to propose some possibilities of where such a genealogy might take us. Finally, I would like us to consider some of the ways in which disciplinary power is at work in development, and how it contributes to the construction of the underdeveloped state.

Otherness

The first question we might want to pose is what is meant by the "other." Here it may be helpful to turn to the works of those scholars writing from what can be termed a postmodern perspective.[3] Postmodernism can be conceived of as a posture, attitude, or conversation. It is not meant to represent a particular period or historical era, necessarily bound by time and space. Rather, it can be viewed as a critical reaction to another discourse: the discourse of modernism. We can look upon modernism as a "grand narrative"—a discourse, if you will, constitutive of a set of attitudes found dominant in Western culture, but not limited to that culture. It is a conversation whose recognized participants situate themselves at the "end of ideology." As Richard Ashley (1987a) has commented:

> [They] know their discourse as the timeless and universal organon of truth, anticipate the transcendence of all fragmentary tradition-bound experience, and interpret their history as a progressive unfolding of universalizing reason and social harmony, via science, technology, philosophy, law and the state.

In effect, modernism is a discourse in which every practice, every theoretical principle, is disciplined by a commitment to what Jacques Derrida calls "logocentrism."

Logocentrism is both a strategy and orientation for disciplining social behavior. It is an orientation that gives pride of place to some absolute identity, principle of interpretation, or necessary subjectivity. It recognizes a "central and ordinary presence," which is necessary to the interpretation of history, and which is itself regarded as unproblematic and beyond history (Ashley, 1987a, 1987b).

However, it must be noted that this true and central subject has no necessary or natural form. We can envision it as the "rational state;" "economic man;" Marx's "consciousness of the proletariat;" Habermas's "ideal speech situation;" "science;" "God;" or any other absolute identity. What is important is that this subject, this privileged viewpoint, is conceived of as existing within itself, above and beyond history making and political play. It is a center around which history must be organized. It is the origin, the truth, to which all intelligent analysis must ultimately speak.

Logocentrism finds expression in modernism through those plain and practical oppositions that we so often take for granted: male/female, rational/irrational, realism/idealism, continuity/change, modern/traditional, developed/undeveloped, core/periphery, base/superstructure, and so on. Accepting these oppositions as natural, modernist discourse imposes a hierarchy upon them (see, for example, Derrida, 1977; Culler 1982; Ashley, 1987a, 1987b). Participants are disposed to identify with a particular subjective position in which one of the two opposing terms is given priority, that is, conceived of as a "higher reality," belonging to the domain of *logos*—a pure presence in need of no explanation. The other term in the opposition is viewed from the same central interpretive position, but solely in relation to the first pure privileged term.

This logocentric posture imposes a hierarchy in which the "other" is rendered as a complication, negation, manifestation, disruption, parasitic (mis)representation, or fall from the graceful presence of the first (see Culler, 1982: 93). Analysis thus becomes for Derrida (1977) "the enterprise of returning 'strategically,' in idealization to an origin or a 'priority' seen as simple, intact, normal, pure, standard, self-identical in order *then* to conceive of derivation, complication, deterioration, accident, etc." It must be emphasized that this logocentric posture is neither an exception to the rule nor an "incidental tendency" in modernist discourse. Rather, it is part and parcel of the only metaphysics we know—in Derrida's words, a "metaphysics of presence," a pervasive, familiar, and powerful narrative by which we organize our understanding of social reality.

Within this metaphysics of presence, the "other" is relegated to the position of a suspicious derivative. It exists only in its relation to the privileged prior presence. By way of illustrating this point it may be helpful to briefly examine Luce Irigaray's critique of psychoanalysis, in which she argues most persuasively that woman is treated as man's "other," as an aberration of man's presence.

It is not difficult to see in the writings of Freud that femininity is marginalized. As Jonathan Culler (1982: 167) points out:

> To define the feminine psyche in terms of penis envy is an indubitable instance of phallogocentrism: the male organ is the point of reference; its presence is the norm, and the feminine is a deviation, an accident or negative complication that has befallen the positive norm.

In the account Freud gives of infant sexuality he explicitly presents the feminine as a derivative of this masculine norm. He states, "we are now obliged to recognize that the little girl is a little man." Just as a little boy learns how to derive pleasurable sensations from his small penis, so does a little girl with her "still smaller clitoris." To Freud, "It seems that with them all their masturbatory acts are carried out on this penis-equivalent, and that the truly feminine vagina is still undiscovered by both sexes" ("Femininity," vol. 22 of Freud's *Complete Psychological Works*, 1953–1974: 118).

However, even after the discovery of the vagina, woman remains marked by derivation. In Freud's account the vagina is really only something of an "extra," a supplement to her inadequate clitoris/nonpenis. It does not give her any autonomous sexuality. In fact, mature feminine sexuality, according to Freud, while focused upon the vagina, is constituted by the repression of clitoral sexuality, which is essentially male. Woman remains an inadequate version of man; her sexuality can only be defined in terms of the repression of her original maleness.

Much of Freud's theory of sexual difference relies upon the twin metaphors of light and dark (metaphors which are, as Luce Irigaray [1985] reminds us, embedded within "phallocentric" Western philosophy). His discussion centers upon the notion of the visibility of difference. As Irigaray points out, the principal point for Freud is that the male has an obvious (i.e., a visible) sex organ, and the female does not. In essence, when Freud casts his gaze upon woman he sees nothing. Female difference is seen as the absence or negation of the male norm, the phallus. As Irigaray's title, *Ce Sexe qui n'en pas un* (this sex which isn't one) suggests, woman is nothing but a negation of the masculine. She is not a being with her own sexual organ, the vagina, but rather a being without the penis. And she is defined essentially in terms of this lack.

Turning back to the original intent of this chapter, it is not difficult to draw some parallels between Irigaray's reading of Freud and the present reading of modern global politics. Just as Freud presents woman in terms of a visible lack of the male organ, modern global politics in its debates on Third World development presents the underdeveloped state as an aberration, a negation of the norm—the developed First World. This is not difficult to see. In all of the various dichotomies it proposes, development discourse sets up oppositions in which one side of the dichotomy (that referring to the First World, the core) is always recognized as the central and originary presence (that is, conceived of as a "higher reality") and the other term (that associated with the periphery) is rendered as a negation, disruption, or complication of the first. For example: modern/traditional, rational/irrational, efficient/inefficient, dynamic/static, progressive/backward, and developed/un(der)developed. The first term in each of these dichotomies is regarded as unproblematic, necessary to the interpretation of history. The second term is a disruption, a deviation, an anomaly, which must be checked and brought under control if history is to be played out according to plan, if progress is to be achieved. The boundary separating the two sides of each dichotomy represents the necessary limits that modern man knows he cannot transgress. In each of these dichotomies the periphery lacks something the core has: efficiency, dynamism, rationality. In general terms, this is exactly how the Third World is represented in modern global politics—in terms of a lack of capital, skilled labor, technology, management, political stability, health standards, nutrition, literacy, and so on. As such, the underdeveloped, the traditional, is cast in opposition to what is "normal"—the developed First World, which, by the way, possesses all these things. Another way of putting this is that each side of the dichotomy comprises a particular identity, with the second term's identity constructed in relation to the original identity of the first.

But is not the traditional (the underdeveloped) really a residual category where difference abounds—where, as D. A. Rustow (1967) has commented, the Arabian bedouin, the farmer in the Mekong rice paddy, the Bolivian tin miner, and the Greenland Eskimo are all lumped together, acquiring unity only as they are conceptually confronted by the "culture of industrial society"? In other words, it is only through disciplining difference that identity can be created. Only by homogenizing these different activities, and then recategorizing them in terms of levels of development can the identity of development/underdevelopment be constructed—an identity rendered visible through practices of development.

An Outline for a Genealogy of Development

In order to see how development practices have constructed the identity of the underdeveloped subject, it is necessary, at least in broad terms, to sketch an outline of a genealogy of development. I will not attempt a genealogy here, as there is neither time nor space, but I would like to suggest where such a genealogy might take us. Before doing so, let me say a few words about genealogy.

As Foucault tells us in "Nietzsche, Genealogy, History," genealogy opposes itself to the search for "origins" (1984: 77). Rather than reading history in terms of a linear development or in terms of its logical unfolding, genealogy looks to the "exteriority of accidents" in history: "it is to discover that truth or being does not lie in the root of what we know and what we are, but in the exteriority of accidents" (1984: 82).

Genealogy concerns itself with both descent and emergence. An examination of descent allows us to discover, under the unique aspect of a trait or concept, the diverse events through which something was formed. This is not a search for an uninterrupted continuity, but rather an attempt to identify the accidents, reversals, and erroneous calculations that gave rise to those traits that we value: morality, humanity, liberty, development. Emergence, on the other hand, refers to the moment of arising. It is always produced through a particular stage of forces; it designates a place of confrontation in which the repeated play of dominations are staged. It is here that identity is created, and that interpretations are altered, displaced, inverted, and transformed.

A genealogy of development, then, would do at least two things. First, it would set out to study the numberless beginnings, the minute deviations, and the faulty calculations that gave birth to this discipline we call development. Second, it would study the emergence of identity—the emergence of the developed versus underdeveloped nation-state. The following paragraphs sketch out, in general terms, where such a genealogy of development might take us.

The discipline of development emerged in both North America and Western Europe during and immediately following World War II. As many writers have pointed out, it emerged primarily in conjunction with, and was influenced by, the Cold War and the postwar restructuring of the international political economy (see Packenham, 1973). But although development emerged as a full-fledged discipline only after World War II, development itsclf was not new—neither as a concept nor as a collection of practices. The notion of development (if not the word) is probably as old as European attempts to procure natural resources from the "New World." Development practices such as technical assistance in the form of "missions" can be traced back (at least in the United States) to before the Civil War (Curti and Birr, 1954). Other practices such as investment are even older. But although development has this long history, it is not a history of continuity, nor even of progression. It has been characterized by a myriad of practices, opinions, debates, and procedures.

At one level, however, it would be easy to mistake the "development of development" as a progression, for it would appear that over the years the industrialized world's approach to development has become more progressive in the sense that it has become more humane. As we shall see shortly, policymakers from industrialized countries began in the twentieth century to discover (or at least mention with increasing frequency) the "humanity of underdeveloped peoples." As such, development practices became increasingly concerned with the welfare of these populations. Whereas development had previously focused upon developing natural resources by developing colonial and other peripheral territories, development now began to concern itself with the well-being of underdeveloped people (Alcalde, 1987). A shift occurred in which the object of development (territory and natural resources) was transformed. But it would be erroneous to attribute this to "progress," to the increasing enlightenment of modern man. As we shall see, the twentieth century preoccupation with humanity did not represent the elevated ethical stance of man, but rather it served a quite necessary political purpose—that of quieting an agitated and riotous population.

Prior to the twentieth century and up until the 1920s. European countries and the United States sent abroad technical missions and exploratory operations that "featured a simple search for knowledge; and in other cases . . . the advancement of economic interests" (Curti and Birr, 1954: 14). From the Herndon and Gibbon expedition into the Amazon (1851) to Charles Hall's exploration of the Arctic (1870), these missions tended to focus on geographic, geodic, topographic, and/or hydrographic surveys of peripheral regions, primarily in search of natural resources. By way of example, the Brazilian government, several years before the Hartt expedition to Brazil in 1874, had requested U.S. assistance for geographic surveys. On arrival in the country, Hartt and his associates began to conduct some of the first systematic geographic surveys ever taken there. As a result, the Brazilian government set up the Commissao Geologico do Imperio do Brasil. Over the next several decades, this commission, originally headed by Hartt, continued its surveys, making possible the exploitation of natural resources in the black-diamond district (Curti and Birr, 1954: 19).

But the technical missions were not limited to surveys only in the hopes of procuring natural resources. Agriculture also received its share of attention. In 1882, the U.S. Department of Agriculture sent John C. Banner to Brazil with the purpose of collecting entomological and other data relating to cotton culture. A similar mission was sent to Mexico ten years later. However, neither of these missions was concerned, except perhaps in the most marginal of ways, with improving the agriculture in those countries they visited. Their primary purpose was to collect scientific data with respect to injurious insects, climate, and other conditions that might affect agricultural production in different regions of the world (Curti and Birr, 1954: 20–21).

In most of the missions sent to peripheral regions before the twentieth century, the so-called human factor was not a factor at all. Rather, development took as its object physical territory, typically the exploitation of natural resources. British colonial policy also reflected this practice. The imperial development institutes set up before 1920 tended to focus on either the study of entomology (the Imperial Institute of Entomology, founded in 1909); tropical diseases (the Bureau of Hygiene and Tropical Diseases, founded in 1908); or the promotion of commercial, industrial, and educational interests of the *British Empire* (the Imperial Institute, founded in 1887). The emphasis on the British Empire is important here, for development is not explicitly aimed at the colonies, in the sense of enriching or enhancing them—rather, it is development *of* the colony *for* the Empire. Through development, the mother country, the Crown, the sovereign leaves its mark on the colonial territory.

Merely ten years later, however, a shift occurred in development practices and colonial policies. While technical missions continued to search out natural resources to exploit, the welfare of indigenous people had become an increasing concern of many colonial administrators and other government officials. Both the League of Nation's mandates system and Britain's Colonial Development Act (1929) codify this concern. The Colonial Development Act stated that advances were to be made by loan or grant to governments "for the purpose of aiding and developing agriculture and industry in the colony or territory, and thereby promoting commerce with or industry in the United Kingdom" (Overseas Development Institute, 1964: 14). The Empire was still a beneficiary of development, but development was primarily for the sake of the colony. Debates surrounding this act are testament to this. In opening the debate on the address, H. Snell stated:

> May I say one word on the colonies first of all. The subject peoples of the British Empire are becoming increasingly aware of their position in the human family, and they are not satisfied with it. They are asking with increasing emphasis for the protection of this House against ruthless exploitation, for the protection of their tribal land, for some education, and for some participation in the shaping of their own destinies. These things represent moral responsibility which this

Parliament can neither delegate nor ignore. (Overseas Development Institute, 1964: 15)

Several days later J. H. Thomas concurred with Snell: "As far as our colonies are concerned, we are their main trustees, and a great moral obligation attaches to this country to do all that it can to develop them" (Overseas Development Institute, 1964: 15).

So although the welfare of the Empire remained a concern of policymakers, the well-being of the colonies had begun to slip into development discourse. The League of Nation's mandate system bears this out:

> To those colonies and territories which as a consequence of the late war have ceased to be under the sovereignty of the States and . . . inhabited by peoples not yet able to stand by themselves under the strenuous conditions of the modern world, there should be applied the principle that the well-being and development of such peoples form a sacred trust of civilization and that securities for the performance of this trust should be embodied in this Covenant. (*Mandate Articles of the League of Nations Covenant*, art. 22, sect. 1, quoted in Wright, 1930)

What should be noted here is the differentiation the mandate made between development and well-being. In fact, at the time the covenant was written there was much discussion over how these two conditions were related and whether or not they were even compatible, and whether or not development should be subordinated to native welfare (Wright, 1930). The distinction, however, became blurred over the years as the well-being of underdeveloped people became an increasingly important focus of development discourse. It was not until several years later that H. Myint (1954) argued once again for a distinction to be made between "backward people" and "underdeveloped countries."

As mentioned previously, it would be a mistake to assume that the post-1920 concern with welfare was an indication of humanitarian progress in development policies. What is perhaps truer is that the humanity of underdeveloped peoples was constructed by colonial administrations and others involved in development practices for the sake of controlling those very populations. This was apparent as early as the mandate system. Article 23 of the covenant states that members of the League ought to endeavor to secure fair and humane working conditions for people throughout the world. But as Javier Alcalde points out, the basic aim of this was to raise the standard of *labor's* working conditions, not *people's* living conditions. It was an attempt to avoid class-oriented conflict and revolutionary agitation, as well as unfair competition in international trade (Alcalde, 1987: 12). Moreover, if one looks at how welfare was to be promoted in the mandated territories, it was primarily through the "prohibition of abuses such as the slave trade, the arms traffic, and the liquor traffic" (Art. 22, sect. 5). This in itself is a negative conception of welfare, but one that is quite productive in that it produces a particular representation of what the underdeveloped person as a member of humanity should be. He should be moral, upstanding, sober, and above all free—free to labor in order to better both himself and all of humanity.

Over the next couple of decades the importance of human welfare as a component of development grew. Humanity was not only a result of development practices, it had also become its major instrument. The emphasis on promoting the well-being of colonies and other peripheral societies had become an important component in the battle against Soviet revolutionary influence and local agitation. But the question of how welfare was best promoted was left unanswered.[4] This, for the time being, was a nonproblem. The assumption was that economic progress, in terms of tackling concrete technical problems, would just naturally lead to welfare. In fact, this is an assumption that also carried quite a bit of weight in postwar development policies.

Prior to World War II, the two decipherable practices associated with development were (1) development of natural resources and productive capacities, the object of which tends to be physical territory and increasingly economic infrastructure; and (2) the well-being of underdeveloped people, who are represented in terms of their membership in humanity. Often these practices were set in opposition to one another, but at other times they were manipulated in such a way as to work in unison, creating the very image of "development."

Within this discursive and practical space, which had already been carved out by previous development practices, the postwar discipline of development emerged. But the object that development now took was different from what had previously been the case. It was now neither territory nor the symbol of humanity (although these have remained important concerns). Rather, what emerged as the object of development was the nation-state—in particular, the underdeveloped state. This transformation became possible for several reasons, most importantly the decolonization of vast peripheral regions, the Cold War, and postwar restructuring of the international political economy.

On the one hand, there was a population—a massive wandering population: the newly independent countries. On the other hand, there was fear and danger. If there was anything that policymakers and academics knew, it was the fear associated with the economic collapse during the Depression and the danger associated with the rise of the Soviet Union to superpower status. Both of these presented a threat to the image the Western industrialized world had constructed of itself: liberal, progressive, enlightened. Moreover, it was acknowledged that the newly independent countries were particularly susceptible to these threats, for they had not progressed to the stage at which the "developed countries" found themselves. These new countries had to be made aware of the threats. They had to be shown that the threats were alien to what they were, and to what it meant to be responsible, developed nation-states. So "development" then took as its objectives the transformation of these adolescent states into mature, developed nation-states. But doing this required that these new states be conscious of who they were, what their potentialities were, and what they must do to fulfill their potential. And this required that they speak out and make themselves heard, so that they can denounce the threat, but also so that any trespass, any transgression on their part can be heard by those acting on behalf of the enlightened, responsible, developed First World, and therapeutic correction administered at once. In other words, development necessitated the construction of the underdeveloped state so that this large wandering population—the recently decolonized—could be brought under control (so that contagion, the threat, would not spread). And while we can see that the underdeveloped state is the result of development practices, it is also one of its primary instruments. For it is through the underdeveloped state that development agencies and practitioners extend their control: without underdevelopment there could be no development.

How is it then that the Third World is controlled—by what means is it both subjected and made a subject in development discourse? The answer to this question can be found in the practices associated with disciplinary power, to which we will now turn.

The Instruments of Disciplinary Power

The primary function of disciplinary power is to train:

> It separates, analyzes, differentiates, carries its procedures of decomposition to the point of necessary and sufficient single units. It "trains" the moving, confused, useless multitude of bodies and forces into a multiplicity of individual elements—small, separate cells: organic autonomies; genetic identities and continuities; combinatory segments. Discipline "makes" individuals: it is the specific technique of a power that regards individuals both as objects and as instruments of its exercise. It is not a triumphant power, which because of its own excess can pride itself on its omnipotence: it is a modest, suspicious power, which functions as a calculated but permanent economy. (Foucault, 1984: 188)

As such, disciplinary power can be contrasted with those "majestic rituals" of sovereignty and great state apparatuses. It is humble, deriving its strength from the use of simple instruments—hierarchical observation, normalizing judgment, and the examination.

Hierarchical Observation

The exercise of disciplinary power presupposes some mechanism that coerces by the means of observation "an apparatus in which the techniques that make it possible to see induce effects of power and in which, conversely, the means of coercion make those on whom they are applied clearly visible" (Foucault, 1984: 189). Architecture was no longer built simply to be seen, or to observe some exterior space (e.g., the fortress built to look out), but to permit an internal control, to render visible those who are inside. More generally, this entails an architecture that would work to transform individuals "to act on those it shelters, to provide a hold on their conduct, to carry the effects of power right to them, to make it possible to know them, to alter them" (Foucault, 1984: 189).

The old and simple scheme of confinement and enclosure—thick walls and heavy gates to prevent one from coming or going—began to be replaced by the calculation of openings, of filled and empty space, and of passages and corridors. In this way, hospitals were gradually organized as instruments of medical action, schools as instruments of training, and prisons as instruments of reform. The "new architecture" was to allow for a better observation of patients, students, and criminals so as to better calibrate treatment.

In short, these disciplinary mechanisms secreted a machinery of control that functioned somewhat like a microscope of conduct. The detailed analytical divisions that they created formed around women and men an apparatus of observation, recording, and training. The perfect disciplinary apparatus is one that would make it possible for a single gaze to see everything at once: a perfect eye from which nothing would escape and a center toward which all gazes would turn—the panopticon (Foucault, 1984: 192).

Normalizing

The most significant effect of disciplinary power is its ability to normalize behaviors, attitudes, and speech. In this respect it brings five distinct operations into play. First, it refers individual actions to a "whole" that is at the same time a field of comparison, a space of differentiation, and a principal rule to be followed. Second, it differentiates individuals from one another in terms of minimal threshold, the average to be respected, or an optimum toward which one must move. Third, it measures quantitatively, and hierarchizes in terms of value, the abilities, levels, and "nature" of individuals. Fourth, it introduces through this value-giving measurement a constraint of conformity that must be achieved. And finally, it sets a limit that will "define difference in relation to all other differences": the frontier of the abnormal. In short, disciplinary power compares, differentiates, hierarchizes, homogenizes, and excludes: it *normalizes*.

The normal is established throughout modern society. It is established within the school, within the prison, within the factory, and within the home. Normalization indicates a dual process. On the one hand, normalization procedures indicate membership within a homogenous social body: citizens, workers, students, nation-states. On the other hand, they play a part in the classification, hierarchization, and the distribution of the rank (Foucault, 1984: 196): the poor student, sick patient, hysterical woman, Third World nation. Normalization procedures both impose homogeneity and individualize by making it possible (and desirous) to measure gaps, to determine levels, and to render differences useful by fitting them together.

The Examination

The examination combines the techniques of surveillance (i.e., hierarchical observation) and normalizing judgment. It is, as Foucault, says, a "normalizing gaze, a surveillance that makes it possible to qualify, classify, and to punish" (Foucault, 1984: 197). It is the deployment of force and the establishment of truth. It manifests in itself the subjection of those who are perceived as objects and the objectification of those who are subjected. The examination is the comparison of each and all that makes it possible to measure and judge. It occurs in the schoolroom, the doctor's office, the prison, and international agencies like the International Monetary Fund.

The examination links the exercise of power to the formation of knowledge in three ways.

1. The examination has transformed the economy of visibility into the exercise of power. Whereas traditionally power has relied on being visible for its strength, casting the object of its force into the shadows, the examination reverses the order. Disciplinary power is exercised precisely through its invisibility, but at the same time it forces its subjects into the light. In discipline it is the subjects who must be seen. Only their visibility will assure the hold that power has on them, the objectification through which they become subjects.

2. The examination introduces individuality into the field of documentation. The examination, which would place the individual within a field of surveillance, would also place the individual within a network of writing. It captures and fixates. Documentation, or disciplinary writing, opens up two possibilities. First, it makes possible the constitution of the individual as a describable, analyzable object, in order to maintain the individual within the power structure of the system of knowledge. Second, it makes possible the constitution of a whole, a comparative system that makes possible disciplinary power itself.

3. Finally, the examination, with all its documentary techniques, makes each individual a "case." Description here has become a means of control and

method of domination. It is no longer the chronicle of the hero, but the documentation of everyday people. As such, it functions as a procedure of objectification and subjection.

In summary, disciplinary power can be perceived as a system of knowledge. It seeks to know the individual as an object to be known in relation to others who can be known. It sets up a system in which there is a norm, an optimum point to be reached. It then would designate as abnormal those "cases" that deviate from this norm. The abnormal case, the anomaly, would then be subject to corrective or therapeutic techniques that would reform, fix, or rehabilitate it. However, rehabilitation can never be fully attained, for the logic of the system depends upon the existence of both the normal and abnormal.

Political Development and Disciplinary Power: An Appraisal

Political development as characterized by modernization theory postulates a dichotomy between developed and underdeveloped, modern and traditional (Banfield, 1958; Binder, 1966; Black, 1966; Inkeles, 1966; McLelland, 1966). Broadly speaking, traditional societies tend to be underdeveloped, and modern societies (nation-states) developed. The prior arrangement is viewed as an unhealthy aberration or deviation from the pure, healthy, and good order of the modern, developed nation-state.

> These were societies with hereditary hierarchical rule, living under the sway of customs rather than that of law. Their economics were static and remained at the same level of limited technology and low income from one generation to the next. Even though some ancient societies exhibited high proficiency in certain directions, they should be termed traditional since they were incapable of generating a regular flow of inventions and innovations and of moving into a phase of sustained economic growth. (Milikan and Blackmer, 1961: 1)

Compare this to the modern nation-state. Much like Alex Inkeles's modern man, the modern nation-state is efficient, democratic, cosmopolitan, and future oriented. It recognizes the importance of science and technology, and is forever expanding its horizons. It is innovative and "advanced": the healthy, good society.

The logic that drives modernization theory is, very simply put, the modern/traditional, developed/underdeveloped dichotomies. Just as the prison has been built upon the logic of the law-abiding citizen versus the criminal, and hospitals upon the healthy versus the sick person, theories of modernization have rested upon a logic of development versus underdevelopment and modern versus traditional. And just as disciplinary power has worked to consolidate the relation among knowledge, power, and truth within the prison and hospital, so it has worked within both theoretical and practical approaches to political development and modernization.

Let us remember that disciplinary power works at two levels. First it would seek to identify and isolate anomalies or deviations: the unhealthy, the impure. In modernization theory, this would be societies that emphasize ascriptive versus achievement orientations, societies that have parochial versus cosmopolitan outlooks, or societies whose governments are inefficient versus efficient. The characteristics of these backward, traditional societies are defined, however, only in terms of their relation to what it is to be modern: the pure and the healthy modern (i.e., Western) nation-state. The modern nation-state is set up as a goal to be achieved, as the norm to which all individual societies must be compared. At another level, disciplinary power works to correct, rehabilitate, and reform. By producing the "truth" of political development, disciplinary power, working through modernization theory, would seek to normalize the abnormal: the traditional society, the underdeveloped country, the Third World. In speaking the truth, it would seek to liberate the modern nation-state held captive within each traditional society. But we can now see that such liberation is impossible, because the traditional and modern are themselves creations of modernization theory. Modernization theory cannot hope to rid itself of the traditional because its very existence depends upon the logical opposition between traditional and modern. There is nothing to be liberated but the arbitrary social construction of the theory itself.

In the following paragraphs I briefly address some of the means by which disciplinary power functions both in modernization theory and more generally in practices of development. For lack of space and time, though, I will merely sketch an outline of some of these practices.

To begin, we review the instruments of disciplinary power. The first instrument is surveillance, that is, hierarchical observation. Foucault has emphasized the role of architecture in this respect, but there remain other means of surveillance that are just as important, for example, the use of statistics. This latter means is perhaps the most widely used technology of surveillance within political development practices. The second instrument of disciplinary power is normalizing judgment. This refers to the techniques and practices that would compare, differentiate, hierarchize, homogenize, and exclude individuals from one another and the social whole. Finally, there is the examination, which is a combination of the previous two instruments; it is a surveillance that makes possible differentiation, classification, and punishment.

The first question we may want to ask is where disciplinary power is located with respect to political development and modernization. Here, much like elsewhere, we find it to be decentered and dispersed. It is located in state agencies, international organizations, university systems, and so-called "think tanks." But it would be wrong to say that these institutions themselves are constituitive of disciplinary power. Rather, it is only through them that power passes. They are important in the fields of power relations, but do not themselves "possess" power (Foucault, 1984: 247). But it is through these institutions that the Third World, developing nations, or, if you will, traditional societies have become known to the outside, Western world. It is through these institutions that something called the Third World is at once objectified and subjected.

After World War II there was a dramatic proliferation in writing on this new Third World. And the writing was of an important kind. Through a variety of organizations—UN agencies, branches of the U.S. government such as the CIA, foundations such as Ford, and numerous Western universities—a mountain of statistics on the Third World began to pile up. These statistics became the window through which the West would view the "new emerging nations" (along with student exchange programs, the Peace Corps, and other programs that would attempt to bring the Third World "into the fold"). Birth rates, death rates, literacy rates, consumption rates, GNPs, urban to rural population ratios, energy consumption rates—all sorts of statistics were compiled on the Third World. And it was through these statistics that we largely came to know the Third World.

Statistics are themselves a special kind of knowledge; they are a feature of disciplinary power. They are, in fact, a means of normalizing judgment. On the one hand, they differentiate with respect to each case's own specific value. But above all, they compare and hierarchize. Statistics allow for a whole range of comparisons. We compare such things as literacy rates, GNPs, industrial growth rates, or energy consumed per capita, and then we classify: high GNP per capita, developed; low GNP per capita, underdeveloped. High literacy rate, developed; low literacy rate, undeveloped. And then we hierarchize. Statistics allow us to measure all sorts of things, and with the right combination of statistics we can even measure such complex phenomena as a nation's position within the world economy: Is it developed or is it developing? Is it newly industrialized (a NIC) or is it less developed (an LDC)? No longer do we have a simple binary opposition between developed and undeveloped, but a whole range of levels of development.

The purpose of hierarchization is simple. It is to normalize behavior. The hierarchy itself points toward the ultimate end, the true good—in this case, the modern developed nation-state. Those states achieving this goal become good, responsible and productive forces within the world economy and the world system. Those that do not are isolated and punished. But the punishment is such as to reform, or rehabilitate, the delinquent party. Much like the prison would rehabilitate the criminal to become a useful and productive citizen, agencies of political development—the IMF, the World

Bank, the UN, the Ford Foundation, and university systems—would seek to reform the undeveloped state, the traditional or backward society, in order to change it into a productive, modern nation-state.

The means by which such anomalous or deviant states are reformed or corrected vary. Let us remember that the primary function of disciplinary power is to train. It is through "training" that deviant aberrations are normalized (or at least the attempt is made). Within the practical applications of political development, we find several strategies or technologies that would train or normalize. We find them in, for example, educational systems and foreign aid agreements.

Education

Alex Inkeles (1966), in "The Modernization of Man" professes that modernization must include the attainment of popular education. Modern man is an educated man. Within the educational system of the Third World it is possible to identify several potential strategies of normalization. First, we could look at the curriculum of universities. An emphasis placed upon technical training, conventional economics, and public planning and administration within university curricula, much in accordance with Western "models," would signal such a normalizing strategy.

> But whatever else the universities may be teaching, it is not an indigenous traditional culture. They teach modern science and technology, modern economics and social science, and the modern methods of studying traditional indigenous culture. . . . When they teach and study indigenous languages, they do so by modern methods. These new kinds of knowledge and technique are almost exclusively foreign creations. . . . The universities of the new states are almost entirely dependent upon imported culture for the substance of their teaching. They teach very little that has been generated or been created in their own countries, and they also teach relatively little about their own country's history, society and culture. (Shils, 1966: 91)

The curricula of Third World universities homogenize Third World students. They are brought into a relation with a global process—a process that would establish the norm for all university training. In order to become productive forces within the world system, undeveloped Third World nations must introduce curricula within their universities that will properly train their indigenous student population. It is only with a properly trained population that a nation-state can become a responsible, productive member of the international community.

Foreign Aid Agreements

Foreign aid agreements are perhaps one of the more obvious and direct normalizing techniques. IMF stabilization agreements and World Bank loan contracts can be viewed, in essence, as "examinations" performed upon, in this case, Third World countries. The IMF and the IBRD (International Bank for Reconstruction and Development) become the doctor, the teacher, the warden, and underdeveloped countries become the patient, the student, the delinquent.

IMF policies and stabilization agreements represent a normalizing gaze, a surveillance that makes it possible to qualify, classify, and punish (Foucault 1984: 196). They open up and make visible the subject who must be seen. Funds would not be made to one who hides in the shadows. Disciplinary power, which flows through the IMF and its stabilization agreements, does so by making the subject visible for all to see.

In addition, IMF policies both homogenize and differentiate. They differentiate insofar as they analyze and describe whoever would apply for funds in order to maintain that person's individuality under the powerful gaze of the "system of knowledge"—the IMF or, more broadly, the international financial community. But they also homogenize: they create the whole system of relations that makes it possible to differentiate, classify, and compare. They establish what constitutes the behavior of the good, the rational, modern nation-state. It is a state that, broadly speaking, controls spending and values the idea of the free market. Any state that strays from these norms has deviated and must be brought into line, that is, rehabilitated. Thus the IMF ties strings to its fund packages: devaluation, the removal of import restrictions, and cuts in public spending. This is not merely the negative reflex of power (i.e., repression), but rather a positive expression of what is to be expected of the modern, developed, good nation-state.

In essence, disciplinary power produces both the modern, developed nation-state and the traditional underdeveloped state. It does so by disciplining difference and creating identity; by erecting norms and establishing deviations; and finally by rendering the delinquent, the patient, the underdeveloped visible. In this way it has constructed the Third World as underdeveloped—as "other" to the developed First World.

Conclusion

By way of conclusion, I offer a supplement to the preceding text. A supplement (Derrida, 1977, 1978; Culler, 1982) is something that is both other to and at the same times necessary to the text it accompanies. It stands apart from the core text, but also completes that text, thus rendering the core text incomplete without it. The effect of such supplementary logic is to render problematic any construction of an originary self-presence. I follow this strategy primarily for two purposes. The first is to point to (at least in one possible reading) a lack, so to speak, in the original core text—a lack made visible by the supplement. In essence, although the preceding pages would appear sufficient unto themselves, there is a deficiency that this supplement will point out. The second reason for offering a self-conscious supplement as a conclusion is that I want to reinforce the supplementary logic at work in modern practices of development, including theoretical practices.

The preceding pages are lacking. There is a deficiency. This is particularly true insofar as they talk about "identity," "presence," "marginality," "difference," and other deconstructive terms. The primary problem is that, if given too hasty a reading, the above text appears to tell only one side of the story. The side of the story told is how the so-called Third World gets constructed in history as "other" to the developed First World. This in and of itself is interesting, but it is not, I would argue, the most significant side to the story. What is most significant, even compelling, is how that region of the globe we call the First World gets constructed as an originary self-presence—an identity in need of no explanation—and how this identity is reproduced in history in the face of so much resistance. That the Third World is viewed as other to the First World is interesting, even provocative. But it is also obvious. It is obvious in the very metaphors we use to describe the phenomenon of international relations: core/periphery (we acknowledge a center and we know where it is); First World/Third World (we know which comes *first*); and even North/South (we know what's on top—the maps tell us). But what isn't so obvious is how the "original" itself gets constructed as a self-presence. How is it that the core gets constructed as "other" to the periphery, constructed in such a way as to be above the periphery, constructed in such a way as to be above political play—an originary self-presence in need of no explanation, relegating to the realm of the periphery all those dangers and contingencies that must be brought under control in the name of the core, the center? This question, for the most part, is not addressed in the previous pages. But if we are going to take seriously the supplementary logic at work in practices of development, this is the very question on which we will need to focus.[5]

In focusing our attention on questions such as the above, in examining the nature of supplementarity found in development practices (including theoretical practices), we will be changing the way we envision international political economy, particularly in its application to Third World development. So far, theories of development (both conventional and more "radical") have attempted to uncover the truth about underdevelopment—what it is, why it is, and what may be done to remedy it. But in their analyses, they presuppose the very distinction they seek to examine. They accept as natural and necessary the distinction between First and Third Worlds, between core and periphery, between developed and underdeveloped. Both conventional and more radical theories, while at variance with one another over what the problem is, assume as already to be solved the better part of the problem they state: the problem of developing in an environment inhospitable to development.

Because both theoretical traditions share a common foundation in modernist discourse, they have been deeply influenced by a vision of progress—a vision in which reason, history, economic development, and/or political struggle make possible a promised land of freedom and plenty. Within this modernist discourse there are many variations upon this theme of progress, but the theme itself remains all pervasive.[6] With respect to either humanity or the state, the possibility of progress in history has acted as a kind of guarantee of the possibility of emancipation in politics. Development thus becomes a practical problem, something which needs to be solved and is always in the process of the solution—a solution that would, in the end, set us free. But the problem itself, and the necessity of addressing it as a problem, remains invisible. Third World development and the logical opposition it entails remain unproblematized. But by acknowledging the supplementary logic at work within development practices we can render problematic these very distinctions, no longer accepting them as natural and necessary, but as arbitrary social constructions reproduced via a number of theoretical and more self-consciously political practices. The effect of all this is critically consequential to the study of international political economy, for it renders problematic any analysis of a global political economy that would be beyond making history and above political play—"a political economy" continually being produced and reproduced via a multiple of theoretical practices.

Notes

1. These dichotomies are not reducible to one another. They each have their own particular histories. Moreover, the particular theoretical positions they represent are often at odds with one another. The dichotomy I focus on in this chapter is the developed/underdeveloped dichotomy (and more generally, First World/Third World). When the term periphery is used, it will be in order to signify more generally those marginalized regions of the world that in postwar discourse have been constructed as underdeveloped.

2. The chapter is very general in terms of any type of genealogy. Subsequent archival research will allow me to fill in this sketchy outline.

3. This includes people who are writing across a wide range of disciplines. For example, feminist critics such as Julia Kristeva and Luce Irigaray; literary critics such as Edward Said and Jacques Derrida; and international relations theorists such as Richard Ashley, James DerDerian, and Rob Walker. This is not to claim that all these persons wholeheartedly embrace what has been termed postmodernism, but merely to show that at least some of their works exhibit a concern for the "other" as it is variously constituted in Western culture.

4. Actually, during the 1920s and 1930s there was much debate over this issue, especially in Britain between the Conservative and Labour parties. But eventually the hardships of the depression and the measures used to combat them ended resistance to the technological approach to welfare (see Alcalde, 1987).

5. For one way in which this question may be addressed, look at

"Representation and Modernity: Development and the Construction of Peripheral Man" (Johnston, 1990).

6. See for example, William Connolly (1988) on a discussion of modernity and the theme of progress in political theory. Also, it is important to acknowledge that progress also entails sacrifices—the limits which we must know not to transgress. See "What Is Enlightenment?" by Michel Foucault (1984).

8

African International Political Economy: An Assessment of the Current Literature

W. Ofuatey-Kodjoe

The study of African international political economy (AIPE) is relatively new. It emerged in the late 1960s as a response to the problem of underdevelopment in Africa. A concern with underdevelopment was a logical consequence of the rhetoric of the independence struggle. Independence was supposed to bring material well-being. More important, the new African governments quickly realized that their economic performance was closely related to the security of their regimes. At the same time, European and North American governments were becoming concerned about Communist influence in the Third World and, thus, were interested in finding development strategies that would compete with the "Communist path" (Stanley, 1961: 3–4). This accounts for the many development studies and area studies programs that emerged in the West and the multiplicity of government-sponsored books that were written at that time.[1] Whatever the motivation, the search for theories and strategies of development led to the study of African international political economy, for it was clear that it is impossible to analyze African development without considering the *international* relations of the African countries, such as trade, foreign investment, and foreign aid.

At the outset three paradigms emerged: orthodox, Marxist, and dependency. All three originated outside Africa. The Marxist theory of development has been applied to Africa to only a limited extent.[2] However, the orthodox and dependency paradigms have been used by Africans so extensively they have become the poles of the African international political economy literature.

The purpose of this chapter is to explore the current state of this literature, and specifically to present the basic assumptions, diagnoses, and prescriptions of the two dominant paradigms; to discuss the main issues with which they have dealt and the ways they have done so; and to discuss their continued relevance to the African situation. I make this assessment conscious, as all African scholars are, of the continent's devastating economic crisis. I hope that this chapter will contribute to an understanding of the logic behind the analyses and policy recommendations of writers, particularly Africans, trying to confront that crisis.

In this type of overview, it is often necessary to present a composite of many views as a school of thought. I shall attempt to accomplish this without doing serious violence to either the central logic of the two paradigms or the integrity of the views of their main adherents. Within the short space of this review, it will not be possible to engage in the type of in-depth analysis of these paradigms that has been done elsewhere.[3] Rather, I will concentrate on presenting the African adaptation of these paradigms and ways in which they have been applied to the analyses of the major issues of AIPE: relations between Africa and Europe, regional integration in Africa, and the African economic crisis.

A Review of the Orthodox, Marxist, and Dependency Paradigms

The orthodox, or "modernization," paradigm views underdevelopment as the original condition of all societies from which some societies developed into modern countries, whereas some failed to develop and therefore remain underdeveloped and backward. These backward societies, of which the African countries are examples, are "dual societies," with a modern sector and a backward sector. The reason for their underdevelopment is the persistence in their backward sector of certain norms, values, and institutions that resist modernization (Wilber and Jameson, 1988: 8). In order to develop these countries, the traditional sector has to be modernized by the diffusion of modern values and institutions from the modern sector, which is in contact with the modern societies. In the economic sphere, this modernization through diffusion has two major objectives: (1) the expansion of the modern sector through international trade, and (2) the development of "pioneer industries" by direct foreign investment, thus producing profits, savings, and reinvestment leading to the achievement of self-sustained industrial and economic growth (Oxaal, et al., 1975: 39).

The Marxist perspective on underdevelopment is that it is the stage that preceded the capitalist stage in the evolution of human societies toward socialism. In opposition to the orthodox approach, however, this developmental process comes through long struggle in which each phase contains contradictions, and the resolution of these contradictions moves society to the next higher level (Wilber and Jameson, 1988: 15). According to this paradigm, the passage from precapitalist to capitalist society in the developed countries was accomplished by a social revolution that destroyed the old feudal social order and brought to the fore a new class that was able to accumulate capital, which it reinvested for productive use and, hence, development. In the underdeveloped countries this process has not occurred. The failure of this process to take place is due to the fact that capitalism was introduced into those areas in its monopoly form (through imperialism), and therefore its development in those areas has not been accompanied by the rise of a strong capitalist class. Rather, the classes that have emerged in the underdeveloped countries have neither been able to accumulate the capital required for social transformation, nor been willing to spearhead social change, for fear of losing their power and way of life. Based on this analysis, traditional Marxists argue that the way to development is to take up the struggle against the capitalist social order, overthrow it, and replace it with a socialist order (Wilber and Jameson, 1988: 18–19).

The dependency paradigm emerged in Latin America in the 1960s as a framework for explaining underdevelopment in that region. It was a reaction to the orthodox explanation of underdevelopment, which was considered economically naive, culturally biased, normatively pernicious, and practically ineffective (Oxaal, et al., 1975: 1). The central point in the dependency paradigm is that the underdevelopment of Latin American countries can be explained only in the context of the relationship between the metropoles and their satellites (cores and their peripheries) within the world capitalist system. As the argument goes, underdevelopment was generated by the same process of global capitalist expansion that generated economic development in the metropoles (Frank, 1988: 111). This process of capitalist expansion through trade, imperialism, and direct foreign investment led to the asymmetrical incorporation of the peripheries into the international capitalist system as exporters of raw materials and importers of manufactured goods. This situation produced financial, technological, commercial, and cultural dependency of the peripheries on the core, leading the peripheries to underdevelopment (Frank, 1988: 113) or distorted, dependent development (Cardoso, 1972: 89, 94).

AIPE Orthodoxy

The first development analysis that appeared on the African scene came from the orthodox paradigm as a product of the "civilizing mission" of colonialism. This analysis was inherited at independence by the new African governments that "have proceeded with full speed to apply its prescription in the planning and execution of development policy" (Nyang'oro, 1989: 30). The fact that the African governments have adopted the orthodox paradigm and its development strategy of modernization is due in part to the influence of the Western powers. The modernization paradigm was important for the colonial powers because it was consistent with their justification for colonialism. But it has also provided the justification for Western aid to compete with Soviet offers to assist socialist development in Africa (Preston,

1988: 18). And promoting the orthodox paradigm also served Western interests because accepting the paradigm meant accepting the current international division of labor (Nyang'oro, 1989: 36).

Thus, the original purveyors of the modernization theories of development were the advisors left in Africa by the colonial powers, many of whom continued to maintain official connections with their former employers (Manning, 1988). Later, the Western powers concluded a variety of neocolonial bilateral and multilateral agreements, which have tended to reinforce the acceptance of the orthodoxy by the African governments (Asante, 1986: 192). African governments have also adopted policies based on the orthodox paradigm due to the influence of the international financial institutions: the IBRD (World Bank) and the IMF (Nyerere, 1985: 8–9). African governments, feeling the desperate need for large infusions of capital to save their economies from total collapse, have had to accept the orthodox policies of the World Bank and IMF as a condition for receiving loans and positive credit reports that allow borrowing from other international lenders such as the Paris Club (Jaycox, 1989: 338; Fearon, 1988: 122–123).

Acceptance of the orthodoxy in Africa is not all just tactical. The modernization perspective is part of the "corporate-liberal" worldview, which is shared by international capitalists and their junior partners, elements of the African ruling classes (Becker, 1988: 14). Among the components of this broader worldview are a hostility to domestic regulation and a commitment to the idea that international corporations work for the global good (Becker, 1988: 15). In addition to this ideological commitment, the African ruling classes often see their interests in capital accumulation and their own self-reproduction as being achieved through the introduction of private foreign investment and industrialization for export (Becker, 1988: 16).

The most powerful institutional supporters of the further articulation of the orthodox paradigm are the IMF and the World Bank. The *IMF Staff Papers* exert a powerful influence on the staff of the African central banks, which are also beneficiaries of numerous IMF seminars and workshops. An even more powerful purveyor of orthodox thinking is the World Bank through its annual *World Development Report* and other publications. The Bank's eagerness to propagate its theories is evident in its training conferences. In 1985, the Bank organized eleven "Senior Policy Seminars," nineteen "Trainers' Seminars," and forty-six "Direct Training Seminars" for senior employees of Third World governments (Hodd, 1987: 340). Other sources of orthodox theory are centers of higher education and research in the United States and Europe, "where neo-classical economic theory is the almost universal starting point for analysis of the operation of markets and assessment of the efficiency of economic systems" (Hodd, 1987: 341). Undoubtedly, these are the training centers for the U.S. and British personnel, who still fill a disproportionate number of the senior posts at the Bank and IMF. In addition, practically all the African officers at the Bank have had at least some university training in the West (Schoenholtz, 1987: 413). Finally, other sources of orthodox analyses are the publications of the OECD and the EC, and other official European publications.

Since their attainment of independence, most of the African countries have followed the export-led development strategy presented by the Western powers and the international financial institutions. The results have been disastrous. The African economies have not only not developed, but in most cases they have stagnated and in many cases they are actually in decline. The response of orthodox theorists is basically that the economic crisis of Africa is primarily due to the persistence of constraining conditions within the African countries and domestic policy mistakes (IBRD, 1981: 4). As a concession to the recognition of the advance effects of international political and economic factors on the African economies, such as higher energy prices, "stagflation" in the industrialized countries, and the decreasing international demand for primary products, orthodox theorists have advocated some international action like the EC's STABEX arrangement to stabilize primary product incomes (Asante, 1986: 199). But the orthodoxy's basic recommendation has been the adjustment of the African economies to the harsh international environment through the reduction of internal prices, services, consumption, and government expenditure (Berg and Whitaker, 1986).

Dependency Analysis in AIPE

In the early 1970s, at the very beginning of the current crisis, a number of African intellectuals and Western Africanists began to adapt the dependency paradigm to the analysis of the international political economy of Africa, linking it to earlier African analyses of neocolonialism (Nkrumah, 1964). This move was triggered not only by the manifest failure of the modernization paradigm and its prescriptions to make any significant contribution to political and economic development in Africa, but also by the theory's ethnocentric and racist overtones, which offended the new-found racial pride of the Africans. The dependency paradigm provided an alternative that Marxism could not provide due to the relative lack of currency of Marxist analyses among African intellectuals and the relative abundance of Latin American dependency analyses that African scholars could easily adapt to their own situation. Thus the first African dependency theorists have acknowledged their intellectual debt to Frank, Dos Santos, Cardoso, and other Latin American writers (Ake, 1981; Rodney, 1972). The dependency perspective had great appeal to African progressives. They enthusiastically accepted Walter Rodney's statement that the purpose of his *How Europe Underdeveloped Africa* was, "to provide Africans with the historical bases of and ideology for liberations" (Rodney 1972: viii). Rodney's book, which deserves the most credit for bringing the dependency perspective to a larger African audience, also marked the emergence of a theoretical and ideological collective—the Dar es Salaam school—which became the center of radical African scholarship in the 1970s.

From Dar es Salaam, the community of African dependency theorists has spread throughout the continent. In the past few years, several centers of scholarly activity associated with the dependency approach have emerged. The Department of International Relations of the University of Ife has produced a number of edited volumes, most of them from conferences, on a variety of topics including regionalism in Africa, relations between Africa and Europe, African foreign policies, and Africa and the New International Economic Order (NIEO). The core of the Ife Group—Aluko, Fasehun, Ojo, Onwuka, Feray, and others—maintain a collaborative relationship with scholars like Ake, Adeniran, and Nweke from other Nigerian campuses. Other loci of dependency research and analysis are African research institutes: the Nigerian Institute of International Studies, the University of Dar es Salaam Institute of Development Studies, and the Council for the Development of Economic and Social Research in Africa (CODESRIA) based in Dakar. One of the leading research institutes is the Africa Bureau of the Third World Institute, also based in Dakar, under the directorship of Samir Amin. At the Africa Bureau, Amin and his colleagues are at work on a research program entitled "Strategies for the Future of Africa," in collaboration with the United Nations University's project on Africa, which was set up to "explore a wide range of problems besetting Africa today and outline possible alternatives to the prevailing development models which have proven to be inadequate" (Amin et al., 1987). A final locus of dependency research is based at the Universities of Zimbabwe and Zambia and other southern African campuses where scholars like Ibbo Mandaza, Derrick Chitala, and Thandika Mkandawire work mainly on regional issues.

Many of these universities and institutes maintain working relationships with non-African organizations that are supportive of African aspirations, such as the Scandinavian Institute of African Studies, the Swedish Agency for Research Cooperation with Developing Countries, and the International Development Research Center of Canada. The Center for African Studies at Dalhousie University under the directorship of Tim Shaw has been a collaborator of a number of African universities and international organizations. This center has had a particularly active working relationship with the Ife Group, with which it has cosponsored several conferences and coproduced many edited books.

One of the most important "official" sources of dependency research has been the Economic Commission for Africa (ECA), and, to a lesser extent, the Organization of African Unity (OAU). In 1973 the ECA and OAU collaborated on a *Declaration on Cooperation, Development, and Economic Independence*, which set out what became the African demands for the New

International Economic Order. Since 1975, when he became the executive secretary of the ECA, Adebayo Adedeji has moved vigorously to be a major advocate of African development and a propagandist for African positions on the NIEO, regionalism, and self-reliant development. In this effort the ECA, along with the OAU, has held conferences and symposia and produced a veritable mountain of reports, studies, recommendations, and policy papers. In 1979, the ECA and OAU held a symposium in Monrovia and subsequently prepared the draft for the *Lagos Plan of Action*, about which much more will be said below.

Whatever their institutional affiliation, all African dependency theorists argue that the explanation for Africa's underdevelopment lies in the incorporation of the African countries into the global capitalist system through a process completed only when Africa was "actually made the periphery of the World Capitalist System in its imperialist stage" (Amin, 1976: 106; see also Rodney, 1972: 82; Ake, 1981: 135). The effect of this process in the African countries is such distortion of their economies that they became disarticulated, dependent, and underdeveloped (Amin, 1976: 292).

The underdevelopment of the African countries means that their economies can respond only to developments in the core. African economies grow or stagnate in response to economic changes in the core. This pattern of underdevelopment is reproduced over time by the "unequal exchange" of goods, which causes a transfer of surplus to the core, leading to a drain of internally generated investment funds, the reproduction of the limited internal market, and further underdevelopment (Wilber, 1988: 160). The social consequence of underdevelopment is increasing inequality between a local petty bourgeoisie, which basically performs the function of a comprador class, and the laboring classes of peasants and proletarians who are increasingly victims of unemployment and progressive pauperization (Amin, 1987: 1138).

The political economies of the African peripheral countries are beset with a variety of contradictions—contradictions among different factions of the local capitalist class, between international capital and indigenous capital, and between indigenous capital and the impoverished masses (Ake, 1981: 138). The major contradiction is between the world bourgeoisie (the nucleus of which is located in the core of the world capitalist system) and the world proletariat located in the periphery (Ake, 1981: 162). These contradictions are deepened by the fact that the exploitation and attendant repression of the masses are intensified by the smallness of the exploitable surplus in any African society, the primitiveness of the accumulation, and the need to use political power as the main mechanism for accumulation (Ake, 1981: 179).

As a result of these contradictions, African governments remain in a perpetual crisis of legitimacy, due to the generation of revolutionary pressures (Ake, 1981: 174), which the ruling classes attempt to solve by a combination of ideological, political, and economic containment, with increasingly limited success (Amin, 1987: 1144). Finally, due to these failures, the African ruling classes have, "accepted the pursuit of development through economic subordination to the core," thus perpetuating their role as comprador subordinates (Amin, 1987: 1146).

Although African dependency theorists tend to share the same analysis of Africa's past and present, they have divergent views about Africa's future. Walter Rodney believed that there was a possibility of a revolution led by "marginal sectors," the outcome of which would be "victory for the workers and the peasants." The timing of this revolution would be determined by "the extent to which sections of the petty bourgeoisie attach themselves to and actually transform themselves into workers" (Rodney, 1972: 68). On the whole, however, Rodney believed that the petty bourgeoisie has no revolutionary potential because it members tend to align themselves with imperialist capital rather than commit class suicide.

Alternatively, according to Amin, the consequences of the global expansion of capital is increasing social inequality, political despotism, and increasing inter-African conflicts (Amin, 1987: 1155). This condition is not likely to change. The international bourgeoisie, except where they are limited by competition among themselves, will continue to transfer enough resources to Africa to keep the international division of labor intact. As for the African bourgeoisie, they have already surrendered to the "*diktat* of transnational capital, reorganized around the IMF, the World Bank and the consortium of the big western banks" (Amin, 1987: 1146).

For Claude Ake, the structural features of the African countries have built in resistance to change. However, a revolutionary situation exists in Africa due to the radicalization of the subordinate classes and the tendency of factions of the ruling class to "scramble leftward" in order to win the intraclass competition for power (Ake, 1981: 187). In spite of this, in the near term Africa will see neither capitalist nor socialist development. Persistent stagnation will lead to paranoia among the ruling class and extremism among the subordinate classes. This will, in turn, lead to the politics of anxiety. Fascism, a protracted stalemate in which the state will depend on loyalty, patriotism, discipline, and summary treatment of "enemies of the state" would be the most likely outcome (Ake, 1981: 189).

Whatever their interpretation of the likely future for Africa, dependency theorists would prefer radical transformation through an alternative development model, "informed by a creative vision of the types of societies we want to create in Africa" (Onimode, 1988: 219). However, their visions are not uniform. For instance, Ake advocates a socialist solution. He argues that the solution of the problem is to overturn the existing relations of production, which can be achieved by the transition to socialism (Ake, 1981: 188). He admits, however, that the prospects for such a transformation are nil. First, there is little evidence of real socialist movement in Africa.

Second, even if a socialist revolution occurs, very little success against underdevelopment is likely due to the underdeveloped state of productive forces, the subversion by international capital, and the pressure of the advanced socialist countries on African states to adopt inappropriate policies. Rodney and Amin call for disengagement (Rodney, 1972: vii) and "delinking" (Amin, 1990) from the capitalist world economy. Amin's delinking refers to the submission of foreign relations to the logic of an internal popular strategy of development, as opposed to the strategy of "adjusting" internal development to the constraints of the global expansion of capitalism (Amin, 1987: 1140). Onimode has proposed an alternative development strategy with the objective of achieving "self-reliance and effective integration at national and regional levels." Such a strategy, he argues, will include a radical restructuring of the African economies from their external dependence to a national, subregional, and regional self-reliance orientation, which will terminate foreign domination (Onimode, 1988: 219). Similarly, Nyang'oro advocates a new development strategy in Africa that will "restructure Africa's relationship with the international economy—inevitably moving toward less association" (Nyang'oro, 1989: 156).

The diversity of views apparent among African dependency writers has increased the popularity of the paradigm. By the early 1980s the dependency paradigm had become synonymous with *the* African paradigm—not only the dominant paradigm in African intellectual circles, but also the only one most intellectuals would consider to be *pro-African.*[4] In this sense, they see dependency analysis as the proper (and actual) theoretical underpinning for all policies that were considered to be supportive of African liberation, empowerment, and autonomous development, and the basis for negotiating agendas for demands for more equitable treatment of African countries such as the call for a New International Economic Order (Murphy, 1983: 68). At the same time, the orthodox perspective had become identified by most African scholars as the "Western" paradigm for at least three reasons. First, the West was the initial and is the continuing source of that paradigm and the policy recommendations that flow from it. Second, the major institutional purveyors of the paradigm—the World Bank and the IMF—were and remain manifestly Western in terms of ideology and personnel; they represent Western interests (Hodd, 1987: 338; Schoenholtz, 1987: 413). Third, the orthodox paradigm provided the West's ideological defense against any suggestion that it owed the Third World something for past imperial exploitation (Murphy, 1983: 67), and thus the orthodox paradigm provided the most persuasive intellectual justification for the intransigence of the OECD, the European Community, the Paris Club, and other Western groups during international economic negotiations (Hart, 1983: 103–122). As a result, in the debates over African international political economy, the orthodox and dependency paradigms have become something more than just alternative research programs. They have become, for many African scholars, rival worldviews: one European, the other African; one anti-African, the other pro-African.

Let me now consider the alternative perspectives provided by these two paradigms on the three central issues of contemporary AIPE: Africa's relationship with Europe, the prospects for regional integration in the continent, and, most significantly, strategies for dealing with the contemporary crisis.

Africa and Europe

The oldest of the debates that demonstrates the fundamental opposition between the orthodox and dependency perspectives focuses on the relations between Europe and Africa during the colonial period and thereafter. According to the orthodox perspective, the European motivation for the colonization of Africa was to civilize Africans.[5] During the colonial period, the argument goes, the metropoles played the paternalistic role of orchestrating the religious, social, economic, and political development of the colonial territories (Gann and Duignan, 1967). Throughout decolonization, the metropoles continued their benign modernizing role by overseeing the "diffusion" of Western values and institutions to the colonies (Apter, 1955). After independence, the metropoles still assisted in the development of the new African states through the expansion of trade (based on the principle of comparative advantage) and through the infusion of capital and technology into the new states via direct investment and development assistance.

Dependency theorists see the European motivations for colonization as desires to acquire better investment opportunities, sources of raw materials, and markets for European goods (Nabudere, 1978: 101–143; Ake, 1981: 26–29; Rodney, 1972: 135–145). They see the major effect of colonialism as the underdevelopment of African countries through their incorporation into the global capitalist system as exporters of raw materials and importers of manufactured goods. Dependency theorists argue further that the metropoles, after first resisting decolonization (but failing), established neocolonial relationships with their former colonies—relations through which the same basic patterns of domination could be maintained (Nkrumah, 1964). Britain, for example, in its overall orientation to the management of the international political economy and in its bilateral relations with African countries since independence has been concerned the most with the protection of its trade and investment and with securing new markets for its exports (Bangura, 1983: 160). Similarly, after France's colonies had achieved independence, she expanded her trade with, and aid and investments in, those countries in order to create a political, economic, financial, and cultural ensemble that would restore "France's weight in the concert of nations" (Bach, 1986: 76). The neocolonial pattern is repeated by other OECD countries as well (Ofuatey-Kodjoe, 1989: 3).

The pattern is also repeated in relations between the European Community and the African countries under the Lome regimes. Of course, these relations are perceived differently by the adherents of the modernization paradigm. The Lome conventions have been characterized by orthodox writers as a departure from the exploitative colonial relationship (Gruhn, 1986: 14), or as "an enlargement of old colonial links in a way that can no longer be characterized as colonial" (Frey-Wouters, 1980: 253). In contrast, dependency theorists hold that the Lome regimes represent an attempt by the European countries to maintain and expand their markets in Africa and the other Third World regions, thereby assuring Europe secure supplies of raw materials, protecting European investments, and generally preserving the existing international division of labor (Asante, 1984: 188; Shaw, 1989: 182). Thus, the dependency theorists argue that it is not surprising that the Lome conventions have failed to address Africa's major problems directly through the transfer of technology or generalized debt relief; the purpose of the conventions is only to lock African countries into the role of suppliers of raw materials (Asante, 1984: 188; Nyang'oro, 1989: 62).

Regionalism in Africa

Despite the fundamental disagreement about the external sources of Africa's current economic problems, there is general agreement across the two paradigms that "the Balkanization of Africa is one of the major constraints to the economic transformation of the continent" (Adedeji, 1985: 77). Consequently African policymakers and political economists alike share a strong commitment to the idea that continental as well as subcontinental integration schemes can be important instruments in development, as well as tools for achieving greater political and economic independence for Africans (Mazzeo, 1984: 225; Onwuku and Sesay, 1985: ix). Indeed, regional integration has been enshrined in the *Lagos Plan of Action* as one of the most important instruments through which Africans can reduce dependency and develop in a self-reliant manner (Shaw, 1989: 81; Adedeji, 1985: 66).

Not surprisingly, there have been many attempts to analyze the many integration efforts on the continent, both from the orthodox viewpoint and from the radical or dependency perspective. Most of the literature has been devoted to the continent-wide Organization of African Unity and the two most prominent existing regional organizations, the Economic Community of West African States (ECOWAS) and the Southern African Development Coordination Conference (SADCC).

In analyzing these organizations, writers from both perspectives generally agree that they have been less than successful. However, the reasons that they provide for the failure of these organizations are quite different.

The OAU

The orthodox approach to the OAU has concentrated on the classical structural analysis of the organization, emphasizing its objectives, principles, structures, and resources. Viewed as an exercise in collective diplomacy, it has been evaluated in terms of its performance in the areas of decolonization, maintenance of peace and security, and advocacy of African interests in international forums (Cervenka, 1977: 185).

The dependency approach to the analysis of the OAU has been less concerned with the structural aspects of the organization and more interested in the ability of the organizations to assist in a more fundamental transformation of the continent: higher levels of political integration, empowerment of the continent vis-à-vis other international actors, reduction of dependency, and the elimination of underdevelopment (M'bunyinga, 1982; Ofuatey-Kodjoe, 1986: 402).

Both the orthodox and the dependency theorists recognize the failures of the OAU. However, the orthodox theorists consider these failures of diplomacy. On this basis, they consider the mere continued existence of the organization as a measure of success. Dependency theorists are less charitable. They tend to blame the failures of the organization on the ideological symbiosis between the African ruling class and international capitalism, which predisposes African leaders to be more interested in their neocolonial relationship with Europe than with inter-African cooperation. On this basis, African dependency theorists have expressed misgivings about the continuation of the organization. For instance, Sam Ikoku notes that:

> The OAU as presently constituted will never allow us to achieve African political union. And because it cannot evolve in this direction the OAU will tend to degenerate into an organization protecting the existing regimes in various African countries. (Quoted in Ofuatey-Kodjoe, 1986: 402)

ECOWAS

ECOWAS, too, has been disappointing to both orthodox and radical scholars, but, again, for different reasons. Both camps agree that ECOWAS has not achieved its goals of trade liberalization, a customs union, monetary cooperation, and free movement of labor.

Writers from the orthodox perspective argue that the main obstacles to success are problems internal to the region: inadequate transport and communication systems, low levels of industrialization, lack of complementarity of national economies, and foreign debt. The attributes, the argument goes, make it difficult for the African countries to take the risks and bear the possible costs of economic integration (Lancaster, 1982: 5).

For dependency theorists, the most important criterion for evaluating the merits of ECOWAS is the extent to which it can assist in the reduction of dependency and underdevelopment. For instance, Yansane states that the purpose of his analysis is to determine

> to what extent African regional cooperation can be of assistance in building economic foundations that . . . would generate self-sufficiency, integrated economies, decolonization, and the reduction of dependency resulting from inherited institutional structures. (Yansane, 1977: 63)

His judgment is that

> regional integration schemes that do not break away from the colonial patterns of development will be establishing new forms of dependency which will not end the inequities of the existing structures, but replace alien firms with national entrepreneurs who could exploit their fellow Africans. (Yansane, 1977: 84)

Thus, he argues, ECOWAS is unlikely to overcome underdevelopment and dependency because of the economic and political interests of international capital and the local ruling classes attached to it. ECOWAS would be useful only if it could help create new structures that do not replicate colonial and neocolonial relationships.

SADCC

Some orthodox theorists have suggested that the SADCC approach to regional integration, which, unlike that of ECOWAS, emphasizes sectoral coordination and the primacy of national decisionmaking, may have a salutary effect on the generation of workable development projects, the security of development project funds from abroad, and, ultimately, the success of the organization. A similar assessment states that SADCC "offers an alternative approach to regionalism, one which is better grounded in the realities of the African situation, and which draws on the past experience of failed regional schemes" (Ravenhill, 1985b: 221).

From the point of view of dependency theorists, however, the real issue is how the organization relates to underdevelopment. As a result, the massive funding that SADCC has received from the European Community, which orthodox scholars see as a sign of the organization's success, becomes a point of concern for the radical scholars. Apart from the increasing possibility of donor manipulation, the situation is perceived as imposing a pattern of investment and trade that will continue to limit the potential of these countries for independent development by locking them into the role of producer of raw materials for Europe, importing European manufactured goods in exchange. Furthermore, a massive increase in SADCC dependence on European countries would defeat its declared objective of reducing its dependence on South Africa, because the South African and European economies are so intertwined (Mandaza, 1987a: 214). According to this mode of analysis, the most optimistic prospect for SADCC would be some sort of dependent development. Such a policy would, in fact, be consistent with the aspirations of the political and economic elites of the Southern African regions, as well as the interests of the European Community (Ofuatey-Kodjoe, 1990: 168).

In all three cases, the gloomier assessment of regional integration schemes offered by dependency scholars can be linked to the extent to which the organizations, as institutions of the African ruling class, are guided by orthodox views and, thus, not even directed toward the fundamental problems of Africa's underdevelopment.

The African Economic Crisis

Nevertheless, there are situations in which African state policy is influenced as much by the dependency perspective as by the orthodoxy. This is the case with regard to official African responses to the protracted economic crisis of the 1970s and 1980s and Africa's response to the proposals offered by the orthodoxy to deal with it. A key starting point for the debate about the African crisis is 1981, when the World Bank published its *Accelerated Development in Sub-Saharan Africa: Agenda for Action*, known as "the Berg Report" (IBRD, 1981), and the UN Economic Commission for Africa and the OAU published *The Lagos Plan of Action* (ECA and OAU, 1981). The debate has been sustained by a host of subsequent ECA and World Bank reports[6] and a number of commentaries (e.g., Ravenhill, 1987; Bourne and Cummings, 1984).

The *Lagos Plan* proposed a program for the elimination of illiteracy, the provision of self-sufficiency in food production, the realization of integrated industrial development, the development of indigenous technical manpower, in addition to cooperation in the preservation of the environment and the integration of development with African sociocultural values. The objective of this strategy was supposedly the establishment of an African economic community and integrated sectoral development. The strategy of the *Lagos Plan*, and all subsequent ECA documents, was based on the dependency explanation of the African crisis as a consequence of the vulnerability of the dependent and underdeveloped African economies to new conditions in the world economy, including the transnationalization of capitalist production and the resulting new international division of labor, which further marginalized the region (Onimode, 1988: 14).

The Berg Report, in contrast, reflects orthodox assumptions. Its diagnosis of the African problem is reminiscent of the attributes that had been advanced as obstacles to modernization. Its list of "formidable constraints to development" include "lack of human resources, political fragility, ill-suited institutions, dualistic and underdeveloped economies, insufficient basic infrastructures, a climate and geography hostile to development, and rapid population growth" (IBRD, 1981: 4). In addition, after a passing remark about negative external factors, the Berg Report notes that the basic reasons for poor economic performance in Africa, over and above the formidable constraints, have ben ill-conceived policies, specifically the overvaluation of national currencies, the neglect of peasant agriculture, and the overextension of the state sector in the economy. Consistent with its diagnosis, the prescriptions offered by the World Bank reflect the liberal orthodox solutions involving the reduction of state intervention in the productive and distributive sectors of the economy and their restriction to the creation of an institutional and policy framework conducive to the mobilization of private enterprise in order to give free play to internal and external market forces.

As the debate between the ECA and World Bank dragged on throughout the 1980s, many African governments and observers came to recognize an underlying compatibility between the seemingly opposed positions, with the orthodoxy accepted as the immediate guide for action—the World Bank's blueprint could be viewed as a statement of "what should be done now and in the next few years to achieve the longer term objectives of the Lagos Plan of Action" (Please and Amoako, 1987: 132).

Meanwhile, the catastrophic decline of many African economies forced many governments to adopt structural adjustment programs (SAPs) mandated by the World Bank, suggesting, perhaps, that the newly recognized compatibility between the ECA and Bank positions involved making virtue of a necessity. The demands that the SAPs made on African governments represented "the consensus that has grown among Western donors and the World Bank since the extremity of Africa's problems became clear" (Berg and Whitaker, 1986: 1), and were basically the same as those made by export-led development programs advocated by orthodox theorists in the early 1960s: reduction of public expenditures, reduction of state economic activity, liberalization of trade, promotion of exports, and promotion of foreign investment.

African governments have accepted the terms of their SAPs, but they have also continued to support the ECA's attempt to outline an alternative. ECA economists have remained reluctant to concede any deep compatibility between their analysis and the Bank's, suggesting, for example, that the right mix of *short-term* policies for most African states includes land reform, taxation of luxury imports, and a number of measures geared toward popular participation in economic and political decisionmaking (ECA, 1989b). These are not policies demanded in most SAPs. Nor, however, are they policies that most African elites would accept, which suggests that the ECA's link to state policymaking may be a bit weaker than it was at the time of the *Lagos Plan* itself.

Summary and Conclusions

The orthodox (modernization) and radical (dependency) perspectives on African international political economy are based on fundamentally different assumptions about the relationship between international political and economic linkages and about development. The orthodox paradigm sees the free market and international trade based on comparative advantage as the engine of economic growth and prosperity. The dependency alternative sees the international system of capitalist trade as a system of exploitation, shifting economic surplus from the periphery to the metropole. As a result, whereas the orthodox theory sees development as the modernization of backward countries through the infusion of advanced capitalist institutions, technology, and values, dependency theory sees real development as a process of structural change toward capital retention and, thus, autonomous growth for the satisfaction of popular needs.

Since independence, the African countries (with very few and, then, very temporary exceptions) have been trying to develop through the orthodox strategy of exporting raw materials (reflecting their supposed comparative advantage), attracting foreign investment, and using foreign assistance to build infrastructure and begin a few local industries, often only industries producing exports. As a response to the dramatic failure of these policies most governments, with the help of the Western donor community, have redoubled their efforts to be more faithful to the orthodoxy and carry out the same policies more faithfully. The orthodox remedies to the crises in African economies have been directed toward assuring that Africa can continue to play its traditional role in the international division of labor as a producer of primary commodities (Higgott, 1986: 295). Critics have questioned these remedies on the grounds that they ignore both the ubiquitous historical role of the state in development and Africa's increasingly subordinate position in the global political economy as a result of the new international division of labor (Nyang'oro, 1989: 44; Higgott, 1986: 288).

Unfortunately, although dependency theory can show the flaws of the orthodoxy (demonstrating that underdevelopment is maintained in a vicious spiral by the very forces that the orthodoxy holds to be so essential for development), the policy advice it offers is also inadequate. Although African dependency theorists have a theory of underdevelopment, they do not have a theory of *development*. Neither Ake's call for revolution nor Amin's call for delinking (Amin, 1990) has been presented with sufficient specificity to provide policy guidelines for concrete political actors. Other proposals seem to dissolve into acts of faith and wishful thinking. For instance, Onimode declares with obvious frustration: "The people must instill into their leaders that they must build for posterity, especially in view of limited resources and of the infrastructural inadequacies yet to be rectified in the face of deepening crisis" (Onimode, 1988: 22).

Yash Tandon does not exhort the masses. He just shows his confidence in their revolutionary potential:

> The indomitable will of the people, and the fact that imperialism will not yield easily, indicate that Africa has still a long way to go, but the African peoples will inexorably travel the path of victory . . . A power will arise from the social bowels of Africa, led by the working masses, which will stand up to the superpowers and call a halt to the continuing pillage and immiseration of the peoples of Africa. (Tandon, 1984: 50–51)

But as Africa's economic crisis continues we must recognize that a theoretical perspective that would provide the basis for practical solutions to the crisis has yet to be found. The World Bank's solutions have not worked, and even if they had been effective in stabilizing African economies, it is doubtful that would provide fundamental solutions to the problem of underdevelopment. As a result, the orthodoxy has lost a great deal of its credibility (Shaw, 1989: 5), which is one reason African governments continue to support the ECA's efforts to present alternatives. Yet, those few policies informed by a dependency perspective that African states have followed in the past have not proven any more useful; consider the international solutions that African states have attempted to negotiate by calling for the NIEO (Hart, 1983) and by taking a similar position on reforming the Lome convention (Ravenhill, 1985a), both of which came to nothing. The World Bank and the Western donors at least offer some short-term incentives if African governments adhere to the orthodoxy. Thus, even without considering the specific interests of the African ruling classes, it is not surprising that African governments are influenced more by the perspective of Berg and the World Bank than by Rodney, Amin, or Ake, or even the ECA.

This situation represents a crisis in African international political economy. The orthodox paradigm provides an unsatisfactory theory of development and underdevelopment. The dependency paradigm "does explain how international domination and exploitation are maintained in a world where a global capitalist system coexists with a political order based on state sovereignty" (Becker, 1988: 3), but it provides no strategic theory of development. In order to break out of this crisis, it would be necessary to advance toward a more nuanced theory of development, one that would go beyond a broad explanation of the origins of the African condition toward the establishment of causal relationships between clearly defined development outcomes and their national and international policy antecedents (Becker, 1988). It is not within the scope of my abilities to direct such an enterprise. However, it may be worthwhile to suggest two key attributes of the resulting theory:

- a definition of "development" as constant improvement in the quality of people's lives, including their ability to maintain the integrity of their values
- identification of social forces in conflict over development policy and identification of strategies for progressive forces.

I agree with Becker (1988: 25 ff) that we should eschew investigation of grandiose, and (necessarily) rather abstract "revolutionary" strategies in favor of more incremental programs designed to expand the scope of democratic participation.

What following these principles means in practical terms will have to be determined by African theorists and policymakers, and it will take time. This means that the present generation of African dependency theorists must reproduce themselves, or, more precisely, they must produce a new generation of thinkers who will continue the search for theory. This is not a simple task. As Shaw argues, Africans must "rebuild the physical and intellectual infrastructure so that a viable longer-term programme of readjustment and recovery can be commenced" (Shaw, 1989: 3).

Unfortunately, this need comes at a time when higher education in Africa is in dire straights. One of the consequences of the economic crisis in Africa has been a serious deterioration of educational and research institutions. Furthermore, the African governments, especially under the constraints of the SAPs of the 1980s, do not have the resources to reverse the deterioration of academic facilities or the resulting brain drain.

As we have seen earlier, many of the African intellectuals of this generation have developed AIPE with the material assistance and intellectual support of the United Nations (the United Nations University and the ECA) and some sympathetic Western institutions. However, in the end, the bulk of the intellectual work must be done by Africans, and the only reliable support for such work will come from Africans, who, after all, are the ones at risk. Like everything else in Africa today, the struggle to advance African international political economy promises to be long and difficult.

Notes

1. The fact that many of the books produced in the late 1950s and early 1960s were motivated by consideration of competing with the Soviet bloc in the Third World is obviously evident in the title of Rostow's (1960) *The Stages of Economic Growth: A Non-Communist Manifesto*.

2. This is due to the relative lack of Marxist training in African academia and the fact that Africa was a low priority research area for non-African Marxists. As Jewslewicki (1989: 30–43) points out, "penetration of Marxism in African studies is slight." There are a few Marxists who have written on African development. The best known of these is Mohammed Babu. In 1980, the late Emmanuel Hansen and a few colleagues started the *Journal of African Marxists*. Also, the *Review of African Political Economy*, which is published in Sheffield, has legitimate radical credentials with some Marxist affiliations and occasional articles by African Marxists. Beyond this, there is very little organized Marxist analysis by African Marxists.

3. See, for example Chilcote (1984), Blöstrom and Hettne (1984), Dupe (1988), and Kay (1975).

4. Of course, there are some African writers who espouse the orthodox approach (for example, Ahiakpor, 1985). However, these writers are definitely in the minority among African scholars.

5. The fact that the "civilizing mission" was the official ideology of colonialism is borne out by the following resolution of the 1944 Brazzaville Conference, "the aims of the civilizational work by France in her colonies rule out all idea of autonomy and all possibility of development outside the French Empire" (quoted in Deschamps, 1970: 253).

6. ECA (1983, 1985, 1986, 1987, 1988a, 1988b, 1989a, 1989b); IBRD (1983, 1984, 1986, 1989a, 1989b, 1989c).

9

On the Fringes of the World Economy: A Feminist Perspective

J. Ann Tickner

International political economy should give us tools to help us understand how global economic welfare and security can be maximized, and it should help us think about the contemporary global problems of militarism, economic injustice, and environmental degradation. The most basic tools that IPE offers are ideas—key concepts like "rationality," "security," and "power"—the building blocks of explanation.

In *The Political Economy of International Relations*, Robert Gilpin (1987: ch. 2) describes what he calls the three constituting ideologies of international political economy: liberalism, nationalism, and Marxism. Gilpin defines an ideology as a belief system that includes both scientific explanations and normative prescriptions. Because none of these ideologies discusses *gender*, we must presume that they are to be considered gender neutral, meaning that they claim that the interactions between states and markets (which is the limited way that Gilpin defines political economy) can be understood without reference to gender distinctions. Feminists would disagree with this claim; just as Marxists have argued that the world economy cannot be understood without reference to class, feminists make similar claims about gender. Ignoring gender distinctions hides a set of social and economic relations characterized by inequality between men and women. Feminists would argue that in order to understand how these unequal relationships affect the workings of the world economy and their consequences for both women and men, an approach that makes gender relations explicit must be constructed.

In this chapter I shall investigate whether liberalism, nationalism, and Marxism are indeed gender neutral, with respect to their explanations and their normative prescriptions. I shall examine the individual, state, and class, the central unit of analysis for each of these perspectives, to see whether they evidence a masculine bias both in the way they are described and the interest they represent. If this is the case, then it is legitimate to ask whether and how gender has circumscribed each perspective's understanding of the workings of the world economy. If there is evidence of a masculine bias in these representations, we must ask whether the normative preferences and policy prescriptions of each of these perspectives will serve the interests of men more than those of women.

Having critiqued each ideology from a feminist perspective, I shall attempt to begin to construct a feminist understanding of international political economy that will necessarily take us out of Gilpin's oppositional tricotomy. I do so by specifying a wider set of fundamental concepts and by employing a feminist perspective to redefine some of the core concepts that are contested within the three perspectives. Because there is very little literature on gender and international relations, I shall draw on feminist literature from different disciplines and approaches. I am aware that it is impossible to speak of one feminist approach—feminist theory is interdisciplinary and encompasses a broad ideological spectrum. Feminist theorists define themselves variously as liberals, radicals, socialists, Marxists, and post-modernists, and it would be impossible to do justice to all of them. Nevertheless, there are common themes in much of the feminist literature suggesting that any feminist perspective on international political economy would start with very different assumptions about the individual, the state, and class from those at the foundations of Gilpin's three ideologies. Whereas different feminist literatures respond to the needs and concerns of different groups of women—middle class or poor, Western or Third World—feminism shares a common opposition to gender inequality and the oppression of women and a commitment to building a world in which women and men are equal participants in all aspects of society.

Throughout this chapter I shall be using the terms "masculine" and "feminine" to refer to a set of socially constructed categories that vary in time and place rather than to fixed biological determinants of sex. In the West, conceptual dichotomies such as objectivity versus subjectivity, reason versus emotion, mind versus body, culture versus nature, autonomy versus relatedness, and public versus private have typically been used to describe male/female differences. Although many feminists object to this type of dichotomization, arguing that it tends to devalue the characteristics associated with femininity, psychological tests performed in the United States confirm that in that country, at least, both men and women recognize these dichotomous characteristics as masculine and feminine, respectively (Broverman et al., 1972). Not only do individuals perceive these dichotomies as gender related, but the characteristics associated with masculinity are more highly valued by men and women alike.

A Feminist Critique of IPE Liberalism

I shall begin with a feminist critique of liberalism, the dominant view in Western international political economy in the twentieth century. Although its proponents present it as a scientific theory with universal and timeless applications, liberalism, which arose together with modern capitalism in the eighteenth century, has generally been the ideology preferred by theorists from rich and powerful states. I shall first examine whether the construct "rational economic man," used as a basis for liberals' explanations of the workings of the economy, is gendered, and then whether liberal prescriptions for maximizing human welfare may be biased toward rewarding men more than women.

Liberal theory takes the individual as the basic unit of analysis. According to liberals, human beings are by nature economic animals driven by rational self-interest. Rational economic man is assumed to be motivated by the laws of profit maximization. He is highly individualistic, pursuing his own economic goals in the market without any social obligation to the community of which he is a part. Liberals believe that this instrumentally rational market behavior, even though it is driven by selfish profit motives, produces outcomes that are efficient or beneficial for everyone even though they acknowledge that not everyone will benefit to the same extent. The detrimental effects of economic growth and market behavior, such as dwindling resources and environmental damage, are generally not considered.

A feminist critique of liberalism should begin with an examination of rational economic man, a construct that, although it extrapolates from roles and behaviors associated with Western men and assumes characteristics that I have described as masculine, has been used by liberal economics to represent the behavior of humanity as a whole. Nancy Hartsock (1983: 47) suggests that rational economic man, appearing coincidentally with the birth of modern capitalism, is a social construct based on the reduction of a variety of human passions to a desire for economic gain. Sandra Harding contrasts this type of behavior with what she calls an "African" worldview, in which the economic behavior of individuals is embedded within a social order. She claims that this communal orientation, seen as deviant by neoclassical economic theory, contains some striking parallels with the worldview of Western women (Harding, 1986: 167–179).

For Hartsock, Harding, and other nonliberal feminists, the highly individualistic, competitive market behavior of rational economic man could not be assumed as a norm if women's experiences were taken as the prototype for human behavior. Women in their reproductive and maternal roles do not conform to the behavior of individual instrumental rationality. Much of women's work in the provision of basic needs takes place outside the market, in households or in the subsistence sector of Third World economies.

Moreover, when women enter the market economy, they are disproportionately represented in the caring professions as teachers, nurses, or
social workers—choices that are generally not made on the basis of profit
maximization but on the basis of values that are emphasized in female
socialization. If this is the case, we must conclude that most women's, as
well as some men's, motivations and behavior cannot be explained using this
model of rationality.

Rational economic man is extrapolated from assumptions about human
nature that have their origins in Western liberal political theory. Rational
economic man is a Hobbesian man whose passions have been tamed by the
rational pursuit of profit. Liberal contract theories about men's origins depict
a state of nature where individuals exist prior to and apart from the
community; they come together not out of any desire for community but out
of the need for a protected environment in which they can conduct their
economic transactions more securely. Hartsock argues that, given its
dependence solely on economic exchange, any notion of community in
liberal theory is fragile and instrumental. She claims, however, that this
liberal assumption that the behavior of individuals can be explained apart
from society is unrealistic because individuals have always inhabited and been
a part of society (Hartsock, 1983).

Even though early liberal theorists were explicit in their assertion that
their theories about human behavior applied to the behavior of men and not
women, this distinction has since been lost as contemporary liberals assume
this type of behavior for humanity as a whole. Feminists take issue with this
theory of human behavior, claiming that it is biased toward a masculine
representation. Harding claims that for women, the self is defined through
relationship with others rather than apart from others (Harding, 1986). Alison
Jaggar argues that liberalism's individualistic portrayal of human nature has
placed excessive value on the mind at the expense of the body. Because, in
our sexual division of labor, men have dominated the intellectual fields
whereas women have been assigned the tasks necessary for physical survival,
Jaggar concludes that given this sexual division of labor, women would be
unlikely to develop a theory of human nature that ignored human
interdependence or to formulate a conception of rationality that stressed
individual autonomy. If the need for interdependence were taken as the
starting point, community and cooperation would not be seen as puzzling and
problematic (Jaggar, 1983: 40–48).

Generalizing from rational economic man to the world economy, liberals
believe that world welfare is maximized by allowing market forces to operate
unimpeded and goods and investment to flow as freely as possible across
national boundaries according to the laws of comparative advantage. Critics
of liberalism question this liberal belief in openness and interdependence,
claiming that it falsely depoliticizes exchange relationships and masks hidden
power structures. They challenge the notion of mutual gains from exchange

by focusing on the unequal distribution of gains across states, classes, and factors of production, arguing that gains accrue disproportionately to the most powerful states or economic actors. For example, Marxist critics argue that liberal economic theory obscures the unequal power relations between capital and labor. Because capital is mobile across interstate boundaries and controls strategic decisions about investment and production, it is being rewarded disproportionately to labor, a trend that was on the rise in the 1980s when labor was becoming increasingly marginalized in matters of economic policy (Gill and Law, 1989: 364).

If capital is being rewarded disproportionately to labor in the world economy, then men are being rewarded disproportionately to women; a 1981 Report to the UN Committee on the Status of Women states that although women represent one-half of the global population and one-third of the paid labor force, and are responsible for two-thirds of all working hours, they receive only one-tenth of world income and own less than one percent of world property (Jaggar, 1983: 138). Although much of women's work is performed outside the formal economy, even when they enter the market economy these data suggest that women are not being rewarded to the same extent as men; earning lower wages and owning an insignificant proportion of the world's capital puts women at an enormous disadvantage in terms of power and wealth.

This claim has been examined in some detail in studies of Third World women and development. The UN Decade for the Advancement of Women (1975–1985) assumed that women's problems in the Third World were related to insufficient participation in the process of modernization and development. But recent studies of women and development suggest that in many parts of the Third World the position of rural women may actually decline as they become assimilated into a global market economy and that development aid can actually reduce the status of women relative to men. It is often the case that women's access to land and technology actually decreases as land reform is instituted and agriculture is modernized. Land reform, traditionally thought to be a vital prerequisite for raising agricultural productivity, often reduces women's control over traditional use rights and gives titles to male heads of households. Agricultural mechanization in the Third World has also reduced women's control over agricultural production as men take over the mechanized part of the production process. The modernization of agriculture, which often leads to a dualism in agricultural production, tends to leave women behind in the traditional sector (Sen and Grown, 1987).

Liberals have generally supported export-led strategies of development. But, because states that have opted for export-led strategies have often experienced increased income inequalities and because women are disproportionately clustered at the bottom of the economic scale, such strategies may have a particularly negative effect on women. The harsh effects of structural adjustment policies imposed by the International Monetary Fund on Third World debtor nations fall disproportionately on women as providers of basic needs as social welfare programs in areas of health, nutrition, and housing are cut. When government subsidies or funds are no longer available, women in their roles as unpaid homemakers and care providers must often take up the provision of these basic welfare needs.

Recent studies of Third World development and its effects on women are beginning to document evidence that demonstrates that liberal strategies to promote economic growth and improve world welfare may have a differential impact on men and women. Because women's work more generally often takes place outside the market economy, a model based on instrumentally rational market behavior does not capture all the economic activities of women. Nor can we assume that the prescriptions generated by such a model will be as beneficial to women as they are to men.

A Feminist Critique of IPE Nationalism

The intellectual roots of the nationalist approach date back to the mercantilist school of sixteenth-, seventeenth-, and eighteenth-century Europe—the period coincidental with the rise of the nation-state. The contemporary version of nationalism, associated with the realist school of international relations, became popular in the United States in the 1970s at the same time as its proponents became concerned with what they perceived as the U.S. hegemonic decline (Gilpin, 1987; Krasner, 1982a). The nationalist approach takes the state and its behavior in the international system as its basic unit of analysis. All nationalists ascribe to the primacy of the state, of national security, and of military power in the organization and functioning of the international system (Gilpin, 1987: 31).

Nationalism in orthodox IPE emerged as a critique of liberalism, but its explanation of state behavior is quite close to the liberals' explanation of the behavior of rational economic man. States are assumed to be behaving as rational profit maximizers pursuing wealth, power, and autonomy in an anarchic international system devoid of any sense of community. In a conflictual world, states are striving to be economically self-sufficient. Their participation in the world economy is an attempt to create an international division of labor and resource allocation favorable to their own interests and those of groups within their national boundaries. Arguments against extensive economic interdependence are justified in the name of national security. Strategic domestic industries are to be given protection, especially when they produce military-related goods. National security and national interest are, therefore, the overriding goals of policy (Gill and Law, 1988: 367).

A feminist critique of the nationalist approach must begin by asking whether the state, the central unit of analysis, is a gendered construct with respect to both its historical origins and its contemporary manifestations. In spite of advances in the legal rights of women in many states, none of the known forms of state politicizes women's roles in such a way as to give them de facto equality with men (Moore, 1988: 150). In all states, institutions of state power are dominated by men, particularly in the realm of foreign policy and the military. Because most foreign-policymakers and theorists who have explained the origins of states and state behavior in the international arena have been men, we might assume that this could influence not only the behavior of states and the prioritizing of certain statist goals, such as power and autonomy, but also the theoretical explanations of that behavior. We might also assume that prescriptions for maximizing state power might work more to the advantage of men than women.

The consolidation of the modern state system and the rise of modern science, from which the Western social sciences trace their origins, both occurred in the seventeenth century, a time of dramatic social, economic, and political upheaval well documented in Western history. Less well documented is the fact that the seventeenth century is also associated with the intellectual origins of Western feminism. According to Juliet Mitchell, this is not coincidental; women in the seventeenth century saw themselves as a distinct sociological group completely excluded from the new society rising out of the medieval order (Mitchell, 1987: 31). Seventeenth-century feminists, such as Mary Astell, lamented that the new spirit of equality did not apply to women. At such moments of great historical change, usually identified with progress, feminist historians claim that women are often left behind economically or even made worse off. In the seventeenth century, concepts of gender were shifting; definitions of male and female were becoming polarized in ways that were suited to the growing division between work and home required by early capitalism but not necessarily to the interests of women. The notion of housewife began to place women's work in the private domestic sphere as opposed to the public world of the market inhabited by rational economic man.

Although these new economic arrangements were synonymous with the birth of the enlightenment, "female" became associated with what enlightenment knowledge had left behind. The persecution of witches, who were defending female crafts and medical skills of a precapitalist era against a growing male professionalism, reached new heights in the sixteenth and seventeenth centuries. Jean Bodin (1530–1596), a French mercantilist and founder of the quantitative theory of money as well as the modern concept of national sovereignty, was one of the most vocal proponents of the persecution of witches. According to Bodin's mercantilist philosophy, the modern state must be invested with absolute sovereignty for the development of new wealth necessary for warfighting; to this end the state needed more workers and thus must eliminate witches held responsible for abortion and other forms of birth control (Mies, 1986: 83).

Sovereignty and rationality were part of an enlightenment epistemology, committed to the discovery of universal objective or "scientific" laws—an epistemology bent on discrediting superstition often portrayed as "old wives tales." As mentioned earlier, notions such as objectivity and rationality, central to the definition of the modern natural and social sciences in the West, have typically been associated with masculine thinking. In her study of the origins of modern science in the seventeenth century, Evelyn Fox Keller claims that modern scientific thought is associated with masculinity. Keller bases her claim on psychological theories of gender development, which argue that the separation of subject from object is an important stage of childhood masculine gender development, a separation that is never completely made by girls. According to Keller, Western cultural values simultaneously elevate what is defined as scientific and what is defined as masculine (Keller, 1985: ch. 3 and 4).

Beginning in the seventeenth century, the economy was placed in the public domain of men and of rational scientific knowledge. The nationalist approach, particularly its contemporary neorealist version, has taken the liberal concept of rational economic man, which grew out of this enlightenment knowledge, and used it to explain the behavior of states in the international system (Waltz, 1979). Using game theoretic models, such explanations of states' behavior draw on the instrumentally rational market behavior of individuals. Because international economic interactions rarely result in winner-take-all situations, neorealists have focused on Prisoners Dilemma games to explain states' behavior in the international system. Where international cooperation is seen to exist, it is explained not in terms of international community but rather in terms of enlightened self-interest in an environment that is essentially anarchic (Axelrod, 1984; Keohane, 1984: 67–84).

In her feminist critique of this application of game theory, Birgit Brock-Utne (1989) cites recent research to support her claim that men and women exhibit different types of behavior when playing Prisoners Dilemma games. Challenging a research finding that suggests that men may be more cooperative than women because, in single-sex Prisoners Dilemma games, men choose a cooperative strategy more often than women do. Brock-Utne claims that this is because men are more interested than women in strategic considerations of winning the game. When given a choice, men prefer games of skill, whereas women prefer games of chance. Prisoners Dilemma is a game of skill, so this may explain why women tend to lose interest when playing such games and fail to figure out the best strategy to maximize gains. Recent research findings suggest that women may be more influenced by the interpersonal situation, such as getting along with the other players, than by strategic considerations associated with winning the game (Brock-Utne, 1989). If, as Brock-Utne suggests, women tend to find this type of game based on instrumental rational behavior uninteresting, it is unlikely that they would have selected this methodology for explaining the behavior of states in the international system.

Using game theoretic models to explain states' behavior in the international system, nationalists portray states as unitary actors: concentrating at the interstate level, nationalists do not generally focus their attention on the internal distribution of gains. But, if, as I have argued, women have been peripheral to the institutions of state power and are less rewarded economically than men, the validity of the unitary actor assumption should be examined from the perspective of gender. We must question whether women are gaining equally to men from nationalist prescriptions to pursue wealth and power. In all states, women tend to be clustered at the bottom of the socioeconomic scale; in the United States in the 1980s, 78 percent of all people living in poverty were women or children under 18 (Seager and Olson, 1986: 28). When they enter the labor market, women tend to be ghettoized in low-paying jobs or face wage discrimination in the form of lower wages for the same jobs as men (Seager and Olson, 1986: 18–21). Moreover, in societies where military spending is high, women are often the first to feel the effects of economic hardship when social welfare programs are sacrificed for military priorities. As mentioned above, for nationalists the military/industrial complex is an important part of the domestic economy entitled to special protection. For women, however, the trade-off between military and economic security can be particularly acute.

I have shown that the nationalist explanation of states' behavior in the international system that focuses on instrumental rationality may be biased toward a masculine representation. Nationalist prescriptions for maximizing wealth and power may impact negatively on women because women are often situated at the edge of the market or the bottom of the socioeconomic scale.

A Feminist Critique of IPE Marxism

Unlike the liberal and nationalist approaches, which center on explaining the behavior of and prescribing for the interests of advanced capitalist states, the contemporary Marxist approach to international political economy comes out of a perspective of the weak and powerless in the world economy. Writers in the dependency and world systems schools—Marxist approaches that gained some recognition in the West in the 1970s—argue that the world economy operates, through trade and investment, in a way that distorts the economies of underdeveloped states in the Third World and condemns them to permanent marginalization. Their participation in the world capitalist economy is seen as detrimental to their development and as exacerbating domestic inequalities between the rich and poor (Gill and Law, 1988: 54–69). Concepts of core and periphery, which exist both in the world economy and within the domestic economies of states themselves, are used to explain these inequalities: class alliances between capitalists in the Third World and transnational capital contribute to the further marginalization of Third World peripheries (Chase-Dunn, 1982: Galtung, 1971). Therefore, according to Marxists, both the domestic and international political and economic relations of Third World capitalist states are embedded in exploitative structures of a capitalist world economy. Authentic, autonomous development that satisfies the needs of all people can be achieved only by a socialist revolution and by delinking from the world economy.

Because it speaks for the interests of the least powerful in the international system, Marxist theory would appear to be more compatible with a feminist perspective. In fact, much of recent feminist theory owes a strong intellectual debt to Marxism. Like Marxists, radical, socialist, and postmodern feminists see knowledge as historically and socially constructed. Marxists and feminists would agree that knowledge is embedded in human activity. Like much of feminist theory, Marxism rejects the notion of a universal and abstract rationality and objectivity upon which both the liberal and nationalist approaches to specific ways are attributable to patriarchy rather than to capitalism. Second, Marxism rejects that a class analysis ignores women's role in the family. Feminists maintain that women do not have the same opportunities as men when they enter the workforce. Even in the United States, where considerable advances have been made in the economic position of women, full-time working women in 1987 earned an average of 71 percent of the earnings of full-time working men (Okin, 1989: 144). Women frequently experience harassment and intimidation in the workplace, and taking time off for bearing and raising children may impede opportunities for promotion. In many other parts of the world, the position of working women is more critical. Multinational corporations in the Third World prefer to hire young women because they are willing to work for low wages and are more docile than men and therefore easier to control. Such women are often fired if they attempt to unionize or if they marry, since marriage raises the issue of the company's responsibility for maternity benefits (Mies, 1986: 117–136).

It is Marxism's tendency to ignore women in their reproductive roles of which feminists are most critical, however. For classical Marxists, procreation was seen as a natural female process fixed by human biology. Therefore a division of labor, whereby women are primarily responsible for the rearing of children, was also seen as relatively fixed (Jaggar, 1983: 75). Because Marxism assumed that women's roles as caretakers of children was natural, an assumption questioned by many feminists, classical Marxism omitted women's roles in the family from its analysis. Feminists argue that ignoring women in their reproductive and childrearing roles, an omission common to all approaches to political economy, leaves all the unpaid labor that women perform in the family outside of economic analysis. By ignoring women in their domestic roles, Marxists and non-Marxists alike neglect certain issues that are peculiar to women regardless of their class position. In most cases, when married women move into the labor force, they continue to be responsible for most of the housework and childrearing (Okin, 1989: 153). Besides the lack of respect for unpaid housework and the dependence of full-time housewives on the income of their husbands, women, including those in the workforce, usually suffer a severe decline in income should their marriage end in divorce. Economic dependence may force women to stay in marriages in spite of violent and abusive treatment.

Marxist theory has paid insufficient attention to women's private roles in households, and feminist writers also claim that contemporary Marxist analyses do not adequately deal with the position of marginalized women in the Third World. Although they often play a crucial role in subsistence production, increasingly women in the Third World are being defined as dependents (Mies, 1986: 115). Although dependency theory recognizes this type of marginalization as a structural consequence of capitalist development, it does not acknowledge the special position of women among the marginalized nor the fact that the status of women relative to men has been declining in many parts of the Third World. For example, Mies argues that, in India, there has been a steady decline in the proportion of women to men since the beginning of the twentieth century. She attributes this to a high maternal mortality rate. In instances where overall mortality rates have been reduced, there is considerable evidence to suggest that women receive less adequate health treatment and have lower nutritional standards than men (Mies, 1988: 31). Feminists would argue that the particular oppression of women, evident in such data that are generalizable beyond the case of India, can only be explained in social and cultural terms that extend beyond capitalism.

If, as many feminists claim, women's oppression is due to patriarchy as well as capitalism, could the position of women be expected to improve under socialism as Marxists maintain? Socialist feminists agree that the condition of women in socialist states usually improves in areas of social policies, welfare, and legal rights (Molyneux, 1985: 255). The availability of maternity rights, day-care, and other institutional reforms may further improve the position of working women in socialist states. However, a study of Soviet women, who make up 51 percent of the Soviet workforce, finds them disproportionately concentrated in unskilled jobs while they continue to carry most of the domestic workload (Moore, 1988; 141). Since interference in the family as an institution is as much resisted in socialist states as it is in capitalist states, problems of powerlessness and violence that women encounter in families remain. Moreover, writers on women in socialist states generally conclude that even if women's conditions in the workforce are improved, women are as poorly represented in positions of state power and decisionmaking as they are in capitalist states. Feminists conclude, therefore, that, although women may suffer from particular forms of repression under capitalism, the liberation of women through class struggle cannot be assumed. It will come about only when women are equal to men in both the public and private spheres, a condition that will not necessarily be attained in a postcapitalist world.

Toward a Feminist Perspective on IPE

I have shown that the individual, the state, and class, which are the basic units of analysis for the liberal, nationalist, and Marxist approaches to international political economy, respectively, tend to present a narrowly masculine representation. I have also suggested that the prescriptions that each of these perspectives offers for maximizing economic welfare and security may work to the advantage of men more than women. I shall now suggest how we might begin to think about constructing a feminist perspective which could offer us a less gender biased representation of international political economy and could represent the particular interests of women. Such a perspective, coming from the position of those on the fringes of the state and the market, might also help us to think about solutions to contemporary global problems such as militarism, economic injustice, and environmental degradation, which, although they have not traditionally been central to the field of international political economy, are problems with which the state and the market seem increasingly unable to cope.

A feminist perspective on international political economy must be wary of discourses that generalize and universalize from theories based on assumptions taken from characteristics associated with Western men. Because, as I have shown, a masculine perspective is embedded in the epistemological foundations of all three approaches, the construction of a feminist perspective should include efforts to develop a feminist epistemology. Only by so doing can hidden gender relations be brought to light and an approach that takes gender into account both in its scientific explanations and normative prescriptions be constructed. A feminist perspective on international political economy might begin, therefore, by constructing some alternative definitions of concepts, such as rationality, security, and power—concepts that have been central to our understanding of the field but, as I shall argue, have been embedded in a masculine epistemology.

Both the liberal and nationalist perspectives rely on a depersonalized definition of rationality that equates the rationality of individuals and state with a type of instrumental behavior that maximizes self-interest. Both of these approaches assume that rational action can be defined objectively regardless of time and place. Most feminists take issue with this definition of rationality; agreeing with Marxists, they would argue that individuals and states are socially constituted and what counts as rational action is embodied within a particular society. In capitalist societies, rationality is associated with profit maximization; thus, the notion of rationality has been placed in the public sphere of the market and thus distinguished from the private sphere of emotion and the household. Feminists argue that because it is men who have primarily occupied this public sphere, rationality as we understand it is tied to a masculine type of reasoning that is abstract and conceptual. Women, whose lived experiences have been more closely bound to the private sphere of caretaking and childrearing, would define rationality as contextual and personal rather than as abstract. In their caring roles, women are engaged in activities associated with serving others—activities that are rational from the perspective of reproduction rather than production. A feminist definition of rationality would, therefore, be tied to an ethic of care and responsibility. Such a definition would be compatible with behavior more typical of women's lived experiences and would allow us to assume rational behavior that is embedded in social activities that are not necessarily tied to profit maximization. It could be extended beyond the household to include responsibility for the Earth and its resources, a type of rationality that may be necessary if we are to ensure the survival of future generations.

The concept of security is central to the nationalist perspective. For nationalists, security has generally been subsumed under the rubric of power, particularly military power, and is usually associated with the security of the nation-state. National security is a concept that is particularly problematic for women. Betty Reardon believes that, far from protecting women, national security, with its military connotations, can offer particular dangers for women. According to Reardon, sexism and militarism are two interdependent manifestations of social violence (Reardon, 1985: 5). Excluded from the patriotic duty of defending the state, women have traditionally been defined as the protected rather than the protectors, although they have had little control over the conditions of their protection. Moreover, women experience special vulnerabilities within the state as frequent victims of family violence, which often takes place outside the protection of the law. As mentioned above, women are also subject to special economic vulnerabilities in households, in the workforce, and in the subsistence economy. With the growing militarization of many parts of the Third World, fueled by an international arms trade that is becoming an increasingly significant proportion of world trade, women are especially vulnerable to the trade-off between military and economic security. Given these special vulnerabilities of women inside society and households as well as with respect to the international system, security for women is not necessarily synonymous with national security. A more adequate definition of security would be multilevel and multi-dimensional and would include both physical and economic security. A feminist perspective would therefore define security as the absence of violence, whether it be military, economic, or sexual.

Power in international relations, whether it is used to explain the behavior of states or classes, has generally been defined in terms of domination and coercion. Nancy Hartsock argues that this type of power as domination has always been associated with masculinity because the exercise of power has generally been a masculine activity. When women write about power, they stress energy, capacity, and potential, says Hartsock (Hartsock, 1983: 210). Hannah Arendt's definition of power is frequently cited by feminists; Arendt defines power as the human ability to act in concert, or action that is taken in connection with others who share similar concerns (Arendt, 1969: 44). This definition of power is similar to psychologist David McClelland's portrayal of female power, which he describes as shared rather than assertive (McClelland, 1975: 109). Jean Jaquette argues that because women are rarely in positions of economic or political power, they have been more apt to rely on power as persuasion. She compares women's domestic activities to coalition-building activities of weak states (Jaquette, 1984). All of these writers are portraying power not as domination but as a relationship of mutual enablement.

If we were to agree with Marxists that the way in which we describe reality has an effect on the way we perceive and act, and that autonomy and self-sufficiency are unrealistic, then a feminist perspective would assume a connected, interdependent individual whose behavior includes activities related to reproduction as well as production. In order to capture these productive and reproductive activities, the artificial boundaries between the world of rational economic man in the public sphere of production and the activities that women perform outside the economy as mothers, caretakers, and subsistence producers of basic needs must be broken down. Breaking down these barriers would help to reduce the differential value attached to the rational or "efficient" world of production and the private world of reproduction. Were childbearing and childrearing to be seen as more valued activities, it could help to reduce the excessive focus on the productive efficiency of an ever-expanding commodity production—a focus whose utility in a world of shrinking resources, vast inequalities, and increasing environmental damage is becoming questionable. A perspective that takes this redefined individual as its basic unit of analysis could help to create an alternative model of political economy that respects human relationships as well as their relation to nature (Kaldor, 1986: 454).

If a substantial portion of women's productive and reproductive activities are taking place on the peripheries of the world economy in households or in the subsistence sector of Third World economies, a feminist perspective must be concerned with achieving economic justice in these particular contexts. Although agreeing that women's domestic labor should be recognized as work, feminists caution that economic justice for women in households cannot be guaranteed in the family as it is presently constituted. Although the family has been designated as the private sphere of women, the concept of male head of household has ensured that male power has traditionally been exercised in the private as well as the public realm. Okin argues that families are unjust to women or children as long as women continue to bear a disproportionate share of childrearing, have lower expected incomes than men, and are left with primary responsibility for supporting and caring for children if families break up. Only when paid and unpaid work associated with both productive and reproductive labor is shared equally by men and women can the family be a just institution and one that can provide the basis for a just society (Okin, 1989: 171).

As discussed above, Third World development strategies have tended to ignore the subsistence sector where much of women's labor is being performed, with the result that modernization has had a differential impact on men and women and has, in certain instances, actually reduced the position of women. Due to the absence of women from local and national power structures, development programs have tended to support projects in areas of production that are dominated by men. To achieve economic justice for rural women in the Third World, development must target projects that benefit women, particularly in the subsistence sector. Improvements in agriculture should focus on consumption as well as production; in many parts of Africa, gathering water and fuel, under conditions of increasing scarcity and environmental degradation, are taking up larger portions of women's time and energy.

Because women are so centrally involved in basic needs satisfaction in households and in the subsistence economy of the Third World, a feminist approach to international political economy must be supportive of a basic needs approach where basic needs are defined in terms of both material needs and the need for autonomy and participation. Because, as I have argued, Third World development strategies that are export oriented have tended to contribute to domestic inequality and, in times of recession and increasing international indebtedness, have had a particularly detrimental impact on women, a strategy that seeks to satisfy basic needs within the domestic economy may be the best type of strategy to improve the welfare of Third World women. Local satisfaction of basic needs requires more attention to subsistence or domestic food production than to growing crops for export markets. A more self-reliant economy would also be less vulnerable to the decisions of foreign investment whose employment policies can be particularly exploitative of women. A basic needs strategy is compatible with values of nurturance and caring; such a strategy is dependency reducing and can empower women to take charge of their own lives and create conditions that increase their own security.

Women have generally been peripheral to the institutions of the nation-state and transnational capital; therefore, a feminist perspective on international political economy should take a critical stance with respect to these institutions, questioning whether they are effectively able to deal with global problems of militarism, poverty, and the environment—problems that have a particularly negative impact on women. Building a model of political economy that starts at the bottom, with the individual and the local satisfaction of the individual's basic needs, envisages a type of state that is more self-reliant with respect to the international system and more able to live within its own resource limits. Such a state would be less militaristic and give priority to welfare over military considerations. Looking at the world economy from the perspective of those on the fringes of capitalism can help us to think about constructing a model that would be concerned with the production of life rather than the production of things and wealth. Maria Mies argues that the different conception of labor upon which such a model depends could help us adapt our lifestyle at a time when we are becoming increasingly conscious of the finiteness of the Earth and its resources (Mies, 1986: 211 ff.). Such a model would depend on an extended definition of security, which goes beyond a nationalist, militarist focus and begins to speak to the economic and environmental security of individuals and states alike.

In their conclusion to *The Global Political Economy*, Stephen Gill and David Law (1988) call for the formation of a counterhegemonic perspective on IPE, one based on an alternative set of concepts and concerns, which could deal with a series of problems associated with militarism, environmental crises, and the excesses and inequalities of the marketplace that are becoming more acute as we enter the twenty-first century. They suggest that such a perspective might emerge out of transnational linkages between grass-roots social movements concerned with peace, ecology, and economic justice (Gill and Law, 1988; see also Gill and Law, 1989). Because women are represented in much larger numbers in these new social movements than they are in institutions of state power and transnational capital, women would be in a position to make a significant contribution to the formation of this counterhegemonic perspective. Some feminists have argued that women's position outside the structures of power, on the peripheries of the system, gives them a special epistemological standpoint, which can provide a more comprehensive view of reality. At a time when existing political and economic institutions seem increasingly incapable of solving many global problems, a feminist perspective, by going beyond an investigation of market relations, state behavior, and capitalism, could help us to understand how the global economy affects those on the fringes of the market, the state, or in households as we attempt to build a more secure world where inequalities based on gender and other forms of discrimination are eliminated.

Bibliography

Abegunrin, L. (1985) "The Southern African Development Coordinating Conference: Politics of Dependence," in R. Onwuka and A. Sesay, eds. *The Future of Regionalism in Africa.* New York: St. Martins Press.

Adedeji, A. (1985) "Inter-African Economic Cooperation in Light of the Final Act of Lagos," in A. Adedeji and T. M. Shaw, eds. *Economic Crisis in Africa: African Perspectives on Development and Potentials.* Boulder, Colo.: Lynne Rienner Publishers.

Ahiakpor, J. C. (1985) "The Success and Failure of Dependency Theory: The Experience of Ghana." *International Organization* 39, 3: 535–552.

Ake, C. (1976) "Explanatory Notes on the Political Economy of Africa." *Journal of Modern African Studies* 14, 1: 1–23.

———— (1978) *Revolutionary Pressures in Africa.* London: Zed Books.

———— (1981) *A Political Economy of Africa.* New York: Longmans.

Alcalde, J. G. (1987) *The Idea of Third World Development.* Lanham, Md: University Press of America.

Alker, H. R., Jr. (1981) "Dialectical Foundations of Global Disparities." *International Studies Quarterly* 25, 1: 69–98.

Amin, S. (1972) "Underdevelopment and Dependence in Black Africa: Their Historical Origins and Contemporary Forms." *Journal of Modern African Studies* 10, 4: 503–524.

———— (1974) *Accumulation on a World Scale.* New York: Monthly Review Press.

———— (1976) *Unequal Development: An Essay on the Social Formations of Peripheral Capitalism.* New York: Monthly Review Press.

———— (1977) *Imperialism and Unequal Development.* New York: Monthly Review Press.

———— (1987) "Democracy and National Strategy in the Periphery." *Third World Quarterly* 9, 4: 1129–1156.

———— (1990) *Delinking.* London: Zed Books.

Amin, S., D. Chitala, and I. Mandaza, eds. (1987) *SADCC: Prospects for Disengagement and Development in Southern Africa.* London: Zed Books.

Anderson, B. (1983) *Imagined Communities.* London: Verso.

Apter, D. (1955) *The Gold Coast in Transition.* Princeton, N.J.: Princeton University Press.

———— (1987) *Rethinking Development: Modernisation, Dependency and Post-Modern Politics.* London: Sage Publications.

Arendt, H. (1969) *On Violence.* New York: Harcourt, Brace and World.

Arrighi, G. (1989) "The Three Hegemonies of Historical Capitalism." Paper presented at the ESRC Conference on Structural Change in the West, Cambridge, September. Forthcoming in S. Gill, ed. *Gramsci and International Relations*. New York: Columbia University Press.

Arrow, K. (1963) *Social Choice and Individual Values*. New Haven, Conn.: Yale University Press.

———— (1971) "Exposition of the Theory of Choice Under Uncertainty," in C. B. McGuire and R. Radner, eds. *Decision and Organization*. Amsterdam: North-Holland.

———— (1983) *Social Choice and Justice*. Cambridge, Mass.: Harvard University Press.

Asante, S. K. B. (1984) "ECOWAS, the EEC, and the Lome Convention," in D. Mazzeo, ed. *African Regional Organizations*. New York: Cambridge University Press.

———— (1986) "Africa and Europe: Collective Dependence or Interdependence," in A. Sesay, ed. *Africa and Europe*. London: Croom Helm.

Ashley, R. K. (1983) "Three Modes of Economism." *International Studies Quarterly* 27, 4: 463–496.

———— (1984) "The Poverty of Neorealism." *International Organisation* 38, 2: 225–286.

———— (1987a) "Marginalia: Poststructuralism/International Theory." Paper prepared for German-American Workshop on International Relations Theory, Bad Homburg, Federal Republic of Germany, June.

———— (1987b) "Effecting Global Purpose: Notes on a Problematic of International Organization." Unpublished manuscript.

———— (1988) "Untying the Sovereign State: A Double Reading of the Anarchy Problematique." *Millennium: Journal of International Studies* 17, 2: 227–262.

———— (1989) "Imposing International Purpose: Notes on a Problematic of Governance," in C. Z. Czempiel and J. N. Rosenau, eds. *Global Changes and Theoretical Challenges: Approaches to World Politics for the 1990s*. Lexington, Mass.: Lexington Books.

Augelli, E., and C. N. Murphy (1988) *America's Quest for Supremacy and the Third World*. London: Pinter Publishers.

———— (forthcoming) "Gramsci and International Relations: A General Perspective with Examples from the U.S. Policy in the Reagan Era," in S. Gill, ed. *Gramsci and International Relations*. New York: Columbia University Press.

Australian Bureau of Agricultural and Resource Economics (1985) *Agricultural Policies in the European Community: Their Origins and Effects on Protection and Trade*. Canberra, Policy Monograph, No. 2.

———— (1988) *Japanese Beef Policies: Implications for Trade: Prices and Market Shares*. Canberra, Occasional Paper, No. 102.

———— (1989) *U.S. Grain Policies and the World Market*. Canberra, Policy Monograph No. 4.

Axelrod, R. (1984) *The Evolution of Cooperation*. New York: Basic Books.

Axelrod, R., and R. O. Keohane (1985) "Achieving Cooperation Under Anarchy: Strategies and Institutions." *World Politics* 32, 2: 226–254.

Babu, M. A. (1981) *African Socialism or Socialist Africa*. Dar es Salaam: Tanzania Publishing House.

Bach, D. C. (1986) "France's Involvement in Sub-Saharan Africa," in A. Sesay, ed. *Africa and Europe*. London: Croom Helm.

Ball, D. (1987) *Nurrungar: A Base for Debate*. Sydney: Allen and Unwin.

———— (1988) *Pine Gap*. Sydney: Allen and Unwin.

Banfield, E. C. (1958) *The Moral Basis of a Backward Society*. Glencoe, Ill.: The Free Press.

Bangura, Y. (1983) *Britain and Commonwealth Africa: The Politics of Economic Relations, 1951–1975*. Manchester: Manchester University Press.

Becker, D. G. (1988) "Beyond Dependency: Development and Democracy in the Era of International Capitalism." Paper presented to the Conference on Comparative Politics: Research and Practice for the Next Twenty Years, City University of New York, September.

Benedict, R. (1946) *The Chrysanthemum and the Sword: Patterns of Japanese Culture*. Boston: Houghton Mifflin.

Berg, R. J., and J. S. Whitaker, eds. (1986) *Strategies for African Development*. Berkeley: University of California Press.

Bernheim, B. D. (1986) "Axiomatic Characterization of Rational Choice in Strategic Environments," *Scandinavian Journal of Economics* 88, 3: 473–488.

Bertalanffy, L. von (1968) *General Systems Theory*. New York: G. Braziller.

Bhagwati, J. (1971) "The Generalized Theory of Distortions and Welfare," in J. Bhagwati et al., eds. *Trade, Balance of Payments and Growth*. Amsterdam: North-Holland.

———— (1988) *Protectionism*. Cambridge, Mass.: MIT Press.

Bhagwati, J., and T. N. Srinivasan (1969) "Optimal Interventions to Achieve Non-Economic Objectives." *Review of Economic Studies* 36, 1: 27–38.

———— (1983) *Lectures on International Trade*. Cambridge, Mass.: MIT Press.

Binder, L. (1966) "Ideology and Political Development," in M. Weiner, ed. *Modernization: The Dynamics of Growth*. New York: Basic Books.

Binmore, K. (1987) "Modelling Rational Players (Part 1)," *Economics and Philosophy* 3, 2: 179–214.

———— (1988) "Modelling Rational Players (Part 2)." *Economics and Philosophy* 4, 1: 9–55.

Binmore, K., and Brandenburger, A. (1990) "Common Knowledge and Game Theory," in K. Binmore, ed. *Essays on the Foundation of Game Theory*. Cambridge: Basil Blackwell.

Black, C. E. (1966) "Change as a Condition of Modern Life," in M. Weiner, ed. *Modernization: The Dynamics of Growth*. New York: Basic Books.

Blake, D. H., and R. S. Walters (1976) *The Politics of Global Economic Relations*. Englewood Cliffs, N.J.: Prentice Hall.

Block, F. (1977) *The Origins of International Economic Disorder*. Berkeley: University of California Press.

———— (1987) *Revising the State Theory*. Philadelphia: Temple University Press.

Blöstrom, M. and B. Hettne (1984) *Development Theory in Transition*. London: Zed Books.

Boardman, R., T. M. Shaw, and P. Soldatos, eds. (1984) *Europe, Africa, and Lome III*. Lanham, Md.: University Press of America.

Bourdieu, P. (1985) *Distinction*. Cambridge, Mass.: Harvard University Press.

Bourne, R. S., and R. Cummings (1984) *The Lagos Plan of Action Versus the Berg Report*. Washington D.C.: Howard University Press.

Brander, J. A. (1986) "Rationales for Strategic Trade and Industrial Policy," in P. R. Krugman, ed. *Strategic Trade Policy and the New International Economics*. Cambridge, Mass.: MIT Press.

Braudel, F. (1979) *The Perspective of the World—Civilization and Capitalism 15th-18th Century*, vol. 3. New York: Harper and Row.

Bremer, S. A., and B. B. Hughes (1990) *Disarmament and Development: A Design for the Future?* Englewood Cliffs, N.J.: Prentice Hall.

Brittan, S. (1984) "The U.S. Loco No Longer Pulls." *Financial Times*, 13 September.

Brock-Utne, B. (1989) "Gender and Cooperation in the Laboratory." *Journal of Peace Research* 26, 1: 47–56.

Broverman, I. K., S. R. Vogel, D. M. Broverman, F. E. Clarkson, and P. S. Rosenkranz (1972) "Sex-Role Stereotypes: A Current Appraisal." *Journal of Social Issues* 28, 2: 9–78.

Byers, R. A., et al., eds. (1987) *Confidence Building Measures and International Security*. New York: East-West Security Studies Center, Monograph Series, No. 4.

Cafruny, A. (1987) *Ruling the Waves*. Berkeley: University of California Press.

Cairns Group. (1986) *Declaration of Ministerial Meeting of Fair Traders in Agriculture*. Cairns, Australia, August 26.

——— (1987) *Proposal to the Uruguay Round Negotiating Group on Agriculture*. Geneva: GATT Secretariat, UR-87-0322.

——— (1988) *Time for Action: A Proposal for a Framework Approach for Agriculture*. Geneva: MTN. GNG/NG5/W/89 July 13.

——— (1989) *The Cairns Group Plan: A Comprehensive Proposal*. Chiang Mai, Thailand, Ministerial Meeting, November 23.

Camilleri, J. (1980) *Australian-American Relations: The Web of Dependence*. Melbourne: Macmillan.

——— (1987) *ANZUS: Australia's Predicament in the Nuclear Age*. Melbourne: Macmillan.

Cardoso, F. H. (1972) "Dependency and Development in Latin America." *New Left Review* 74: 89–94.

Caves, R., and Jones, R. (1985) *World Trade and Payments*. Boston: Little Brown.

Cerny, P. G. (1982) *Social Movements and Protest in France*. London: Frances Pinter.

Cervenka, Z. (1977) *The Unfinished Quest for Unity: Africa and the OAU*. New York: Africana Publishing Co.

Chase-Dunn, C. K. (1982) "International Economic Policy in a Declining Core State," in W. P. Avery and D. P. Rapkin, eds. *America in a Changing World Political Economy*. New York: Longmans.

Chatterjee, P. (1988) *Nationalism and the Colonial World—A Derivative Discourse*. London: Zed Books the United Nations University.

Chilcote, R. H. (1984) *Theories of Development and Underdevelopment*. Boulder, Colo.: Westview Press.

Chitala, D. (1987) "The Political Economy of SADCC and Imperialism's Response," in S. Amin, D. Chitala, and I. Mandaza, eds. *Prospects for Disengagement and Development in Southern Africa*. London: Zed Books.

Choucri, N., and R. C. North (1975) *Nations in Conflict*. San Francisco: Freeman.

Cohen, B. J. (1990) "The Political Economy of International Trade." *International Organization* 44, 2: 261–281.

Cohen, S., and Zysman, J. (1987) *Manufacturing Matters*. New York: Basic Books.

Connolly, W. (1988) *Political Theory and Modernity*. Oxford: Basil Blackwell.

Connors, T. (1972) *The Australian Wheat Industry: Its Economics and Politics*. Armidale: Gill.

Conybeare, J. (1987) *Trade Wars: The Theory and Practice of International Commercial Policy*. New York: Columbia University Press.

Corden, W. M. (1974) *Trade Policy and Economic Welfare.* Oxford: Oxford University Press.

Cox, R. W. (1979) "Ideologies and the New International Econmic Order: Reflections on Some Recent Literature." *International Organization* 33, 2: 267–302.

—— (1981) "Social Forces, States, and World Orders: Beyond International Relations Theory." *Millennium: Journal of International Studies* 10, 2: 126–155.

—— (1983) "Gramsci, Hegemony, and International Relations: An Essay in Method." *Millennium: Journal of International Studies* 12, 2: 162–175.

—— (1986) "Social Forces, States, and World Orders: Beyond International Relations Theory," in R. O. Keohane, ed. *Neorealism and Its Critics.* New York: Columbia University Press.

—— (1987) *Production, Power and World Order: Social Forces in the Making of History.* New York: Columbia University Press.

—— (1990) "Towards a Counterhegemonic Conceptualisation of World Order." Notes Prepared for the Governance Without Government Workshop, Ojai, CA, February.

Crough, G., and Wheelwright, E. (1982) *Australia: A Client State.* Victoria: Penguin Books.

Culler, J. (1982) *On Deconstruction: Theory and Criticism after Structuralism.* Ithaca, N.Y.: Cornell University Press.

Curti, M., and K. Birr (1954) *Prelude to Point Four.* Madison: University of Wisconsin Press.

Curzon, R., and V. Curzon (1976) "The Management of Trade Relations in the GATT," in A. Shonfield, ed. *International Economic Relations of the Western World,* vol. 1. London: Oxford University Press for Royal Institute of International Affairs.

Dam, K. (1970) *The GATT: Law and International Organization.* Chicago: University of Chicago Press.

Davidoff, L. (1990) "Adam Spoke First and Named the Orders of the World: Masculine and Feminine Domains in History and Sociology," in H. Corr and L. Jamieson, eds. *The Politics of Everyday Life: Continuity and Change in Work, Labor and the Family.* London: Macmillan.

Der Derian, J., and M. Shapiro, eds. (1989) *International-Intertextual Relations: Readings in Post-Modern Politics.* Lexington, Mass.: Lexington Books.

Derrida, J. (1977) *Limited Inc.* Supplement to *Glyph 2.* Baltimore: The Johns Hopkins University Press.

Deschamps, H. (1970) "France in Black Africa and Madagascar between 1925 and 1945," in L. H. Gann and Peter Duignan, eds. *Colonialism in Africa, 1870–1960,* vol. 2. Cambridge: Cambridge University Press.

Destler, I. M. (1986) *American Trade Politics.* Washington, D.C.: Institute for International Economics.

Destler, I. M., et al. (1979) *The Textile Wrangle: Conflict in Japanese- American Relations 1969–1971.* Ithaca, N.Y.: Cornell University Press.

Dos Santos, T. (1970) "The Structure of Dependence." *American Economic Review* 60, 2: 231–237.

Dreyfus, H., and Rabinow, P. (1982) *Michel Foucault: Beyond Structuralism and Hermeneutics.* Chicago: University of Chicago Press.

Drucker, P. (1986) "The Changed World Economy," in *Foreign Affairs* 64, 4: 768–791.

Dunning, J. (1985) "Toward an Eclectic Theory of International Business." Mimeo, Reading University.

Dupe, S. C. (1988) *Modernization and Development: The Search for Alternative Paradigms*. London: Zed Books.

ECA and OAU (1981) *Lagos Plan of Action for Economic Development of Africa, 1980–2000*. Addis Ababa: ECA and OAU.

——— (1983) *ECA and African Development, 1983–2008: A Preliminary Perspective Study*. Addis Ababa: ECA.

——— (1985) *African Priority Programmes for Economic Recovery, 1986–1990*. Addis Ababa: ECA.

——— (1986) *OAU/ECA Africa's Submission to the Special Session of the United Nations General Assembly on Africa's Economic and Social Crisis*. Addis Ababa: ECA.

——— (1987) *African Statement on the Challenge of Economic Recovery and Accelerated Development in Africa*. Addis Ababa: ECA.

——— (1988a) *Beyond Recovery: ECA Revised Perspective of African Development, 1988–2008*. Addis Ababa: ECA.

——— (1988b) *The African Framework for Structural Adjustment Programmes: An Issue Paper*. Addis Ababa: ECA.

——— (1989a) *Statistics and Policies: ECA Preliminary Observations on the World Bank Report, "Africa's Adjustments and Growth in the 1980s."* Addis Ababa: ECA.

——— (1989b) *Africa's Alternative Frameworks to Structural Adjustment Programmes for Socio-Economic Recovery and Transformation*. Addis Ababa: ECA.

Elster, J. (1989) *The Cement of Society*. Cambridge: Cambridge University Press.

Emmanuel, A. (1972) *Unequal Exchange: A Study of the Imperialism of Trade*. New York: Monthly Review Press.

Evans, G. (1989a) "Australian Foreign Policy: Priorities in a Changing World." *Australian Outlook: The Australian Journal of Foreign Affairs* 43, 2: 1–5.

——— (1989b) *Australia's Regional Security*. Canberra: Department of Foreign Affairs and Trade.

Evans, P. B., B. Reuschmayer, and T. Skocpol, eds. (1985) *Bringing the State Back In*. Cambridge: Cambridge University Press.

Fallows, J. (1989) *More Like Us*. Boston: Houghton Mifflin.

Fearon, J. D. (1988) "International Financial Institutions and Economic Policy Reform in Sub-Saharan Africa." *Journal of Modern African Studies* 26, 1: 113–137.

Foster-Carter, A. (1976) "From Rostow to Gunder Frank: Conflicting Paradigms in the Analysis of Underdevelopment." *World Development* 4, 3: 167–180.

Foucault, M. (1977) *Discipline and Punish: the Birth of the Prison*. New York: Pantheon Books.

——— (1978) *Writing and Difference*. London: Routledge and Kegan Paul.

——— (1980) *The History of Sexuality*, vol. 1. New York: Vintage.

——— (1984) *The Foucault Reader*, ed. by P. Rabinow. New York: Pantheon Books.

Frank, A. G. (1969) *Latin America—Underdevelopment or Revolution*. New York: Monthly Review Press.

——— (1988) "The Development of Underdevelopment," in C. K. Wilber, ed. *The Political Economy of Development and Underdevelopment*, 4th ed. New York: Random House.

Freud, S. (1953–1974) *Complete Psychological Works*. London: Hogarth Press.

Frey, B. S. (1984) *International Political Economics*. Oxford: Basil Blackwell.

Frey-Wouters, E. (1980) *The European Community and the Third World*. New York: Praeger.

Frieden, J. (1987) *Banking on the World: The Politics of American International Finance.* New York: Harper and Row.

Gallagher, P. (1988) "Setting the Agenda for Trade Negotiations: Australia and the Cairns Group." *Australian Outlook: The Australian Journal of International Affairs* 44, 1: 3–8.

Galtung, J. (1971) "A Structural Theory of Imperialism." *Journal of Peace Research* 8, 2: 81–117.

Gann, L. H., and P. Duignan, eds. (1967) *The Burden of Empire.* New York: Praeger.

GATT (1979) *The Tokyo Round of Multilateral Trade Negotiations.* Geneva: GATT.

George, J. (1988) "International Relations and the Positivist/Empiricist Theory of Knowledge: Implications for the Australian Discipline," in R. A. Higgott, ed. *New Directions in International Relations: Australian Perspectives.* Canberra: Australian National University, Canberra Studies in World Affairs, No. 23.

———— (1989) "International Relations and the Search for Thinking Space." *International Studies Quarterly* 33, 3: 269–279.

Giddens, A. (1981) *A Contemporary Critique of Historical Materialism,* vol. 1. Berkeley: University of California Press.

———— (1985) *The Nation State and Violence,* vol. 2 of *A Contemporary Critique of Historical Materialism.* Cambridge: Polity Press.

———— (1987) *Social Theory and Modern Sociology.* Cambridge: Polity Press.

Gill, S. (1986) "American Hegemony: Its Limits and Prospects in the Reagan Era." *Millennium: Journal of International Studies* 15, 4: 311–336.

———— (1988) "The Rise and Decline of Great Powers: The American Case." *Politics* 8: 3–9.

———— (1990) *American Hegemony and the Trilateral Commission.* Cambridge: Cambridge University Press.

Gill, S., and D. Law (1988) *The Global Political Economy: Perspectives, Problems and Policies.* Baltimore: The Johns Hopkins University Press.

———— (1989) "Global Hegemony and the Structural Power of Capital," *International Studies Quarterly* 33, 4: 475–499.

Gilpin, R. (1975) *United States Power and the Multinational Corporation.* New York: Basic Books.

———— (1981) *War and Change in World Politics.* Cambridge: Cambridge University Press.

———— (1984) "The Richness of the Tradition of Political Realism." *International Organization* 38, 2: 287–304.

———— (1987) *The Political Economy of International Relations.* Princeton: Princeton University Press.

Goffman, E. (1967) *Interaction Ritual: Essays on Face-to-Face Behavior.* New York: Pantheon.

———— (1974) *Frame Analysis: An Essay on the Organization of Experience.* New York: Harper and Row.

Goldstein, J. (1988) *Long Cycles: Prosperity and War in the Modern Age.* New Haven: Yale University Press.

Gramsci, A. (1971) *Selections from the Prison Notebooks.* Q. Hoare and G. N. Smith, trans. New York: International Publishers.

Greico, J. M. (1990) *Cooperation Among Nations: Europe, America and Non-Tariff Barriers to Trade.* Ithaca: Cornell University Press.

Grossman, G. M. (1986) "Strategic Export Promotion: A Critique," in P. R.

Krugman, ed. *Strategic Trade Policy and the New International Economics.* Cambridge, Mass.: MIT Press.

Gruhn, I., (1986) "Lome Convention Renegotiations: Litmus Test for North-South Relations," in R. Boardman et al. *Europe, Africa, and Lome III.* Lanham, Md.: University Press of America.

Gunell, J. G. (1968) "Social Science and Political Reality: The Problem of Explanation." *Social Research* 35, 1: 159–201.

Hall, S. (1982) "The Rediscovery of Ideology," in M. Gurevitch et al., eds. *Culture, Society, and the Media.* London: Methuen.

Hamilton, C., and Whalley, J. (1989) "Coalitions in the Uruguay Round," *Weltwirtschafliches Archive* 125, 3: 547–562.

Hampson, F. O. (1990) "Climate Change: Building Coalitions of the Like-Minded." *International Journal* 45, 1: 36–74.

Hansen, E., ed. (1987) *Africa: Perspectives on Peace and Development.* London: Zed Books.

Harding, S. (1986) *The Science Question in Feminism.* Ithaca, N.Y.: Cornell University Press.

Harris, S. (1989) "Regional Economic Cooperation, Trading Blocs and Australia's Interest." *Australian Outlook: The Australian Journal of International Affairs* 43, 2: 16–24.

—— (1990) "Economic Change in the International System: Implications for Australia's Prospects," in C. Bell, ed. *Agenda for the Nineties: Australian Choices in Foreign and Defence Policy to the End of the Century.* Melbourne: Longmans.

Harrod, J. (1972) *Trade Union Foreign Policy.* Garden City, N.Y.: Anchor Press.

Harsanyi, J. (1977) *Rational Behaviour and Bargaining Equilibrium in Games and Social Situations.* Cambridge: Cambridge University Press.

Hart, J. A. (1983) *The New International Economic Order.* New York: St. Martins Press.

Hartsock, N. C. M. (1983) *Money, Sex and Power: Toward a Feminist Historical Materialism.* Boston: Northeastern University Press.

Helpman, E., and P. Krugman (1989) *Trade Policy and Market Structure.* Cambridge, Mass.: MIT Press.

Henderson, H. (1949) "The Havana Charter." *American Economic Review* 39, 4: 605–617.

Herrick, B., and C. P. Kindleberger, eds. (1983) *Economic Development,* 4th ed. New York: McGraw Hill.

Higgott, R. A. (1986) "Africa and the New International Division of Labor," in J. Ravenhill, ed. *Africa in Economic Crisis.* New York: Columbia University Press.

—— (1987a) "The Dilemmas of Interdependence: Australia and the New International Division of Labor," in J. Caporaso, ed. *The New International Division of Labor.* Boulder, Colo.: Lynne Rienner Publishers.

—— (1987b) *The World Economic Order and the Trade Crisis: Implications for Australia.* Canberra: Australian Institute of International Affairs.

—— (1988a) "Trans Regional Coalitions and International Regimes: The Cairns Group and Agricultural Trade." *The Australian Quarterly* 60, 4: 415–434.

—— (1988b) *New Directions in International Relations: Australian Perspectives.* Canberra: Australian National University, Canberra Studies in World Affairs, No. 23.

—— (1989a) "The Ascendancy of the Economic Dimension in Australian American Relations," in J. Ravenhill, ed. *No Longer an American Lake:*

Alliance Problems in the South Pacific. Berkeley: University of California, Institute of International Affairs.

—— (1989b) *The Evolving World Economy: Some Alternative Security Questions for Australia.* Canberra: Strategic and Defence Studies Centre, Australian National University, Papers on Strategy and Defence, No. 51.

Higgott, R. A., and Cooper, A. F. (1990) "Middle Power Leadership and Coalition Building: Australia, the Cairns Group and the Uruguay Round of Trade Negotiations." *International Organization.* 44, 4: 591–632.

Higgott, R. A., and George, J. (1990) "Tradition and Change in the Study of International Relations in Australia." *International Political Science Review.* 11, 4: 423–438.

Hill, J., and J. Mendez (1983) "Factor Mobility and the General Equilibrium Model of Production." *Journal of International Economics* 15, 1: 19–25.

Hirschleifer J. (1985) "The Expanding Domain of Economics." *American Economic Review* 75, 6: 53–68.

Hirschmann, A. O. (1985) "Against Parsimony," *Economics and Philosophy* 1, 1: 7–21.

Hodd, M. (1987) "Africa, the IMF, and the World Bank." *African Affairs* 86, 344: 331–342.

Hoffmann, S. (1977) "An American Social Science: International Relations," *Daedelus* 106, 3: 41–60.

—— (1989) "What Should We Do in the World?" *The Atlantic,* October: 84–96.

Hyden, G. (1980) *Beyond Ujamaa in Tanzania: Underdevelopment and an Uncaptured Peasantry.* Berkeley: University of California Press.

—— (1983) *No Shortcuts to Progress: African Development Management in Perspective.* Berkeley: University of California Press.

IBRD (1981) *Accelerated Development in Sub-Saharan Africa: Agenda for Action.* Washington, D.C.: IBRD.

—— (1983) *Sub-Saharan Africa: Progress Report on Development Prospects and Programs.* Washington, D.C.: IBRD.

—— (1984) *Towards Sustained Development in Sub-Saharan Africa: A Joint Program of Action.* Washington, D.C.: IBRD.

—— (1986) *Financing Adjustment with Growth in Sub-Saharan Africa.* Washington, D.C.: IBRD.

—— (1989a) *Beyond Adjustment: A Participatory Program for Sustainable Growth with Equity in Sub-Saharan Africa.* Washington, D.C.: IBRD.

—— (1989b) *Africa's Adjustment and Growth in the 1980s.* New York: UNDP and the World Bank.

—— (1989c) *Adjustment Lending: An Evaluation of Ten Years Experience.* Washington, D.C.: IBRD.

IMF (1988) *Issues and Developments in International Trade Policy,* Occasional Papers 68, Washington, D.C.: IMF.

Inkeles, A. (1966) "The Modernization of Man," in M. Weiner, ed. *Modernization: The Dynamics of Growth.* New York: Basic Books.

Jagger, A. (1983) *Feminist Politics and Human Nature.* Totowa, N.J.: Rowman and Allanheld.

Jaquette, J. S. (1984) "Power as Ideology: A Feminist Analysis," in J. H. Stiehm, ed. *Women's Views of the Political World of Men.* Dobbs Ferry, N.Y.: Transnational Publishers.

Jaycox, E. V. K. (1989) "Structural Adjustments in Sub-Saharan Africa: The World Bank's Perspective." *Issue.* 18, 1: 36–40.

Jervis, R. (1988) "Realism, Game Theory and Cooperation." *World Politics* 40, 3: 317–349.

———— (1989) *The Meaning of Nuclear Revolution: Statecraft and the Prospect of Armageddon.* Ithaca, N.Y.: Cornell University Press.

Jervis, R., R. N. Lebow, and J. G. Stein (1986) *Psychology and Deterrence.* Baltimore: The Johns Hopkins University Press.

Jessop, B. (1982) *The Capitalist State: Marxist Theories and Methods.* New York: New York University Press.

Jewslewicki, B. (1989) "African Historical Studies: Academic Knowledge as 'Usable Past' and Radical Scholarship." *African Studies Review* 23, 3: 1–76.

Johnson, C. (1982) *MITI and the Japanese Miracle.* Stanford, Calif.: Stanford University Press.

Johnson, H. G. (1960) "The Cost of Protection and the Scientific Tariff." *Journal of Political Economy* 68, 4: 327–345.

Johnston, D. (1990) "Representation and Modernity: Development and the Construction of Peripheral Man." Paper presented at the annual meeting of the International Studies Association, Washington, D.C., April.

Jones, R. (1965) "The Structure of Simple General Equilibrium Models." *Journal of Political Economy* 73, 6: 557–572.

———— (1971) "A Three-Factor Model in Theory, Trade and History." in J. Bhagwati et al., eds. *Trade, Balance of Payments and Growth.* Amsterdam: North-Holland.

Kaldor, M. (1986) "The Global Political Economy." *Alternatives* 11, 4: 431–460.

Kay, G. (1975) *Development and Underdevelopment: A Marxist Analysis.* New York: Cambridge University Press.

Keeley, J. (1989) "Towards a Foucaldian Analysis of Regimes." *International Organization* 44, 1: 83–106.

Keller, E. F. (1985) *Reflections on Gender and Science.* New Haven, Conn.: Yale University Press.

Keohane, R. O. (1984) *After Hegemony: Cooperation and Discord in the World Political Economy.* Princeton, N.J.: Princeton University Press.

———— (1986a) "Theory of World Politics: Structural Realism and Beyond," in R. Keohane, ed. *Neorealism and Its Critics.* New York: Columbia University Press.

———— (1986b) "Reciprocity in International Relations." *International Organization* 40, 1: 1–27.

———— (1988) "International Institutions: Two Approaches." *International Studies Quarterly* 32, 4: 379–396.

———— (1989) *International Institutions and State Power: Essays in International Relations Theory.* Boulder, Colo.: Westview Press.

Kindleberger, C. (1973) *The World in Depression: 1929–1939.* London: Allen Lane.

Kornai, J. (1986) *Contradictions and Dilemmas.* Cambridge, Mass.: MIT Press.

Krasner, S. D. (1976) "State Power and the Structure of International Trade," *World Politics* 28, 3: 317–347.

———— (1979) "The Tokyo Round: Particularist Interests and Prospects for Stability in the Global Trading System." *International Studies Quarterly* 23, 4: 491–553.

———— (1982a) "American Policy and Global Economic Stability," in W. P. Avery and D. P. Rapkin, eds. *America in a Changing World Political Economy.* New York: Longmans.

———— (1982b) "Structural Causes and Regime Consequences: Regimes as Intervening Variables." *International Organization* 36, 2: 185–206.

—— (1982c) "Regimes and the Limits of Realism: Regimes as Autonomous Variables." *International Organization* 36, 2: 497–510.

——, ed. (1983) *International Regimes*. Ithaca, N.Y.: Cornell University Press.

—— (1985) *Structural Conflict: The Third World Against Global Liberalism.* Berkeley: University of California Press.

—— (1989) "Realist Praxis: Neo-Isolationism and Structural Change." *Journal of International Affairs* 43, 1: 143–160.

Kratochwil, F. V. (1989) *Rules, Norms, and Decisions*. Cambridge: Cambridge University Press.

Kratochwil, F., and J. G. Ruggie (1986) "International Organization: A State of the Art on the Art of the State." *International Organization* 40, 4: 753–775.

Krugman, P. R., ed. (1986) *Strategic Trade Policy and the New International Economics*. Cambridge, Mass.: MIT Press.

—— (1990) *Rethinking International Trade*. Cambridge, Mass.: MIT Press.

Lake, D. (1988) *Power, Protection and Free Trade*. Ithaca, N.Y.: Cornell University Press.

Lancaster, C. (1982) "ECOWAS: Problems and Prospects." *CSIS Africa Notes* 4.

—— (1985) "Africa's Development Challenges." *Current History* 84, 501: 146–186.

Lapid, Y. (1989) "The Third Debate: On the Prospects of International Theory in a Post-Positivist Era." *International Studies Quarterly* 33, 3: 235–254.

Larrain, J. (1983) *Marxism and Ideology*. London: Macmillan.

Leaver, R. (1990a) "The Future of Northeast Asian Growth: The Regionalist Alternative," in J. L. Richardson, ed. *Australia and the Northeast Asian Ascendancy*. Melbourne: Longmans.

—— (1990b) "International Political Economy." Mimeo, Australian National University, Peace Research Centre.

Little, D. (1985) *The Scientific Marx*. Minneapolis: University of Minnesota Press.

Luke, D. F., and T. M. Shaw, eds. (1984) *Continental Crisis: The Lagos Plan of Action and Africa's Future*. Lanham, Md.: University Press of America.

McClelland, D. C. (1966) "The Impulse in Modernization," in M. Weiner, ed. *Modernization: The Dynamics of Growth*. New York: Basic Books.

—— (1975) "Power and the Feminine Role," in D. C. McClelland, ed. *Power, the Inner Experience*. New York: Wiley.

McCubbins, M., and T. Sullivan, eds. (1987) *Congress: Structure and Policy*. Cambridge: Cambridge University Press.

McGuiness, P. P. (1990) *An Asia Pacific Economic Cooperation Organisation*. Sydney: Pacific Security Research Institute.

Maclean, J. (1981) "Political Theory, International Theory, and the Problem of Ideology." *Millennium: Journal of International Studies* 10, 2: 102–125.

Mandaza, I. (1987a) "Perspective on Economic Cooperation and Autonomous Development in Southern Africa," in S. Amin et al. *SADCC: Prospects for Disengagement and Development in Southern Africa*. London: Zed Books.

—— (1987b) "Conflict in Southern Africa," in E. Hansen, ed. *Africa: Perspectives on Peace and Development*. London: Zed Books.

Mann, M. (1986) "Autonomous Power of the State: Its Origins, Mechanisms and Results," in J. A. Hall, ed. *States in History*. Oxford: Basil Blackwell.

Manning, P. (1988) *Francophone Sub-Saharan Africa, 1880–1985*. Cambridge: Cambridge University Press.

Marx, K. (1971) *Grundrisse*, ed. by D. McLellan. Harmondsworth: Penguin.

Mayer, T. F. (1989) "In Defense of Analytical Marxism." *Science and Society* 53, 4: 416–441.

Mayer, W. (1982) "Endogenous Tariff Formation." *American Economic Review* 74, 5: 970–985.

Maynard Smith, J. (1982) *Evolution and the Theory of Games*. Cambridge: Cambridge University Press.

Mazzeo, D. (1984) *African Regional Organizations*. Cambridge: Cambridge University Press.

M'buyinga, E. (1982) *Pan-Africanism or Neocolonialism: The Bankruptcy of the OAU*. London: Zed Books.

Meyer, F. V. (1978) *International Trade Policy*. London: Croom Helm.

Michalet, C.-A. (1976) *Le Capitalisme Mondaile*. Paris: Presse Universitaires de France.

———— (1982) "From International Trade to World Economy," in H. Makler, A. Martinelli, and N. Smelser, eds. *The New International Economy*. London: Sage.

Mies, M. (1986) *Patriarchy and Accumulation on a World Scale: Women in the International Division of Labor*. London: Zed Books.

Miliband, R. (1969) *The State in Capitalist Society*. New York: Basic Books.

Milikan, M. F., and D. L. M. Blackmer (1961) *The Emerging Nations: Their Growth and United States Policy*. Boston: Little, Brown.

Millennium: Journal of International Studies. (1988) "Philosophical Issues in International Relations." 17, 2: 189–348.

Mitchell, J. (1987) "Women and Equality," in A. Phillips, ed. *Feminism and Equality*. Oxford: Basil Blackwell.

Mkandawire, T. (1987) "Dependence and Economic Cooperation: The Case of SADCC," in E. Hansen, ed. *Africa: Perspectives on Peace and Development*. London: Zed Books.

Molyneux, M. (1985) "Mobilization Without Emancipation? Women's Interests, State and Revolution in Nicaragua." *Feminist Studies* 11, 2: 227–254.

Moore, H. (1988) *Feminism and Anthropology*. Minneapolis: University of Minnesota Press.

Morera, E. (1990) *Gramsci's Historicism*. London: Routledge.

Murphy, C. N. (1983) "What the Third World Wants: The Development and Meaning of the New International Economic Order Ideology." *International Studies Quarterly* 27, 1: 55–76.

———— (1984) *The Emergence of the NIEO Ideology*. Boulder, Colo.: Westview Press.

Myerson, R. (1986) "An Introduction to Game Theory," in S. Reiter, ed. *Studies in Mathematical Economics*. Washington, D.C.: Mathematics Association of America.

Myint, H. (1954) "An Interpretation of Economic Backwardness," *Oxford Economic Papers* 6, 2: 132–163.

Nabudere, D. (1978) *The Political Economy of Imperialism*. London: Zed Books.

Nau, H., ed. (1989) *Domestic Trade Politics and the Uruguay Round*. New York: Columbia University Press.

Nelson, D. (1987) "The State as a Conceptual Variable: Another Look." Mimeo, Washington University, St. Louis, Mo.

———— (1989a) "The Domestic Political Preconditions of U.S. Trade Policy: Liberal Structure and Protectionist Dynamics." *Journal of Public Policy* 9, 1: 83–108.

———— (1989b) "On The High Track to Protection: The U.S. Automobile Industry,

1979–81," in S. Haggard and C. Moon, eds. *Pacific Dynamics: The International Politics of Industrial Change*. Boulder, Colo.: Westview Press.

Neumann, J. von, and O. Morgenstern (1944) *The Theory of Games and Economic Behaviour*. Princeton, N. J.: Princeton University Press.

Nivola, P. S. (1986) "The New Protectionism: U.S. Trade Policy in Historical Perspective." *Political Science Quarterly* 109, 4: 577–600.

Nkrumah, K. (1964) *Neocolonialism: The Last Stage of Imperialism*. London: Panaf Publishers.

Nordlinger, E. (1981) *On the Autonomy of the Democratic State*. Cambridge, Mass.: Harvard University Press.

North, R. C. (1990) *War, Peace, and Survival*. Boulder, Colo.: Westview Press.

Nyang'oro, J. (1989) *The State and Capitalist Development in Africa*. New York: Praeger Publishers.

Nye, J. S. (1990) *Bound To Lead: The Changing Nature of American Power*. New York: Basic Books.

Nyerere, J. (1985) Speech at the Royal Commonwealth Society, March 20.

Ofuatey-Kodjoe, W., ed. (1986) *Pan-Africanism: New Directions on Strategy*. Lanham, Md.: University Press of America.

—— (1988) "United States Economic Policy Towards Sub-Saharan Africa: Sources and Impact." *TransAfrica Forum* 5, 2: 3–16.

—— (1989) "The Economic Policies of the OECD Countries Toward Sub-Saharan Africa." Paper presented at the Italo-African Institute Conference, "Which Cooperation with Africa in the 1990s?," Rome, April.

—— (1990) "The SADCC and the Frontline States: Viewing Their Performance: A Comment," in H. Glickman, ed. *Toward Peace and Security in Southern Africa*. New York: Gordon and Breach.

Okin, S. M. (1989) *Justice, Gender and the Family*. New York: Basic Books.

Onimode, B. (1988) *A Political Economy of the African Crisis*. London: Zed Books.

Onwuku, R. T., and O. Aluko, eds. (1985) *The Future of Africa and the New International Economic Order*. New York: St. Martins Press.

Onwuku, R., and A. Sesay, eds. (1985) *The Future of Regionalism in Africa*. New York: St. Martins Press.

Overbeek, H. (1990) *Global Capitalism and Britain's Decline*. London: Routledge.

Overseas Development Institute (1964) *Colonial Development*. London: Overseas Development Institute.

Oxaal, I., et al., eds. (1975) *Beyond the Sociology of Development: Economy and Society in Latin America and Africa*. London: Routledge.

Packenham, R. (1973) *Liberal America and the Third World: Political Development Ideas in Foreign Aid and Social Science*. Princeton, N.J.: Princeton University Press.

Pijl, K. van der (1988) "The Socialist International and the Internationalisation of Capital." Occasional Papers, University of Amsterdam, Faculty of Political and Social Sciences.

—— (1984) *The Making of an Atlantic Ruling Class*. London: Verso.

Please, S., and K. Y. Amoako (1987) "OAU, ECA, and the World Bank: Do They Really Disagree?" in J. Ravenhill, ed. *Africa in Economic Crisis*. London: Macmillan.

Polanyi, Karl (1944) *The Great Transformation*. New York: Rinehart.

Pratt, C., ed. (1990) *Middle Power Internationalism: The North-South Dimension*. Montreal: McGill University Press.

Preston, P. W. (1988) *New Trends in Development Theory: Essays in Development and Social Theory.* London: Routledge.

Prestowitz, C. (1988) *Trading Places.* New York: Basic Books.

Putnam, R. (1988) "Diplomacy and Domestic Policies: The Logic of Two-Level Games." *International Organization* 42, 3: 427–461.

Pye, L. (1966) *Aspects of Political Development.* Boston: Little, Brown.

Rapoport, A. (1962) *Fights, Games, and Debates.* Ann Arbor: University of Michigan Press.

Ravenhill, J. (1985a) *Collective Clientalism.* New York: Columbia University Press.

———— (1985b) "The Future of Regionalism in Africa," in R. J. Onwuku and A. Sesay, eds. *The Future of Regionalism in Africa.* New York: St. Martins Press.

———— (1987) *Africa in Economic Crisis.* New York: Columbia University Press and London: Macmillan.

Reardon, B. A. (1985) *Sexism and the War System.* New York: Teachers College Press.

Resnick, S. A., and R. D. Wolff (1987) *Knowledge and Class.* Chicago: University of Chicago Press.

Richardson, J. D. (1989) "The Political Economy of Strategic Trade Policy," *International Organisation* 44, 1: 107–135.

Rodney, W. (1972) *How Europe Underdeveloped Africa.* London: Bogle-l'Overture Publications.

Roemer, J. (1982) *A General Theory of Exploitation and Class.* Cambridge: Cambridge University Press.

Rosecrance, R. (1986) *The Rise of the Trading State.* New York: Basic Books.

Rosenau, J. (1986) "Before Cooperation: Hegemons, Regimes and Habit Driven Actors." *International Organization* 40, 4: 849–894.

Rostow, W. W. (1960) *The Stages of Economic Growth: A Non-Communist Manifesto.* Cambridge: Cambridge University Press.

Rothstein, R. L. (1977) *The Weak in the World of the Strong.* New York: Columbia University Press.

———— (1979) *Global Bargaining: UNCTAD and the Quest for an NIEO.* Princeton, N.J.: Princeton University Press.

———— (1984) "Regime Creation by a Coalition of the Weak: Lessons from the NIEO and the Integrated Program for Commodities," *International Studies Quarterly* 28, 3: 307–328.

Russett, B. M. (1985) "The Mysterious Case of Vanishing Hegemony: Or Is Mark Twain Really Dead?" *International Organization* 39, 2: 207–231.

Rustow, D. A. (1967) *A World of Nations: Problems of Political Modernization.* Washington, D.C.: Brookings Institution.

Sandbrook, R. (1985) *The Politics of African Economic Stagnations.* Cambridge: Cambridge University Press.

Schoenholtz, A. I. (1987) "The IMF in Africa: Unnecessary and Undesirable Western Restraints in Development." *Journal of Modern African Studies* 25, 3: 403–434.

Seager, J., and A. Olson (1986) *Women in the World: An International Atlas.* London: Pan Books.

Sen, G., and C. Grown. (1987) *Development, Crises and Alternative Visions: Third World Women's Perspectives.* New York: Monthly Review Press

Sesay, A., ed. (1986) *Africa and Europe: From Partition to Interdependence of Dependence.* London: Croom Helm.

Shaw, T. M. (1986) "The African Crisis: Debates and Dialectics over Alternative

Development Strategies for the Continent," in J. Ravenhill, ed. *Africa in Economic Crisis*. New York: Columbia University Press.

―――― (1989) "The Revival of Regionalism in Africa: Cure for Crisis or Prescription for Conflict?" *Jerusalem Journal of International Relations* 11, 4: 79–105.

Shaw, T. M., and O. Aluko, eds. (1984) *The Political Economy of African Foreign Policy*. New York: St. Martins Press.

Shepsle, K. (1979) "Institutional Arrangements and Equilibrium in Multidimensional Voting Models." *American Journal of Political Science* 23, 1: 27–59.

Shils, E. (1966) "Modernization and Higher Education," in M. Weiner, ed. *Modernization and the Dynamics of Growth*. New York: Basic Books.

Shiviji, I. (1976) *Class Struggles in Tanzania*. Dar es Salaam: Tanzania Publishing House.

Skocpol, T., and K. Finegold (1982) "State Capacity and Economic Intervention in the Early New Deal." *Political Science Quarterly* 97, 2: 255–278.

Skocpol, T., and G. J. Ikenberry (1983) "Political Formation of the Welfare State in Historical and Comparative Perspective." *Comparative Social Research* 6: 87–148.

Snape, R. H. (1989) "A Free Trade Agreement with Australia?" in J. J. Schott, ed. *Free Trade Areas and U.S. Trade Policy*. Washington D.C.: Institute for International Economics.

Snidal, D. (1985) "The Limits of Hegemonic Stability Theory." *International Organization* 39, 4: 579–614.

Spero, J. E. (1985) *The Politics of International Economic Relations*, 3rd ed. New York: St. Martins Press.

Srinivasan, T. N. (1987) "The National Defense Argument for Government Intervention in Foreign Trade," in R. Stern, ed. *U.S. Trade Policies in a Changing World Economy*. Cambridge, Mass.: MIT Press.

Stanley, E. (1961) *The Future of the Underdeveloped Countries: Political Implications of Economic Development*, rev. ed. New York: Harper and Row.

Stigler, G. (1975) *The Citizen and the State: Essays on Regulation*. Chicago: University of Chicago Press.

Stopford, J. (1972) *Managing the Multinational Corporation*. New York: Basic Books.

Strange, S. (1971) *Sterling and British Policy*. London: Oxford University Press for the Royal Institute of International Affairs.

―――― (1985) "International Political Economy: The Story So Far and the Way Ahead," in L. Hollist and L. Tullis, eds. *An International Political Economy*. Boulder, Colo.: Westview Press.

―――― (1976) *International Monetary Relations*, vol. 2 of A. Schonfield, ed. *International Economic Relations in the Western World 1959–71*. London: Oxford University Press for the Royal Institute of International Affairs.

―――― (1982) "*Cave! Hic Dragones*: A Critique of Regime Analysis." *International Organization* 36, 2: 479–497.

――――, ed. (1984) *Paths to International Political Economy*. London: Frances Pinter.

―――― (1986) *Casino Capitalism*. Oxford: Basil Blackwell.

―――― (1987) "The Persistent Myth of Lost Hegemony." *International Organization* 41, 4: 551–574.

―――― (1988) *States and Markets: An Introduction to International Political Economy*. London: Pinter Publishers.

Strange S., and R. Tooze (1981) *The Politics of International Surplus Capacity.* London: Allen and Unwin.

Takayama, A. (1982) "On Theorems of General Competitive Equilibrium of Production and Trade: A Survey of Some Recent Developments in the Theory of International Trade." *Keio Economic Studies* 19, 1: 1–38.

Tan, A. (1971) "Optimal Trade Policies and Non-Economic Objectives in Models Involving Imported Materials, Inter-Industry Flows and Non-Traded Goods." *Review of Economic Studies* 38, 113: 105–111.

Tandon, Y. (1984) *Argument with African Marxists: The Dar es Salaam Debates.* London: Zed Books for the *Journal of African Marxists.*

Tooze, R. (1988) "The Unwritten Preface: 'International Political Economy' and Epistemology." *Millennium: Journal of International Studies* 17, 2: 285–294.

———— (1990) "International Political Economy: An Interim Assessment," in R. A. Higgott and J. L. Richardson, eds. *International Relations: Global and Australian Perspectives on a Changing Discipline.* Canberra: Australian National University.

Toye, J. (1987) *Dilemmas of Development: Reflections on the Counter-Revolution in Development Theory and Policy.* Oxford: Basil Blackwell.

Tuchman-Mathews, J. (1990) "Redefining Security: An Environmental Perspective." *Dialogue* 1: 3–8.

Tussie, D. (1986) *The Less Developed Countries and the World Trading System: A Challenge to the GATT.* London: Pinter Publishers.

UNCTAD (1989) *Trade and Development Report.* Geneva: UNCTAD.

UNCTC (1973) *Multinational Corporations in World Development.* New York: UNCTC.

———— (1988) *Transnational Corporations in World Development.* New York: UNCTC.

Vandendorpe, A. (1974) "On the Theory of Non-Economic Objectives in Open Economies." *Journal of International Economics* 4, 1: 15–24.

Varynyen, R., et al. (1988) *International Relations Research in Finland: A Centre-Periphery Perspective.* Williamsburg, Va.: World Assembly of International Studies Associations.

Vasquez, J. A. (1983) *The Power of Power Politics: A Critique.* London: Frances Pinter.

Vernon, R. (1977) *Storm over the Multinationals.* London: Macmillan.

Viner, J. (1937) *Studies in the Theory of International Trade.* New York: A. M. Kelley.

Wallerstein, I. (1974) "Dependence in an Interdependent World: The Limited Possibilities of Transformation Within the Capitalist World Economy." *African Studies Review* 17, 1: 1–26.

———— (1976) "The Three Stages of African Involvement in the World Economy," in P. C. W. Gutkind and I. Wallerstein, eds. *The Political Economy of Contemporary Africa.* London: Sage.

Waltz, K. N. (1979) *Theory of International Relations.* Reading, Mass.: Addison-Wesley.

Webb M. and S. D. Krasner (1989) "Hegemonic Stability Theory: An Empirical Assessment." *Review of International Studies* 15, 2.

Weber, M. (1922) *Economy and Society.* Berkeley: University of California Press.

Wendt, A. E. (1987) "The Agent-Structure Problem in International Relations Theory." *International Organisation* 41, 3: 335–370.

Wilber, C. K., ed. (1988) *The Political Economy of Development and Underdevelopment.* 4th ed. New York: Random House.

Wilber, C. K., and K. P. Jameson (1988) "Paradigms of Economic Development and Beyond," in C. K. Wilber, ed. *The Political Economy of Development and Underdevelopment.* 4th edition. New York: Random House.

Winham, G. (1986) *International Trade and the Tokyo Round Negotiations.* Princeton, N.J.: Princeton University Press.

———— (1989) "The Pre-Negotiation Phase of the Uruguay Round." *International Journal* 44, 2: 280–303.

Wolfers, A. (1962) *Discord and Collaboration: Essays on International Politics.* Baltimore: The Johns Hopkins University Press.

Wood, B. (1990) "Towards North-South Middle Power Coalitions," in C. Pratt, ed. *Middle Power Internationalism: The North-South Dimension.* Montreal: McGill University Press.

Wright, Q. (1930) *Mandates Under the League of Nations.* Chicago: University of Chicago Press.

Yansane, A. (1977) "The State of Economic Integration in North West Africa South of the Sahara: The Emergence of the Economic Community of West African States (ECOWAS)." *African Studies Review* 20, 2: 63–87.

————, ed. (1980) *Decolonization and Dependency.* London: Sage.

Young, O. (1989) "The Politics of International Regimes Formation: Managing Natural Resources and the Environment." *International Organization* 43, 3: 349–375.

———— (1990) "Political Leadership and Regime Reform: The Emergence of Institutions in International Society." Paper presented at the annual meeting of the International Studies Association, Washington D.C., April.

Zartman, I. W. (1976) "Europe and Africa: Decolonization or Dependency?" *Foreign Affairs* 54, 2: 325–343.

About the Contributors

Stephen Gill is associate professor of political science at York University in Ontario and was Hallsworth Fellow in Political Economy at Manchester University in 1989–1990. He is coauthor, with David Law, of *The Global Political Economy* and author of *American Hegemony and the Trilateral Commission*.

Richard Higgott is reader in international relations at the Research School of Pacific Studies of the Australian National University. He is currently president of the Australian Political Science Association and vice-president of the International Studies Association. He has written widely on north-south relations, African state policy, and international political economy, and is completing a comprehensive study of Australia in the world political economy.

Deborah Johnston is completing her doctorate in political science (international relations) at Arizona State University.

Craig N. Murphy is associate professor of political science at Wellesley College. A past president of the International Studies Association's IPE Section, he has written extensively on international economic institutions and north-south relations. His most recent book, coauthored with Enrico Augelli, is *America's Quest for Supremacy and the Third World*. He is completing a study of international institutions and economic change since the industrial revolution.

Douglas Nelson is assistant professor of economics at Syracuse University. He is book review editor of the journal *Economics and Politics*. His research on the political economy of trade policy has appeared in numerous journals including the *American Economic Review* and the *American Journal of Political Science*.

W. Ofuatey-Kodjoe is professor of political science at Queens College and the City University of New York Graduate Center, where he directs the Ralph Bunche Fellows Program. He has written widely in comparative foreign policy, international law, and international organization. His recent work focuses on African political economy and strategies for an effective Pan-Africanism.

Susan Strange is professor of political science at the European University Institute in Florence. As professor of international relations at the London School of Economics, a cofounder of the British International Studies Association, and past vice-president of the International Studies Association, she pioneered the study of IPE in Britain. She has written widely on the international economy and international finance and is author of the popular textbook *States and Markets: An Introduction to International Political Economy.*

J. Ann Tickner is associate professor of political science at the College of the Holy Cross and president of the International Studies Association's Northeast Region. Author of *Self-Reliance Versus Power Politics: The American and Indian Experience in Building Nation States,* she is currently completing a book on feminist theory and international relations.

Roger Tooze is professor of international studies at Nottingham Polytechnic and chair of the IPE research section of the British International Studies Association. He has published widely in the field and is currently completing a book on theory and international political economy.

Diana Tussie is a member of the Facultad Latinoamericana de Ciences Sociales (FLASCO) in Buenos Aires. A past recipient of the International Studies Association IPE Section's Younger Third World Scholar award, she is the author of *The Less Developed Countries and the World Trading System: A Challenge to the GATT.*

Index

About the Book

The short-lived "neorealist/liberal" synthesis in Anglo–North American international political economy suffered from a number of epistemological problems, most notably its inability to apprehend or explain social institutions and facts. This volume explains those problems and introduces the nonstructuralist Marxist, eclectic, feminist, and postmodern alternatives that are now emerging. Illustrating the degree to which both the old IPE and some newer approaches remain parochial, the authors also present alternative syntheses.